Structural Adjustment and the Environment

STRUCTURAL ADJUSTMENT AND THE ENVIRONMENT

EDITED BY
David Reed
WWF–International

Westview Press

BOULDER • SAN FRANCISCO • OXFORD

This Westview softcover edition is printed on acid-free paper and bound in library-quality, coated covers that carry the highest rating of the National Association of State Textbook Administrators, in consultation with the Association of American Publishers and the Book Manufacturers' Institute.

Cover design by Hasten & Hunt, Washington, D.C.

Published in 1992 in the United States of America by Westview Press, Inc., 5500 Central Avenue, Boulder, Colorado 80301-2877, and in the United Kingdom by Westview Press, 36 Lonsdale Road, Summertown, Oxford OX2 7EW

A CIP catalog record for this book is available from the Library of Congress.
ISBN 0-8133-8702-7

Printed and bound in the United States of America

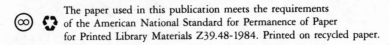

The paper used in this publication meets the requirements of the American National Standard for Permanence of Paper for Printed Library Materials Z39.48-1984. Printed on recycled paper.

10   9   8   7   6   5   4   3   2   1

CONTENTS

Acknowledgments...ix

Foreword..xiii

Introduction 1

1. The Structural Adjustment Experience of the 1980s.......................7
    Genesis of Adjustment Lending.......................................7
    Efforts in Crisis Management 9
    Direct Intervention of the Bretton Woods Institutions.................11
  ◆ Box: Turkey: The SAL Testing Ground 14

2. Diverging Views on the Adjustment Decade.................................21
    Toward Economic Recovery: The World Bank Perspective............22
        Contributions to Improving Growth Rates....................22
        Contributions to Effecting Macroeconomic Reforms 23
        Contributions to Correcting Sectoral Deficiencies...................25
  ◆ Box: Conditionalities of Adjustment Lending......................26
        The Bank's Conclusion: Stay the Course on Adjustment 30
    The Critics' View: Design Failures in Adjustment Lending...........31
        Using Short-term Approaches to Long-term Problems 33
        Overlooking the Impacts of External Conditions 34
        Failure to Create Conditions for Wealth Generation 36
        The Social Dimensions of Adjustment 37
        Ownership of Adjustment Programs 39
    The Sustainability of Adjustment Programs 40

3. Case Study for Côte d'Ivoire **49**
  Macroeconomic History and Broad Pattern of Development 49
    Macroeconomic Setting Prior to Adjustment 49
    Stabilization and Adjustment Program in Côte d'Ivoire 51
  Impacts of Structural Adjustment on the Environment 54
    Land Tenure 55
    Deforestation 57
    Soil Degradation 59
    Pollution 60
  Broad Macroeconomic Policy and Environmental Impacts 61
    Fiscal Policy 61
    Monetary Policy 62
    Trade Policy 63
  Sectoral Policy 63
    Agriculture 64
    Forestry 65
    Industry 68
  Policy Scenarios (Empirical Analysis and Simulation) 69
  Conclusions 71

4. Case Study for Mexico **77**
  Macroeconomic History and Broad Pattern of Development 77
    Overview 77
    Macroeconomic History: From the 1940s to the 1960s 78
    Experiences in the 1970s and Early 1980s 78
    The Oil Boom and the Environment 79
    Economic Policy from 1983 to 1989 80
    The Economy from 1989 to Date 81
  Macroeconomic Policy and the Environment 81
    General Observations 81
    Taxes, Domestic Price Policy, and the Environment 83
    Trade Policy and the Environment 83
  Key Environmental Issues in Mexico 84
    Soil Erosion 84
    Deforestation 87
    Water Resources 90
  Key Areas of Economic Policy and Their
  Environmental Implications 92
    The Maquiladora Program 92
    Energy Pricing 94
    Privatization 95

Conclusions 96

5. Case Study for Thailand 99
Macroeconomic History 99
    Overview..99
    Structural Adjustment Programs......................................100
    Success of Structural Adjustment from a
    Macroeconomic Perspective 101
The Impact of Structural Adjustment on the Environment........102
    Macroeconomic Policies...102
    Conclusions on Macroeconomic Policies............................104
Sectoral Policies 105
    Forestry..105
    Agriculture 107
    Fisheries 111
    Industry 111
    Energy..113
Environmental Impacts of Specific Policy Scenarios...................114
    Reduction of Export Taxes on Rice and Rubber 115
    Increase in Domestic Oil Prices...116
    Increase in Labor-Intensive Manufactured Exports............116
    Increase in Tourism Growth 117
    Reduction in Real Public Sector Investment.....................117
General Themes of Environmental Importance 118
    Pattern of Development 118
    Population Pressure, Poverty, and Income Distribution 120
    Structural Adjustment Policies and Their Impacts on
    Income Distribution, Poverty, and the Environment..........124
    Conclusions 127
Market and Government Policy Failures (Including
Institutional and Infrastructure Constraints).............................129
    Policy Failures 130
    Market Failures 133
Conclusions..136

6. Conclusions...139
The Development Process over Time: Has a Path of
Sustainable Development Been Followed?...................................140
The Relationship of Debt and Environmental Degradation........143
Is There an Environmental Kuznets Curve? 146

The Impacts of Structural Adjustment Programs on the
Environment 148
    The Interaction Between Inherent Market Failure and
    Government Policy Failure 149
• Box: What Are the "Right Prices"? 153
    The Link Between Poverty and Environmental
    Degradation 154
    The Political Economy of Adjusting Countries and
    Environmental Degradation 157
    Structural Adjustment and Institutional and
    Social Constraints 159

7. Recommendations **161**
    Changing the Policy Focus of Structural Adjustment 162
    Institutional Reforms 167
    Reforming the Practices of Official Lending Agencies 168
        Integrating the Environment into Development Planning 169
        Establishing an Operational Directive on Sustainability 171
        Strengthening Implementation Capacity 173
        Strengthening an International Environmental
        Incentive Structure 175
    Changing the Foundations of Adjustment's Political
    Dimension 176

**Annex A: Methodologies Used in the Analysis of
Macroeconomy-Environmental Links** **181**
    Models for Analyzing Economy-Environment Links 181
        Input-Output Models 181
        General Equilibrium Models 182
        Macroeconomic Models 183
    Applications in the Three Case Studies 184

Annex B: Summary Tables **187**
    Macroeconomic and Structural Adjustment Policies 187
    Environmental Impacts of Adjustment

Bibliography **199**

ACKNOWLEDGMENTS

A publication having a provocative avocation, as does this book, is possible only with the support and sharp minds of many dedicated professionals. Contributions from colleagues on five continents enabled this research endeavor to mature from an urgent although poorly formulated idea some three years ago to a serious study of the environmental impacts of policy-based lending. It is nothing short of a privilege to have benefited from the dedication and support of so many gifted colleagues who helped steer this study through methodological, political, and logistical thickets of many kinds.

The core team of WWF colleagues, including Kevin Lyonette, Tony Long, Fulai Sheng, and Barry Coates, guided this project from its inception through many controversies to completion. Their innumerable hours spent reviewing texts, discussing conclusions, and sharpening recommendations effected a coherence that reflects the mission of WWF.

The London Environmental Economics Centre (LEEC) team, composed of Anil Markandya, Julie Richardson, and Joshua Bishop, translated the study's objectives into workable methodological approaches adapted to conditions of the three countries. Under Dr. Markandya's guidance, LEEC provided continuous technical and analytical support to the three country research teams.

Local research teams in Côte d'Ivoire, Mexico, and Thailand faced difficult conditions and challenges in carrying out their respective studies. Dr. Joseph Yao, Director of the *Centre Ivoirien de Recherches*

Economiques et Sociales (CIRES), directed a team composed of Kouadio Yao, Joseph Akomian, and Odile Angoran. Dr. Juan Carlos Belausteguigoitia organized and directed a team of researchers from the *Instituto Tecnologico Autonomo de Mexico* (ITAM), including José Carlos Fernandez, Olga Elena Perez, and Carlos Muñoz Piña. Drs. Theodore Panayotou and Chalongphob Sussengkarn from the Thailand Development Research Institute (TDRI) carried out the research program in Thailand. To each of them, we extend our sincere appreciation.

Members of the project's advisory committee were economists and development experts from developing and industrialized societies representing the full spectrum of views on structural adjustment. We extend our gratitude for the many weeks they spent traveling from all over the world to attend planning and review seminars, for the advice and comments on drafts of the book, and for the conviction and eloquence with which they defended their respective views. The committee was composed of Charles Abugre (Agency for Cooperation and Research in Development), Marcos Arruda (*Politicas Alternativas Para o Cone Sul*, Rio de Janeiro), Laurence Hausman (United States Agency for International Development), Manuel Montes (East-West Center), Stanley Please (London), Michel Potier (Organisation for Economic Co-operation and Development), John D. Shilling (the World Bank), and Konrad von Moltke (Dartmouth College), with supporting comments and contributions from Robin Broad (the American University), Bindu Lohani (Asian Development Bank), and Jeremy J. Warford (the World Bank). They were joined by Patrick Murphy, WWF-International, and Eleanor Richter-Lyonette in several of their deliberations. It is important to state that participation on the advisory committee in no way implies endorsement of the study's findings or recommendations.

Drafts of the book greatly benefited from the insights and critical comments offered by Robert Goodland and John D. Shilling, who bear no responsibility for the views expressed herein. Bill Rau made several important contributions regarding development issues and the impact of structural adjustment. Christopher Herman offered numerous helpful suggestions on the recommendations. David Runnalls provided advice and written contributions on a range of environmental issues. The Institute of Social Studies Advisory Services, under the direction of

Anthony Dolman, made important contributions on issues of political economy and provided helpful reviews at several stages of the project. Thanks to Stephen Kelleher (AMEX) for his comments on the Côte d'Ivoire case study.

Monica Chacon, WWF–International, provided invaluable assistance in managing the project on a day-to-day basis over for the better part of two years and in managing production. Allison Rogers, WWF–U.S., handled preparation of the text for the publisher. Many thanks to Sheila A. Mulvihill for her professionalism and patience in editing the book.

—DAVID REED
Director, International Institutions Policy Program
World Wide Fund for Nature, WWF–International

FOREWORD

The deed of foundation and statutes of World Wildlife Fund (WWF), registered in 1961, identify the first objective of the foundation as "world-wide conservation of the natural environment with particular emphasis on the maintenance of essential ecological processes and life support systems and on the preservation of genetic diversity and on ensuring that any utilization of species and ecosystems is sustainable." That same concern for conservation and sustainability was echoed in *The World Conservation Strategy*, issued jointly by WWF, the International Union for Conservation of Nature and Natural Resources (IUCN), and the United Nations Environment Programme (UNEP) in 1980. In keeping with the conservation practice of the time, however, a large part of the work funded or sponsored by WWF concerned the preservation of biodiversity and species per se.

In 1989, the WWF family, which had already changed its name to World Wide Fund for Nature and had taken on a directly operational role in conservation programs, redefined its mission to focus on issues of most importance to conservation in today's circumstances. The mission is:

The conservation of nature and ecological processes by:

- Preserving genetic, species, and ecosystem diversity;
- Ensuring sustainable use of renewable natural resources now and in the longer term for the benefit of all life on Earth; and
- Promoting actions to reduce, to a minimum, pollution and the

wasteful exploitation and consumption of resources and energy.

WWF's ultimate goal is to stop, and eventually reverse, the accelerating degradation of our natural environment and to help build a future in which humans live in harmony with nature.

This refocusing emphasizes the urgency of establishing a balance between the human species and nature or, in other terms, between the environment and development. Development requires the use of natural resources to our benefit. Conservation requires the sustainability of such use.

WWF's mission emphasizes the need for a holistic approach integrating field- and public policy work and linking North and South. The major elements of WWF's mission are forcefully expressed in *Caring for the Earth: A Strategy for Sustainable Living* (Island Press), issued by WWF, IUCN, and UNEP in October 1991 both as a contribution to the work of the U.N. Conference on Environment and Development (UNCED) of June 1992 in Rio de Janeiro and as a plan for action reaching far beyond the conference. *Caring for the Earth* defines sustainable development as "improving the quality of human life while living within the carrying capacity of supporting ecosystems." This definition incorporates both socioeconomic and environmental factors.

In redefining its mission in 1989, WWF pondered a number of questions: What are the effects of structural adjustment on the environmental and natural resource use policies and practices of developing countries? Given that structural adjustment seems to be an instrument of macroeconomic policy that will continue to be used, how can experience influence its basic philosophy, scope, and objectives so that structural adjustment can contribute to both developmental (human) benefits and the environment?

With this rationale and framework, WWF designed a research project with four basic elements:

- Formulation of a methodology for use in selected countries. The London Environmental Economics Centre (LEEC) carried out this task. LEEC's contribution here was to strengthen the macroeconomic expertise and develop the required link between macroeconomics and environmental factors.
- Application of the methodology by local institutes in Côte d'Ivoire, Mexico, and Thailand. These countries were selected for their geographical distribution, the nature of their environmental

problems, their experience with structural adjustment, and the nature of their economies. WWF emphasized the point that local experts, not expatriates, should do the research. Under Dr. Markandya's guidance, LEEC was available for consultation and advice, but analysis and the formulation of conclusions were the responsibility of country experts. In that perspective, agreements were signed in 1991 with the *Centre Ivoirien de Recherches Economiques et Sociales* (CIRES), led by Dr. Joseph Yao in Côte d'Ivoire, the *Instituto de Tecnologico Autonomo de Mexico* (ITAM), led by Dr. Juan Carlos Belausteguigoitia in Mexico, and the Thailand Development Research Institute (TDRI), led by Drs. Theodore Panayotou and Chalongphob Sussengkarn in Thailand. They completed the analysis by late 1991.

■ Scrutiny by an expert advisory group. Members were not bound to support WWF conclusions, but they would critique and advise on the methodology; preliminary reports from CIRES, ITAM, TDRI, and LEEC; final reports; and WWF's draft conclusions. The advisory group, selected to reflect a wide range of expert opinion, included Charles Abugre (Agency for Cooperation and Research in Development), Marcos Arruda (*Politicas Alternativas Para o Cone Sul*, Rio de Janeiro), Laurence Hausman (U.S. Agency for International Development), Manuel Montes (East-West Center), Konrad von Moltke (Dartmouth College), Michel Potier (Organization for Economic Cooperation and Development), and John Shilling (the World Bank).

On various issues, Robin Broad (American University) and Stanley Please (former vice president, the World Bank) gave valuable advice and shared their opinions. The advisory group reviewed and commented on all reports, analyses, and draft conclusions. It met on two occasions, in Divonne-les-Bains, France, in August 1991 and in Morges in November 1991.

■ Publication of this book, which contains a basic analysis of experience with structural adjustment, individual country analyses, overall analyses, WWF conclusions, and our recommendations for future positive use of structural adjustment measures. David Reed, Director of the WWF International Institutions Policy Program located in Washington, D.C., is both the technical coordinator of the project and principal author of this report. LEEC summarized the case studies presented here. Their full texts are available.

In initiating this project, WWF was aware not only that it involved major commitments of resources but also that the issue is of considerable interest to many institutions and agencies throughout the world. These issues do not seem to fall easily within the direct brief of the World Bank, the International Monetary Fund, or bilateral development agencies. But they do fall naturally into the public policy area of a global and autonomous nongovernmental organization such as WWF. In that perspective, WWF is happy to record its appreciation of the support given by the governments of Denmark, the Federal Republic of Germany, Italy, and the Netherlands, because these issues are intrinsic to the major problems of environment and development today and because this kind of study cannot be done without support.

Overall conduct of the work and formulation of conclusions are the sole responsibility of WWF. WWF will use this work as the basis for future policy development and case-study analysis.

The proposals made here regarding the future design and application of macroeconomic interventions such as structural adjustment illustrate the need for integrated action on a variety of principles. We hope they indicate how human needs can be brought into sustainable harmony with the conservation of nature and natural resources.

—K. LYONETTE
Director, Conservation Policy Division
World Wide Fund for Nature, WWF-International

STRUCTURAL ADJUSTMENT
AND THE ENVIRONMENT

INTRODUCTION

by David Reed

I n April 1980, the World Bank's first structural adjustment program, a $200 million loan to Turkey, became effective. Adjustment programs for Kenya and Bolivia, then for as many as a dozen other countries, received funding from the World Bank before the end of 1981. During the ensuing 10 years of adjustment lending, more than $28.5 billion flowed to 64 countries through 187 separate lending operations.[1] That as much as 25 percent of the Bank's annual loan portfolio was committed to adjustment packages reflects the importance of this new policy-based lending in Bank operations during the 1980s. Regional development banks and bilateral aid agencies, following World Bank priorities and policies, shifted their lending and grant-making activities accordingly to support structural reforms in selected countries during the decade.[2]

High interest rates, declining commodity prices, and internal and external imbalances in the industrialized societies created adverse economic conditions for the developing world by the beginning of the 1980s. In addition, developing countries were often beset by deeply rooted economic distortions and inefficiencies that had become widespread in their production, distribution, and financial systems. Faced with difficult international conditions, those structural weakness rendered many developing country economies increasingly dysfunctional in the global economy. In this context, structural adjustment lending sought to strengthen macroeconomic and supply response of the

1

developing countries as they reacted to these adversities. Extensive and often prolonged economic restructuring, whether initiated by countries themselves or under the tutelage of the World Bank, targeted correction of these deeply ingrained structural weaknesses.

Ten years later, however, a broad, often impassioned debate continues regarding the success of structural adjustment lending in stabilizing distressed economies and creating favorable conditions for longer-term economic growth. Proponents of adjustment, while recognizing the long-term, complex process involved in restructuring economies, hold up for comparison the grim social and economic conditions in countries that postponed or aborted adjustment programs and those that embarked on sustained restructuring efforts. Critics cite numerous examples of countries that faithfully pursued adjustment programs for five, even eight years, yet today remain marginal to the world economy, without short-term prospects for renewed economic vitality and burdened by seemingly insurmountable external debt.

The structural adjustment experience of the 1980s was obviously not limited to or synonymous with World Bank adjustment lending. Quite a number of countries, including the subjects of two case studies in this work, Mexico and Thailand, implemented comprehensive adjustment processes that were designed and driven by their own policy makers, not the World Bank. Mexico, one of the principal recipients of World Bank structural adjustment loans, received nine loans, including five sectoral adjustment loans of $500 million each that covered reforms in trade policy, finance, industry, and public enterprises.[3] Despite these staggering sums, the World Bank's contribution was primarily consolidating and expediting reform measures to which successive Mexican governments were committed. World Bank lending also had a minor part in consolidating the economic restructuring process undertaken by the government in Thailand in the early 1980s.[4] Their Bank funding was used more as a political lever to pressure recalcitrant officials resisting the reform process than as a decisive economic tool to bring about structural changes.

Whether its participation was decisive or peripheral, the World Bank, in conjunction with the International Monetary Fund, remained the driving force on a global level in facilitating and guiding economic restructuring in scores of developing countries. Structural adjustment became the lending vehicle by which the official financial institutions gained access to policy makers and, through conditionality, tried to induce profound changes in development policy and economic structures. Because of its determinant role on a global level and its often preponderant role within developing countries, the World Bank's experience is indicative of overall trends and contributions of the adjustment process in the 1980s.

One unquestioned shortcoming of policy lending sponsored by multilateral financial institutions and individual governments during the 1980s is its failure to address environmental deterioration that, when coupled with burgeoning populations, threatened to erode improvements in economic performance brought about by the restructuring process.

Clearly, however, adjustment lending in the 1980s was not intended to address the environmental dimension of development.[5] There are several basic reasons why the World Bank failed to incorporate environmental concerns into the design of policy-based lending.[6] First, the World Bank and other multilateral development banks did not view the environment as a priority investment area at the time. Borrowing countries had not requested financial support to deal with environmental problems; nor had public concern about the global environment reached the point at which policy changes were even considered necessary. In many quarters, environmental degradation was accepted as an inevitable outcome of the growth process.

Second, when a negative environmental impact was identified in a country or was associated with a specific development project, the prevalent assumption was that either inappropriate macroeconomic policy or a sectoral economic policy failure was the cause. Hence the Bank viewed the remedy far too simplistically—as a matter of correcting the economic failure, for instance, by changing the prevailing sectoral incentive structure or "getting the prices right." In essence, it was assumed that correct economic policy could address environmental problems.

A third reason for failing to integrate environmental concerns in adjustment lending is that environmental protection seemed to indicate the need for more budgetary outlays. Increased public expenditures to protect the environment were not acceptable because they would make achieving fiscal balance, a basic purpose of adjustment lending, more difficult. In short, environmental protection would have to wait until the structural adjustment programs helped improve a country's macroeconomic performance; then additional expenditures for the environment could be justified.

A fourth reason is that many quarters viewed macroeconomic crisis and environmental degradation as essentially unrelated problems that had to be treated with separate and essentially unrelated remedies. In consequence, prescribing correct macroeconomic policy for a distressed economy had to follow the logic and priorities of the discipline and should not be diluted by external factors such as environmental impacts.

These reasons, articulated by Bank staff, help explain the failure of the World Bank to anticipate and address the potential environmental impacts of policy-based lending. The underlying theme of this reasoning is that economic growth, unencumbered by ancillary concerns, remains the unquestioned imperative of development strategy and that the benefits derived from economic growth can best provide the means for addressing ancillary concerns, whatever they may be. In the ensuing chapters, the consequences of viewing development in this perspective will become more apparent.

This book focuses on the environmental impacts of structural adjustment in specific developing countries and assesses the contribution of policy-based lending to putting countries on a sustainable development path. But can structural adjustment lending be held accountable to and measured by these countries' environmental performance when the assumptions on which their programs were designed excluded environmental considerations? Is it appropriate to analyze this dimension of policy reform when adjustment programs never considered, not to mention correct, environmental problems? It is appropriate—indeed, urgent—that the international community does so. Economic adjustment programs, whether implemented with the financial support of official lending institutions or with a country's own resources, will remain the principal vehicle for restructuring struggling economies during the 1990s. Failure to understand the environmental impacts risks perpetuating in the 1990s the social and economic trends that have already generated environmental problems of crisis proportions around the globe. Neither humanity nor the planet can afford that risk.

In presenting this complex subject, WWF was immediately aware that an analysis of the environmental impacts of adjustment lending could not be separated from the economic and social impacts of policy-based lending. A decade of adjustment lending has clearly demonstrated that both economic changes and social dimensions of adjustment directly and indirectly influence the ensuing impacts of policy reforms on the natural environment. Consequently, to situate the environmental analysis in a broader context, we introduce this study with a brief review, presented in Chapter 1, of the economic conditions under which adjustment acquired the status of a global policy instrument in the 1980s. This brief review traces the genesis of adjustment lending and examines the intervention of the Bretton Woods institutions as they tried to address the deepening economic decline in the developing world during the 1980s through adjustment lending.

The second chapter presents an assessment of the adjustment lending as viewed by both the World Bank and critics. The World Bank viewpoint draws on five Bank studies. They use conventional economic criteria as their primary measure and assert that, although adjustment has taken longer than anticipated, the reform programs have contributed decisively to fostering growth in adjusting countries. This positive outlook is challenged by other analysts from both governments and community-based groups in adjusting countries. The criticisms they raise challenge the economic contributions of adjustment as well as the social and political impacts of economic restructuring experienced in many developing countries. The chapter closes with a reference to the failure of adjustment programs to consider either the environmental consequences or the impacts on the (non)sustainability of present development strategies.

The following three chapters present the case studies for Côte d'Ivoire, Mexico, and Thailand. The materials presented here are summaries of the research efforts carried out by local research institutes; the summaries were prepared by the London Environmental Economics Centre. The Centre also provided the methodological and technical coordination for the analytical efforts of the national research institutes in the three countries.

Chapter 6 sets forth conclusions drawn from the case studies. It examines the impacts of adjustment on the environment per se and discusses whether the economic restructuring process has helped place the economies of the three countries on a sustainable development path. In explaining how the development approaches have generated excessive and unnecessary environmental damage, the case studies pose the need to reform the basic approach to adjustment lending. The chapter examines the relationship between poverty and environmental deterioration as well as the role of the elites in implementing policies that do not promote environmental protection or sustainable development.

The book concludes with a series of recommendations categorized under development policy, institutional, and political reforms and changes needed within the international financial institutions. Taken as a whole, the recommendations require a fundamental reconceptualization of the purpose and design of adjustment programs to ensure that sustainability is the hallmark of future policy-based lending.

INTRODUCTION ENDNOTES

1. World Bank, *Adjustment Lending Policies for Sustainable Growth* (Washington, D.C., 1990), pp. 69-70.

2. World Bank, *Structural Adjustment Lending: A First Review of Experience* (Washington, D.C., 1986), pp. 78-79.

3. World Bank, *Adjustment Lending Policies for Sustainable Growth*, op. cit., pp. 69-78; World Bank, *Restructuring Economies in Distress* (Washington, D.C., 1991), pp. 509-519.

4. World Bank, *Program Performance Annual Report: First and Second Structural Adjustment Loans* (Washington, D.C., 1988).

5. Box 4.3, page 51, in the World Bank's publication, *Adjustment Lending Policies for Sustainable Growth,* op. cit., identifies seven SALS and SECALS in fiscal year 1989 that "contained conditions directly related to environmental management." The increased financial resources for environmental purposes reflects the growing international recognition of the urgent need to address environmental problems. However, the World Bank's posture regarding the potential environmental impacts of policy lending is expressed in the opening sentence of Box 4.3: "Although adjustment programs have not focused on environmental issues, most of them included measures that, on balance, appear more likely to help than to hurt the environment." This position is repeated in the most recent internal Bank evaluation of structural adjustment, *The Third Report on Adjustment Lending Private and Public Resources for Growth* (Washington, D.C., 1992), p. 24.

6. Interviews with World Bank staff, January-February 1992.

THE STRUCTURAL ADJUSTMENT EXPERIENCE OF THE 1980s

by David Reed

GENESIS OF ADJUSTMENT LENDING

The concept of structural adjustment as commonly used in the 1980s has its origins in the global economic events of 1973-1974 and the first oil shock. The 350 percent rise in oil prices hit developing country economies far more severely than it hit the 22 nations of the Organization of Economic Cooperation and Development (OECD). In many countries, for example, the cost of oil imports rose to one-fifth of total exports. The ensuing 1974-1975 recession led to a 10 percent contraction in world trade and a sharp decline in export prices of many commodities, thus aggravating the ability of many developing countries to meet outstanding financial obligations.[1] A significant, albeit temporary, increase in the volume of exports and improvement in terms of trade, coupled with inflation in OECD countries and a negative real interest rate during the late 1970s, prevented a further decline in economic conditions in many developing countries.[2] In keeping with its division of responsibility with Bretton Woods institutions, the International Monetary Fund (IMF) assumed near-exclusive responsibility during this period for providing short-term stabilization lending to help countries compensate for trade imbalances often caused by additional costs of imported energy sources.[3]

Their response to the difficult economic events of 1973-1974 reflected broader changes taking place in international financial relations.

First and foremost, the disequilibria for which IMF resources were being used were no longer caused primarily by factors internal to borrowing countries; increased drawdowns of IMF funds were required primarily to respond to exogenous factors over which most developing countries had little if any control. Second, the IMF soon ceased being the principal source of balance of payments (BoP) lending. By the mid-1970s, commercial banks, offering easy credit terms as they sought to recycle petrodollars, replaced the IMF, with its more stringent conditionality and more careful country analysis, as the principal lender for BoP problems. Between 1973 and 1981, private financial creditors increased their lending to non-oil-exporting developing countries sixfold, to more than $220 billion. Whereas 66 percent of less developed country debt was owed to official lenders in 1971, 70 percent was owed to commercial banks by 1981.[4]

By the end of the 1970s, additional external factors pushed the international financial system to the point of collapse. The second oil shock of 1979 hiked oil prices 130 percent between 1978 and 1980, again increasing the percentage of developing country exports needed to purchase imported oil. Further, from the late 1970s onward, most commodities exported by developing countries declined in value in relation to imported manufactured goods. This downward trend was typified by the 2.7 percent annual decline in the composite price indices of traded goods between 1980 and 1986 and reflected primarily declines in the real import purchasing power of export commodities and goods.

Growing pressure on the export earnings of most developing countries was aggravated by the monetary policy of the United States, which further stretched the ability of many developing countries to meet their international obligations. To finance that superpower's largest peacetime military build-up, the Reagan administration drew deeply on global savings during the early 1980s, eventually forcing the Federal Reserve Board to increase its discount rate to 16 percent. U.S. commercial lending rates quickly rose to over 18 percent, obliging Third World borrowers to increase significantly their budgetary allocations to service floating-rate notes denominated in dollars. While the costs of servicing outstanding debt increased, commercial credit to developing countries began to dry up.[5] In a few short years, commercial loans were no longer available to finance development projects or to refinance existing short-term obligations.

It is important to point out that internal and international pressures to expand and strengthen the role of military establishments in developing countries continued through most of the 1980s. Tying foreign aid and overseas development assistance to East-West superpower rivalry created an international incentive structure whose impact was to distort further the development policies and social relations of developing countries at the time, quite often to the economic and social detriment of the countries' most vulnerable social sectors.

These external factors intersected with internal economic distortions and political structures in ways that further undermined macroeconomic and social stability in many countries. Economic distortions woven into national economies during previous decades became increasingly apparent. Parastatals and public enterprises often ran at a loss and did not serve either consumers or the national economy. Inefficient financial institutions made loans at well below market rates and otherwise failed to protect financial resources. Banking regulations and marketing boards frequently reflected political pressures, not responsiveness to national and international prices. Internal terms of trade benefiting urban dwellers discouraged investment and expansion of the agricultural sector and contributed to deepening of rural poverty. In addition, public employment and services, expanded through the years in response to social and political pressures, had reached bloated and unsustainable levels in many countries. And military spending reached one and one-half times the level of spending for education and health for all developing countries in 1977.[6]

EFFORTS IN CRISIS MANAGEMENT

By the early 1980s, four major patterns emerged as developing countries struggled to repay debts contracted during the previous decade and to absorb the financial losses caused by falling terms of trade.[7] First, low-income countries, excluding China and India, cut imports 3.2 percent per year in the 1980s. Countries such as Nigeria, Yemen, and Sierra Leone experienced an annual negative growth in imports of over 10 percent while imports of the middle income countries grew at only 0.6 percent per year in the 1980s.[8] Second, while reducing imports, indebted countries tried to increase hard currency earnings by expanding exports. Export volume grew in Latin America and Asia but declined in

Africa in 1980-1985. Despite improvement in the volume of exports, declining terms of trade eroded the total value of export earnings.

The third response in the early 1980s was to seek an increase in official development assistance (ODA). ODA doubled in total nominal flows between 1975 and 1980, but then the rate of growth declined in the first half of the 1980s as OECD countries struggled to deal with their own domestic budgetary problems.[9] Though many developing countries relied initially on external aid flows to finance consumption and investment, that option soon proved inadequate to meet the rising pressure on resources exerted by growing debt service requirements.

A fourth element of response to these pressures was the change in government spending priorities. Often in response to IMF pressure, debt repayment remained a priority, and, as a consequence, internal investment and social expenditures began to fall.[10] For domestic political reasons, many governments preferred to maintain current expenses, notably for public employment, while dramatically reducing capital spending, particularly for infrastructure maintenance and improvements. In a study of 15 countries, the World Bank found that as interest payments jumped to over 40 percent of central government spending, real capital spending fell over 35 percent in the early 1980s. It is worth noting that defense spending suffered significantly smaller reductions than social expenditures and investment.[11] To varying degrees, social expenditures fell in virtually all countries during the early 1980s; the most vulnerable sectors of many societies often experienced the deepest impact of these reductions.[12]

Because these efforts in crisis management failed to staunch the economic decline in many countries, groups rooted in the poor and middle-income sectors questioned whether the prescribed modernization strategy pursued over the several past decades was built on flawed premises. A frequent expression of discontent was: Would pursuit of the development strategy, within the existing configuration of North-South relations, condemn the developing world to perpetual subservience and exploitation? Further, would continued international support for elites, who frequently were antidemocratic, forestall long overdue social and economic reforms demanded by the poor and the middle class? Replacement of numerous military regimes by civilian governments during the 1980s may have attenuated demands for democratization in some countries. But positive political change did not resolve broader economic questions regarding the viability of the development strategy still being pursued in many struggling developing countries.

DIRECT INTERVENTION OF THE BRETTON WOODS INSTITUTIONS

In keeping with its primary function to stabilize the international financial system, the IMF responded to the evolving crisis by widening the range of financing facilities available to member countries. Although drawdowns on credit tranche, followed by the Supplementary Facility, assumed the largest proportion of IMF lending in the early 1980s, the little-used Compensatory Financing Facility covering export shortfalls became an important source of financing. The existing Extended Fund Facilities (EFF) were little used in the mid-1970s, but with the formation of two new EFF programs in 1979 and 1980, they became an additional capital source for lower- and lower middle-income countries.[13] By 1981, increased IMF disbursements represented 33 percent of low-income developing countries' current account deficits. Further, in addition to creating new facilities, IMF temporarily loosened its conditions for borrowers and more frequently overlooked conditionality lapses, a move strongly resisted in previous years. Included in the relaxation of conditionality were acceptance of longer-term program periods, frontloading of loans, and eased requirements for currency devaluation.

Even this broader financial support could not stem the stagnation and decline sweeping much of the developing world. Dwindling financial reserves, uncontrolled inflation, rising debt obligations, declining productivity, declining export earning capacity, and growing social instability typified conditions in scores of countries. The effectiveness of the World Bank's ongoing project lending operations was clearly threatened. Budget reductions were forcing postponement of project investments, and established economic structures could no longer guarantee adequate return on investments. Albeit somewhat reluctantly, the World Bank decided it had little choice but to commit its own resources to help correct the pervasive macroeconomic imbalances.[14]

The Bank's initial approach to structural adjustment lending contained two basic components. In tandem with the IMF, the first component was to stabilize the country's macroeconomic situation by relieving pressure on the BoP. Structural adjustment loans (SALs) were front-loaded, quick-disbursing loans that helped ease the short-term pressure on available capital. This quick infusion of resources was accompanied by immediate measures to reduce domestic demand. Demand reduction was accomplished by drastic cutbacks in public spending and through monetary policies designed to restrain the money supply. In coordination with the IMF, demand reduction was strengthened by realignment of the national currency with international markets. Through devaluation, the country's exports would become more competitive, import costs would rise, and their volume would decline. These changes would thus reduce pressure on foreign reserves.

The second component of World Bank policy lending was designed to increase overall economic efficiency and promote growth objectives by reforming macroeconomic policy and strengthening national institutions. This growth objective was an essential counterweight to the immediate contractionary impact expected from the demand reduction activities required by the IMF and included in World Bank stabilization programs. Admittedly, this second component would work more slowly than stabilization; it would also require policy and institutional reforms on both a macroeconomic and a sectoral level. In short, strengthening the supply response of distressed economies would require major changes in the structure and functioning of virtually all essential sectors of the economy and of corresponding national management institutions. It was this supply component of policy lending, placed under the purview of the World Bank, that contrasted structural adjustment lending with the stabilization policies of the 1970s.

In its first efforts in adjustment lending in the early 1980s, the World Bank encouraged reforms to expand the tradeable goods sector of national economies by increasing efficiencies when the country enjoyed comparative advantages. This reform effort included reducing export taxes and removing import quotas, which previously impeded competition on the global market and created internal economic distortions. Another major feature of early adjustment programs was the reform of public enterprises. From parastatal agricultural marketing agencies to heavy industries and utilities, SALs sought to reduce public expenditures and increase the economic efficiency of often bloated, wasteful enterprises.

The short- and medium-term nature of the early SALs and that of many IMF programs was based on the far too optimistic expectation that the global economy would improve in the near future and thereby contribute to economic recovery in the majority of developing countries. This optimism was reflected in the World Bank's *World Development Report 1980*, which provided extensive projections on trade, fiscal, and economic recovery during the 1980s.[15] As one Bank official admitted, "In 1980, the problem was seen as a medium-term issue, one which many at that time thought would have been resolved by the mid-1980s."[16] Mexico's default on its commercial debt obligations had made it clear by 1982 that the global economic problems were not transitory. Bank staff soon concluded that even BoP improvements, part of the original rationale for adjustment lending, would depend largely on domestic policy and institutional reforms rather than result from an amelioration of the global economic picture. For many in the Bank, this change in perspective was a mixed blessing. On the one hand, adjustment lending could become "a fundamental instrument for dialogue between the Bank and the country on various aspects of development policy and on the nature and scope of change to be supported."[17] But on the other hand, rekindling economic growth primarily, if not exclusively, through domestic structural reforms would require fundamental and sustained reform efforts that would be fraught with obstacles and many unknowns for both borrowers and lenders. After extensive discussion among its shareholders and in spite of the uncertainties, the World Bank made a major commitment of resources to increase support of policy-based lending.[18]

This shift toward a longer-term restructuring effort prompted greater clarification of World Bank and IMF functions in the adjustment process; the Fund would continue to give priority to short-term loan support to stabilize economies. Its primary focus would be to demand constraint measures and currency devaluations. World Bank SALs, while retaining the stabilization component, would focus on restructuring economies through institutional and policy reforms in the medium term to stimulate the medium-term supply response. To reach this objective, the Bank expanded the focus of adjustment from macroeconomic reforms to sectoral reforms, sectoral adjustment loans or SECALs, which, although introduced in 1980, were not a lending vehicle of major importance in the early 1980s. SECALs sought to promote the supply response within specific stagnant or inefficient sectors and thereby

TURKEY: THE SAL TESTING GROUND

Turkey received the first structural adjustment loan (SAL) in 1980. But in mid-1980, the country began to switch to sector adjustment loans (SECALs). By the end of 1990, its 14 adjustment loans totaled $3 billion, including both SALs and SECALs.[1]

After rapid economic growth in the early 1970s, Turkey encountered severe internal and external imbalances, mainly as a result of its continued expansionary policies following the first oil crisis. In 1979, public sector borrowing requirements reached 8.5 percent of gross national product (GNP), compared with only 2 percent in 1973.[2] The deficit rose from 55 billion Turkish lira in 1978 to 138 billion in 1979. The current account deficit jumped from $1.4 billion in 1979 to $3.4 billion in 1980. The foreign exchange reserves were soon depleted, weakening Turkey's ability to import goods essential for industrial production. In 1980 U.S. dollars, the value of Turkey's imports dropped from $9.5 billion in 1977 to $7.2 billion in 1978 and down to $6.4 billion in 1979.[3] The real GNP growth rate fell from a positive 2.9 percent in 1978 to a negative 0.4 percent in 1979 and a negative 1.1 percent in 1980. At the same time, the shortage of inputs drove the general price level up more than 70 percent. These macroeconomic disequilibria contributed to the country's social disturbances.[4]

Faced with overwhelming economic and social difficulties, the government embarked on a comprehensive structural adjustment program in 1980 with a view to restoring economic growth and balancing its external account in the medium term. Whereas most adjustment programs during the 1980s were prescribed by the International Monetary Fund (IMF) in coordination with the World Bank, the government essentially initiated the structural reforms, which IMF and the Bank agreed upon later. Major structural changes, begun in 1980 and expanded over time, took place in several areas:[5]

- *Exchange rate policy.* In real terms, the Turkish lira was depreciated 33 percent in January 1980 and an average of about 4 percent per year from 1981 to 1985.
- *Foreign trade and investment.* Quantitative restrictions on imports and exports were abolished and controls on foreign direct investment substantially eased.
- *Exchange regulations.* Restrictions on foreign exchange transactions were relaxed, and exporting enterprises were allowed to retain a much greater proportion of export earnings.
- *Interest rate policy.* Time deposit rates and lending rates were liberalized, with a ceiling on the former to be set by the central bank every three months to adjust for inflation.
- *Taxation.* The taxation system was rationalized with a reduction in overall personal income taxes and unification of corporate taxes.

- *Public sector.* Preferential financial treatment of state economic enterprises was almost eliminated and their privatization legally authorized.
- *Financial sector.* Banking reform was initiated to reflect costs, and agricultural subsidies were sharply reduced.
- *Wage policy.* Centrally determined wage increments were enforced by the public sector and used as guidelines by the private sector to adjust for inflation.

Turkey's adjustment effort was immediately supported by the Bretton Woods institutions. In April 1980, the Bank approved its first SAL for $200 million.[6] Just two months later, an IMF stand-by arrangement for Special Drawing Rights (SDR) $1,250 million followed. From 1980 to 1985, the Bank provided $1.6 billion in SALs and IMF provided SDR 1.5 billion.[7] Between 1985 and 1989, Turkey received $1.3 billion of SECALS from the Bank.[8] They were designed to support the reforms in agriculture (1985), finance (1986), and energy (1987). The reforms focused on institutional and macroeconomic distortions within each sector. In agriculture, for example, the reforms sought to reduce subsidies on agricultural products and inputs, liberalize agricultural pricing policy, and deregulate agricultural markets.

Consistent with Bank standard practice, both SAL and SECAL proceeds were disbursed in several tranches for general imports after Turkish authorities met specified conditions. Imports were subject to bank guidelines that prohibited importation of luxury consumer products, military weapons, and other items. Using adjustment loans to finance general imports, the Turkish government could carry out the economically costly and politically sensitive adjustment measures while meeting its balance of payments difficulties and minimizing losses in both output and employment.

—*Fulai Sheng*

TURKEY: THE SAL TESTING GROUND ENDNOTES

1. World Bank, *Adjustment Lending Policies for Sustainable Growth* (Washington, D.C., 1990), p. 77.

2. George Kopits, "Turkey's Adjustment Experience, 1980-85," *Adjustment with Growth* (Washington, D.C.: World Bank, 1987).

3. World Bank, *World Tables 1991* (Baltimore: Johns Hopkins University Press, 1991).

4. Kopits, op. cit.

5. Ibid.

6. World Bank, *Adjustment Lending Policies for Sustainable Growth*, op. cit.

7. Kopits, op. cit.

8. World Bank, *Adjustment Lending Policies for Sustainable Growth*, op. cit.

expand the volume and competitiveness of tradeable goods. Reforming the agricultural sector, often disregarded for years, was a priority for many countries. Reforms encouraged improving marketing systems, providing new incentives, and increasing credit availability. Reforming the manufacturing sector received attention during the mid- and late-1980s, with particular emphasis on removing subsidies and increasing efficiency. Toward the end of the 1980s, reform of the financial sector became increasingly important as privatization of state-owned enterprises gained prominence in strategies to attract foreign capital.

In keeping with the World Bank's shifting perspective on the internal causes of macroeconomic disequilibria, SALs were stretched from the original 12-18 months to 3-5 years so that institutional and policy reforms could take root.[19] In addition, although loans continued to be frontloaded to provide substantial resources at the beginning of the loan period, more complex and stringent conditionality was attached to the first tranche. Kenya exemplifies this trend: its first SAL in 1980 had 9 conditions; the second SAL in 1982 had 42. The average SAL during the 1980s carried some 40 conditions or stipulated policy actions, with more conditions attached to SALs than to SECALs. Further, the number of conditions increased from an average of 27 in 1985 to 56 in 1989.[20]

One of the most important changes in SAL design during the 1980s was acceptance, at least nominally, of the need to lessen the impact of adjustment policies on the most vulnerable sectors of adjusting country populations. In the early- and mid-1980s, priority was given to the productive sectors able to improve BoP. Consequently, human resource sectors were essentially ignored. With the increase in protest from popular groups and nongovernmental organizations against the social costs of adjustment, SAL-sponsored reform measures were put in jeopardy in several countries. After protracted and seemingly futile efforts to persuade the IMF to modify its adjustment policies, the United Nations Children's Fund went public with its carefully documented case studies detailing the impact of adjustment on the well-being of children.[21] Its theme of "adjustment with a human face" gained rapid acceptance among organizations concerned with the social dislocations occurring as a result of, and concurrent with, adjustment programs.[22] In response, the World Bank included social mitigation components in some SALs; in other countries such as Bolivia and Ghana, it designed separate projects in loan packages to reduce the "transitional costs" of adjustment. In other cases, SAL conditionality required reallocation of public spending to "priority sectors that most benefit the poor." Nonetheless, the World Bank continued to emphasize the point that adjustment programs necessarily carried transitional costs (mostly for the poor) that had to be accepted before economic growth and enhanced efficiency would generate broader economic improvements.[23]

Although SALs underwent these changes during the 1980s as a result of public pressure, they remained largely instruments designed by World Bank staff in consultation with a small group of national-level policymakers. Bank staff could usually reach agreement on policy changes with this small group, but their policy prescriptions and institutional reforms were frequently ignored, if not blocked, by other ministries and public opposition once their potential impact became known. Late in the decade, Bank staff came to recognize that "ownership" of adjustment programs was critical to program success and, as a consequence, sought broader government support before reform programs became effective.[24]

During a full decade of adjustment lending, the World Bank had made 187 policy loans. The process began with 21 loans in 1980-1982, expanded to an average of 17 loans annually between 1983 and 1985, and then averaged 29 loans in the years thereafter. Sub-Saharan Africa (SSA) received 45 percent of the SALs, Asia 11 percent, Latin America and the Caribbean (LAC) 26 percent, and Europe-Middle East-North Africa (EMENA) 18 percent. In terms of resource commitments, LAC received 36 percent, Asia 15 percent, and EMENA and SSA, approximately 25 percent each. Thus, though SSA countries received the largest proportion of SALs, their average loan was smaller than those received by countries in other regions, in keeping with the SSA countries' size. Of the total 187 loans, including SECALs, a little more than one-third went to only 9countries, including Turkey (10), Mexico (9), Ghana (8) and Jamaica (8).[25]

Chapter One Endnotes

1. William R. Cline and Sidney Weintraub, eds., *Economic Stabilization in Developing Countries* (Washington, D.C.: Brookings Institution, 1981), pp. 53-62.

2. Richard Cooper, *Economic Stabilization and Debt in Developing*

Countries (Cambridge: MIT Press, 1992), p. 11.

3. Paul Mosley, Jane Harrigan, and John Tage, *Aid and Power: The World Bank and Policy-based Lending* (New York: Toutledge, 1991), pp. 27-56.

4. Joyce Kolko, *Restructuring the World Economy* (New York: Random House, 1988), p. 47.

5. Ibid, p. 42.

6. World Bank, *World Development Report 1980* (Washington, D.C., 1980), p. 29.

7. Cooper, op. cit., pp. 1-48, provides an insightful discussion regarding efforts undertaken by different countries to address negative external conditions.

8. World Bank, *World Development Report 1990* (Washington, D.C. 1990), pp. 204-05.

9. Ibid, p. 214.

10. Per Pinstrup-Andersen, "The Impact on Government Expenditure," in Giovanni Andrea Cornia, Richard Jolly, and Frances Stewart, eds., *Adjustment with a Human Face, Vol. 1: Protecting the Vulnerable and Promoting Growth* (Oxford: Clarendon, 1987), pp. 73-89.

11. World Bank, *World Development Report 1988* (Washington, D.C., 1988), p. 113.

12. Giovanni Andrea Cornia, "Adjustment Policies 1980-1985: Effects of Child Welfare," in Cornia *et al.,* op. cit., pp. 48-72.

13. Graham Bird, "Relationships, Resource Uses and the Conditionality Debate," in Tony Killick, ed., *The Quest for Economic Stabilization: The IMF and the Third World* (London: Heinneman Educational Books, 1984), pp. 145-82.

14. Mosley *et al.,* op. cit., pp. 32-56.

15. World Bank, *World Development Report 1980,* op. cit., p. 3.

16. John Holson, "An Overview of Structural Adjustment" (Paper delivered at the International Seminar on Structural Adjustment Policies in the Third World, Dhaka, January 1990), p. 1.

17. World Bank, *Adjustment Lending: An Evaluation of Ten Years of Experience* (Washington, D.C., 1988), p. 56.

18. Mosley *et al.,* op. cit., pp. 32-38.

19. World Bank, *Structural Adjustment Lending: A First Review of Experience* (Washington, D.C., 1988), p. 5.

20. Elliott Berg and Alan Batchelder, "Structural Adjustment Lending: A Critical View," Washington, D.C., 1984, pp. 38-46; World Bank, *Adjustment Lending Policies for Sustainable Growth* (Washington, D.C., 1990), pp. 36-39, 55.

21. Giovanni Andrea Cornia, "Adjustment with a Human Face: A UNICEF Record and Perspective on the 1980s," Milan, 1990.

22. Cornia *et al.,* op. cit.

23. Transitional costs is used by the World Bank in its evaluation to acknowledge the impacts of adjustment programs on the vulnerable sectors of an adjusting country. See, for example, World Bank, *Adjustment Lending Policies for Sustainable Growth*, op. cit., p. 39.

24. See Robin Broad, *Unequal Alliance: The World Bank, the International Monetary Fund, and the Philippines*, University of California, Berkeley, 1988, for an excellent country case study; Holson, op. cit., p. 9.

25. World Bank, *Adjustment Lending Policies for Sustainable Growth*, op. cit., pp. 72-78.

DIVERGING VIEWS ON THE ADJUSTMENT DECADE

by David Reed

I t is widely accepted that postponing or refusing to restructure badly distorted economies would have pushed scores of countries even further into financial insolvency and many more people into poverty. Failure to undertake adjustment would have further distanced many countries from creditors whose capital was needed for economic growth. By the end of the adjustment decade, it was clear that countries that postponed revising their development policies and overhauling institutional structures paid a much higher price in the long run. The frequently cited case of Peru, which refused to embark on policy and institutional reforms for many years, provides stark evidence of the longer-term costs of vacillation.

But the contribution of structural adjustment to ensuring long-term economic growth in developing countries is neither uniform nor unequivocal. In fact, the economic contribution of adjustment programs remains one of the most controversial aspects of the decade of adjustment. Despite their potential institutional bias, the World Bank's assessments are the most comprehensive and exhaustive analytical reviews available. For this reason, these studies are central to understanding the impacts of adjustment lending. Material in the first part of this chapter is drawn from five Bank studies to provide an overview of its institutional perspective on the economic contributions of adjustment lending.[1]

Contributions to Improving Growth Rates

A prevalent conclusion of the studies regarding the overall contribution of adjustment programs could be summarized as follows: "Among countries requiring adjustment, those that have carried out major adjustments have performed better on average in terms of their aggregate economic activity than those that have not.... There is a general and positive connection between adjustment lending and this relative improvement, but the connection is not a tight one and performance varies substantially among the loan recipients."[2] When examining the contribution of adjustment lending to "sustainable growth" and using improvement in savings ratios, investment ratios, and export ratios as its primary indicators of structural change, World Bank studies are more cautious:

> Simple comparisons show that the growth performance of [early intensive-adjustment lending] countries improved relative to other countries, but this effect was statistically significant only when comparing 1985-1988 with 1981-1984. The adjustment lending programs usually increased the ratios of domestic saving and exports to [GDP, or gross domestic product] but reduced the average ratio of investments to GDP, even after explicitly controlling for external shocks, external financing, initial conditions, and determinants of the demand for adjustment programs—with important differences across countries.[3]

The tentativeness of the Bank's assessments diminishes over time. For example, in a study released in 1992, the World Bank categorically states the positive contributions of its policy-based lending to promoting economic recovery:

> Both middle- and low-income countries in the intensive adjustment group had, by the second half of the 1980s, gotten back to the growth rates achieved in the 1970s.... [T]he middle-income countries enjoyed growth four percentage points higher than would otherwise have

occurred, and the low-income group had growth two percentage points higher. As in the 1970s, however, the low-income group was barely growing in per capita terms. Adjustment lending helped secure a recovery for the low-income group, but did not solve the countries' long-run development problems.[4]

Although it has taken far longer than anticipated, the rekindling of growth in many developing countries provides the most important verification for the Bank that its policy-based lending is achieving its stated purposes. This criterion, the single most important indicator of economic well-being, is regarded as the foundation for the alleviation of poverty and for improvements in the standard of living.

Contributions to Effecting Macroeconomic Reforms

First and foremost, the Bank sought to correct a country's macroeconomic imbalances, then to effect sectoral reforms. Efforts to correct macroeconomic imbalances drew on two principal economic instruments: fiscal policy and trade policy. In reestablishing macroeconomic equilibrium, fiscal policy received immediate attention because growing fiscal deficits "have adverse implications for three key macroeconomic targets: debt, inflation, and the growth rate of the economy."[5] The quickest, although not least painful, way of correcting fiscal imbalances has usually been through major reduction in domestic demand, primarily through reduced public expenditures. The ultimate objective was to restore economic growth per capita as conventionally measured.

The 1992 Bank study on adjustment asserts the point that fiscal reforms have generated significant benefits for adjustment countries: "Between the early and late 1980s, average fiscal deficits in the intensive adjustment lending group declined from almost 5 to 3 percent of GDP in the middle-income countries and from over 8 to 5.5 percent of GDP in low-income countries."[6]

What is of particular significance is that the depth and breadth of demand reduction to ease pressure on budget deficits were central in determining not only the short-term reduction in government expenditures but also whether savings and investment, on which subsequent economic growth would depend, would be negatively affected. In this regard, the Bank has recognized that "short-term considerations have dominated the [fiscal] policy measures much to the prejudice of medium-term supply expansion." As a consequence, "the short-term impact of budgetary retrenchment has generally been recessionary, with a fall in investment and growth."[7] While leading to improved allocation of investment resources, this approach generally led to significant cutbacks in public investment programs. As the Bank recognized after a full decade of promoting stringent fiscal adjustment, "In some countries the sharp decline in public investment may be leading to serious infrastructure bottlenecks to development."[8] Further aggravating the impact of demand reduction on savings and investment was the inability of some countries to increase tax revenues through accompanying fiscal reforms because of deep-seated institutional weaknesses.

The second major component of reforms to correct macroeconomic imbalances was trade policy. With unsustainable current account deficits and diminished access to external finance, governments tried to shift resources to the tradeable goods sector. The basic objective of reforming trade regimes was to increase that sector's production efficiency to generate increased foreign currency earnings. Bank-financed adjustment programs sought to improve export performance by devaluing currency and removing export restrictions. Restrictions on imports, specifically those designed to bolster production of export commodities and to reduce the costs and price distortions on inputs for domestic production, were frequently lifted under adjustment lending programs.

A World Bank study on adjustment lending offers a succinct summary: "Overall, implementation of trade policy reform has been moderately significant."[9] Although the contents and results of specific trade reform programs varied significantly among the 24 countries sampled in the study, improvements were noted in placing national currencies in line with their value on international markets and generally reducing restrictions on exports. The study's assessment continues: "Given the strong emphasis on trade policy under adjustment lending, one might expect greater reforms of trade regimes than actually occurred during this period. In particular, four factors have constrained reform: macroeconomic instability, inadequate conviction concerning the benefits of reform and vested interests against reform, weak capacity for implementation, and conflicts in design."[10]

In comparing the first half of the 1980s to the second half, the Bank documents an improvement of almost 8 percent in the export performance as a share of gross domestic product in middle-income adjusting countries. In low-income countries, however, improvement of export performance during that same period is virtually negligible.[11]

Despite the challenges in effecting policy changes in many countries, the Bank attributes improvement in overall economic performance to the high success rate in the countries' respecting conditions of adjustment loans:

> For [intensive adjustment lending countries], the average share of loan conditions fully or substantially implemented by first tranche release was close to 85 percent of all conditions for both low- and middle-income countries. Moreover, there is a strong statistical association between the degree of conditionality implementation and lower fiscal deficits, lower foreign exchange premia, and lower inflation in 1986–1990.
>
> These results indicate that adjustment lending was associated with good policy change, and they support the view that the gains from adjustment in middle- and low-income countries are due to improved policy.12

Contributions to Correcting Sectoral Deficiencies

Challenges to correcting macroeconomic performance extend to reforming central sectors of nations' economies. Here the impact on three sectors, manufacturing, agricultural, and public enterprise, is briefly reviewed.

Manufacturing

Improvement of the industrial sector is central to the "export-led" development strategy underlying the Bank's approach to adjustment lending in the 1980s. An important conclusion of the World Bank studies regarding the contribution of trade reform is that "over time," improvements in the export of manufactured goods, as opposed to primary products and services, made the most significant contribution to export performance.[13] Largely as a result of the decision by policy makers in adjusting countries to support the industrial sector, the World Bank concludes that even during the global recession of 1982-1983, "the

CONDITIONALITIES OF ADJUSTMENT LENDING

After more than a decade of sustained adjustment lending by the World Bank, the issue of conditionality still creates heated debate. On the one hand, conditionality is an important instrument for the Bank to improve both the design and effectiveness of its adjustment programs. Adjustment loans are generally disbursed in several tranches conditional upon the timely fulfillment of preagreed policy targets, thus providing an incentive for sustained commitment to structural reforms. But on the other hand, conditions attached to adjustment loans can be politically sensitive, socially destabilizing, and institutionally overtaxing, and implementing conditions may be extremely difficult.

Imposition of conditionality is certainly justified from a lender's point of view. First, by imposing conditionality, the Bank can help formulate policy changes in recipient countries that lack the institutional capacity to design comprehensive adjustment programs.

Second, when recipient countries initiate policy reforms, imposition of conditionality enables the bank to provide advice and consolidate the reforms in a contractual form.

Third, and most important, tranche release of adjustment loans contingent on fulfillment of preagreed conditions serves as a lever for implementing adjustment programs. For example, disbursement of a structural adjustment loan (SAL) may be conditioned upon completion of a 20 percent currency devaluation. If this condition is not met within the agreed time, the Bank and the borrowing government meet to resolve the difficulties prior to release of subsequent tranches.

Although specific terms and conditions have evolved over time and necessarily vary from country to country, key conditions may be broadly grouped under six major policy areas:

- *Trade policy.* Adopting a competitive real exchange rate and lifting export restrictions to encourage exports; reducing quantitative restrictions on imports and cutting tariffs to strengthen the international competitiveness of domestic industry.
- *Fiscal policy.* Reducing and eliminating fiscal deficits by contraction of public expenditure; increasing prices in the public sector to cover costs and raise revenues; reforming the tax system to improve the efficiency of raising revenues and create new sources of revenue.
- *Public enterprises.* Cutting public investment and shifting resources to infrastructure and social sectors; reforming public enterprises to improve efficiency and profitability; closing or privatizing

unprofitable public enterprises to reduce the government's fiscal burden.

- *Financial sector.* Restructuring institutions to facilitate resource mobilization; improving regulatory framework to restore public confidence; relaxing interest rate ceilings and reserve requirements and diminishing the role of credit allocation to provide incentives for efficient use of resources.
- *Industrial policy.* Reducing protection to make the industrial sector more competitive internationally; liberalizing price controls to improve resource allocation; providing investment incentives for producing domestic value added; devaluating the currency to develop an export-oriented strategy.
- *Agricultural policy.* Adjusting exchange rates and removing industrial protection to eliminate the bias against agriculture; liberalizing agricultural prices; funding agricultural research and improving infrastructure; deregulating agricultural trade to smooth the circulation of agricultural inputs and products.

Although the effectiveness of adjustment programs may be enhanced because of conditionality, implementation of conditions has not been easy. According to a Bank study, nearly 75 percent of all adjustment loans experienced delays in tranche releases owing to fulfillment of conditions, and 40 percent of the conditions were not fully met while the loan was in effect.[1] At least three major factors complicate enforcement of conditions: political sensitivities, social instability, and institutional constraints. Take political sensitivity first. The liberalization of food prices, for example, is often strongly resisted by urban dwellers, who are strongly represented in the political constituency of the government. Second, contraction of public expenditures, which reduces social services, often leads to social discontent that can threaten survival of the borrowing government. Third, too many detailed conditions that find their way into adjustment lending contracts often go beyond the implementation capacity of the borrowers. They also make the conditions appear unnecessarily harsh, rigid, and socially less acceptable.

—Fulai Sheng

CONDITIONALITIES OF ADJUSTMENT LENDING ENDNOTE

1. World Bank, *Problems and Issues in Structural Adjustment* (Washington, D.C., 1990), pp. 40, 42.

manufacturing sector did not shrink relative to the rest of the economy, so in this sense the adjustment costs for manufacturers were contained. The exception was Africa, where rapid deindustrialization took place. Overall, manufacturing value added rebounded in 1984-1986, but in Africa recovery was very slight and growth rates remained negative."[14] The trend in Latin America was just the opposite; though countries of that region experienced deindustrialization during the 1970s, manufacturing went from "a lagging to a leading sector" during the adjustment years.[15] Industrial expansion continued in Asia, northern Africa, and the Mediterranean.

Despite this indicator of positive economic change, it is difficult, as World Bank observers acknowledge, to attribute performance in different regions or even individual countries exclusively to their participation in adjustment programs. A comparison of 15 adjusting countries to 50 developing countries shows that the differences in industrial performance between the groups are "very minor."[16]

Agricultural Policy

Many in the World Bank welcomed agricultural sectoral lending as an opportunity to correct polices that had strongly favored industrial growth to the prejudice of the agricultural sector for several decades. Unfavorable internal terms of trade, taxation of agricultural production, and low agricultural commodity prices in many developing countries resulted in declining rates of agricultural growth. A primary short-term objective of agricultural sectoral adjustment loans was to correct artificially depressed agricultural prices and other sectoral biases. Though it recognized that price corrections could improve efficiency, the Bank sought, in the medium term, to promote policies that would increase agricultural growth rates and thus deliveries to both domestic and international markets.

Recognizing that adjustment policies would require an extended time period, particularly in sectors in which pervasive government intervention had been the rule, a recent World Bank study recognizes that "agricultural adjustment has mixed results in the short run. The evidence on the relation between adjustment operations and agricultural growth is ambiguous."[17] Bank staff identify the "failure to dismantle the old [governmental] apparatus"[18] still used to set commodity prices, to produce and set prices of inputs such as fertilizers, and to establish levels of food subsidies as the principal barrier to effective agricultural reform. These institutional blockages are further complicated by the oligopsonic control of state marketing boards and the weak land tenure regimes needed to expand agricultural production. While not questioning the need to stabilize prices of food commodities to guarantee availability to popular sectors, the World Bank assessment challenges the pervasiveness and excessive presence of subsidies and regulation. These regulatory mechanisms depressed the agricultural sector in favor of the urban middle class and elites for extended periods. Without strong governmental commitment to reduce its role in the agricultural sector, sectoral reforms encouraged through adjustment lending remained hampered in engendering long-term improvements.

Public Enterprise

Public enterprises became a focal point of World Bank sectoral lending in the second half of the 1980s because the efficiency and economic contribution of a great many of those enterprises had fallen far below profitability and original expectations. Internal business mismanagement and factors external to individual enterprises (including macroeconomic instability, unpredictable national budgeting processes, and easy access to concessional lending) undermined the original catalytic role expected of many state enterprises in promoting economic development. Faced with the urgent need to reduce aggregate demand, public enterprises were a principal target in fiscal policy reforms and subsequent sectoral lending.

Known as public enterprise reform loans (PERLS), reforms sought three basic changes: reducing the breadth of public enterprise activity to focus on areas most suitable for government economic intervention and to open more sectors to private sector activity, improving government institutions responsible for managing or rehabilitating its enterprises, and privatizing enterprises in areas in which the private sector could function dynamically and efficiently.

Given the fact that PERLs have been in place for only a short time, results are still inconclusive:

> Progress in these fields is slow and subject to wide variation from country to country. Across the board, but especially in the institutional realm, much remains to be done. There is little information on the performance of firms after they have been

divested and disturbingly little evidence that gains in efficiency have been responsible for the perceived improvement in the financial situation of many enterprises.[19]

Data remain sketchy on whether divestiture has improved efficiency of enterprises now privately owned. The Bank assessment does recognize improvements in stabilizing and often reducing personnel, preventing creation of new public enterprises, and implementing institutional reforms in monitoring and information gathering about enterprise performance. The Bank concludes that continued improvements in the sector remain dependent on strengthening governmental institutional and managerial capability.

The Bank's Conclusion: Stay the Course on Adjustment

These observations from World Bank studies are necessarily limited, but they reflect the Bank's growing confidence in the economic impact of policy-based lending. The criteria used to assess the adjustment lending impacts are primarily conventional measures of economic growth and efficiency. The Bank's analysis associates adjustment with both higher growth rates in middle- and low-income countries and improved policy performance that it believes will help sustain growth in coming years. Aggregate economic improvement for many low-income countries, particularly in Sub-Saharan Africa is viewed by the Bank as "disappointing" but is considered as better than in countries that "avoided reform, or exited from adjustment programs."[20]

Relative to earlier studies, the Bank's more recent analyses give greater emphasis to the impacts of adjustment programs on the poor. Although the studies assert that in the medium term the "poor gain from adjustment policies," they recognize the fact that recessions associated with adjustment "often cause temporary welfare declines for some."[21] The Bank acknowledges that more needs to be done to understand and reduce the impact of adjustment on the poor. In this regard, it identifies restructuring public expenditures to increase investments in human capital development and strengthen social services. Another area identified by the Bank as needing improved program design is the reduction of transitional costs for the poor, for example, by maintaining the earning power of the poor sectors. Despite the admitted shortcomings, the Bank's bedrock conclusion regarding the impact of adjustment programs on the poor is that "adjustment is much better for the poor than nonadjustment, and that distributional effects of well-designed policies often favor the poor."[22]

Discussion of the impact of external factors on the success of adjustment programs is limited although a recent Bank study gives considerable attention to analyzing the lack of external investment, the "investment lag," that has accompanied the implementation of policy reforms in adjusting countries. Bank studies explain that in the initial phase, a contraction is usually experienced and is then followed by "relative stagnation" in the level of investment. Yet the Bank points out that investment, particularly in middle-income countries, increases once the economy stabilizes and policy reforms take hold. The Bank is obliged to admit that the increase in investment is generally slow in materializing and is viewed as particularly "disappointing" in low-income countries.

As in earlier studies, the Bank's latest analysis continues to recognize the unanticipated difficulties and slowness in improving macroeconomic performance. But in light of aggregate economic improvements, the Bank affirms that staying the "course on macroeconomic and pricing reform" is necessary for rekindling "sustainable growth." The disappointing performance of countries that abandoned adjustment programs, such as Côte d'Ivoire, are highlighted to exemplify the longer-term costs of postponing fundamental economic reforms.

THE CRITICS' VIEW: DESIGN FAILURES IN ADJUSTMENT LENDING

The Bank's growing confidence in asserting the success of policy-based lending has been challenged by other analysts examining its aggregate economic impact. One carefully argued study, *Aid and Power*, challenges the breadth of the significance of adjustment lending's impact on restoring growth.[23] Using a common data base but a different analytical methodology, the study asserts that "the measured effect of Bank adjustment lending on growth varies according to the method of analysis chosen and is in any case weak, but there are cases in which adjustment lending appears to be associated with, and to have caused, subsequent growth."[24]

If the impact on growth has been weak in general, the study affirms that the impact of Bank adjustment lending has been to create a "negative investment effect," a result "very different from that which was planned."[25] The study concludes that "there is little systematic relationship between Bank adjustment lending and subsequent inflows of private foreign finance, and possibly as part consequence, investment levels appear to be lower in adjusting countries than in non-adjusting countries."[26] Further, "the influence of structural adjustment programmes on aggregate investment is almost everywhere negative."[27] The study asserts that this negative impact on investment runs counter to one of the basic objectives of adjustment and thereby questions the assumptions on which policy lending was predicated.

The specific criticisms of this one study typify the more general questions raised by critics about the long-term impact of adjustment programs on an adjusting country's economic viability. Those questions are echoed in two basic themes: First, why has adjustment lending led to a decline in investment rates in developing countries? Can adjustment be contributing to long-term economic growth when investment to expand the productive capacity of developing countries remains inadequate? Second, despite pronounced emphasis on addressing BoP problems through expansion of exports, the debt servicing-exports ratio continued to worsen during the 1980s. Can this outcome possibly create economic conditions from which long-term improvement in productivity and living standards will flow? After nearly $30 billion was channeled to developing countries through adjustment lending in the past decade, critics repeat that the results are less than reassuring and the outstanding questions disturbing.

The response of the United Nations Economic Commission for Africa (ECA) to the World Bank's assessment of the contributions of adjustment lending to growth in sub-Saharan Africa raises perhaps an even more fundamental issue.[28] The ECA challenges the Bank's methodology and use of statistics in reaching its positive conclusions. Its report claims that both "selectivity" and "inconsistency" are found in Bank reporting and analysis, giving rise to "misleading" conclusions. The study asserts that "the analysis and conclusions made on the basis of comparison...are arbitrary and exhibit stark manipulation of data to prove a predetermined position."[29] The sharpness of the response to the World Bank study illustrates the difficulty in establishing shared analytical methodologies and common assessments of adjustment's long-term impact.

Critics of adjustment programs have assessed the adjustment decade from many perspectives and have used different approaches to substantiate claims of failure of adjustment programs. The five themes summarized below reflect persistent criticisms of the design of structural adjustment programs as practiced during the 1980s.

Using Short-term Approaches to Long-term Problems

Critics claim that the assumption that demand reduction and supply response improvements could take place within a relatively short period of two or three years proved damaging for many countries. Not only did many resource-poor countries experience severe economic contraction and social dislocations in the short-term, draconian austerity measures had a serious negative impact on the ability of many countries to improve economic efficiency and rekindle growth in the medium and long term. One of the most cogent expressions of this criticism was articulated in the ECA's African Alternative Framework to Structural Adjustment Programmes, which questioned the validity of the orthodox World Bank–International Monetary Fund (IMF) package in disarticulated, poorly structured societies.[30] The ECA proposal sought to overcome the dichotomy between macroeconomic restructuring and long-term development by placing far greater emphasis on developing human potential and strengthening institutions as a way of improving economic performance. This priority is brought into focus by the policy recommendations offered by the alternative proposal:

> Given the structural bottlenecks in African economies, adjustment must be seen as part of a continuous process of transformation rather than as a discontinuous exercise on its own. Consequently, the siege-mentality of ad hoc crisis management approach must yield place to the total immersion of adjustment programmes with the long-term needs of transformation since adjustment policies and measures are unlikely to yield any full and enduring benefits outside the context of transformation.[31]

This general theme was expanded to include not only Africa but countries of the Caribbean and the Pacific as reflected in a report of the Africa, Caribbean, Pacific-European Economic Community: "The short deadlines for the restoration of economic and financial equilibrium fail to take into account the longer time scales for other economic and social adjustment processes.... In general, the pursuit of short-term stabilization has diverted attention from action to attain longer-term economic growth and development goals."[32]

The World Bank came to recognize the limitations of the boiler-plate approach to adjustment design as a result the widespread criticism articulated by governments and social-based organizations alike in adjusting countries. Bank recognition of its failings in this area are reflected more fully in its recent analytical studies, which recognize the fact that structural adjustment loans (SALs) are rather "blunt instruments" with inherent constraints in reforming distorted economies. In this same perspective, the Bank has more openly accepted the fact that the scores of conditions attached to SALs may contribute little to the ultimate success of individual adjustment packages simply because they are too complex and do not correspond to institutional conditions and managerial capacities in an adjusting country.[33]

Overlooking the Impacts of External Conditions

In the early 1980s, two main views were articulated regarding the causes of economic collapse being experienced in many developing countries. The "externalists" laid principal responsibility for economic problems with the historic inequities and austere conditions in the international economy, and "internalists" attributed the problems primarily to internal economic blockages and political bottlenecks within respective developing countries. The predominant view among the architects of adjustment programs early in the decade was that, regardless of the influence of external conditions, reforms internal to the individual developing countries were the primary vehicle for improving performance of distressed economies.

During the course of the adjustment decade, however, the critics sharpened their charges in claiming that historically rooted inequities between North and South weakened the economic vitality of many developing countries and undermined the potential positive impact of adjustment programs.[34] A frequently cited example of this failure in adjustment programs is that they often set supply response objectives, particularly in commodity-exporting countries, that ignored the century-long trend in declining terms of trade between North and South:

> On the whole, rural economies have been unable to respond to incentives to undertake production for export and, with scarce foreign exchange to import capital and severe infrastructure bottlenecks, raising the value of primary products has proven difficult. Instead, [structural adjustment programs] have undermined the food security of rural and urban poor people and increased imbalances in domestic income distribution. With resources effectively funneled to the production and marketing of exports to the exclusion of local needs, large groups of people have been marginalized from the economy.... The deterioration in the terms of trade has effectively undermined export promotion strategies.[35]

By the end of the 1980s, critics of adjustment programs focused their concerns about the impact of external forces on the success of internal reforms on the following issues:

- *Provision of adequate external financing.* Many examples, particularly in sub-Saharan Africa, are cited of adjustment programs that failed because adequate financing was not available. Not only was the total volume inadequate, but poor timing and the conditions under which financing was delivered proved inappropriate.[36] Provision of stable, adequate, and well-designed external support is viewed as indispensable to effect further structural reforms.

- *Reduction of debt overhang.* High debt service ratios threaten the viability of many adjustment programs. Though most countries have been able to meet rescheduled debt obligations in the short term, often owing to IMF pressure, their longer-term ability to expand productive investment is under pressure and threatens to undermine the goals of adjustment programs. Multilateral efforts to alleviate the debt burden, including the Baker and Brady plans as well as unilateral debt cancellation, provided relief in a few important cases. Longer-term success of adjustment programs in many nations requires more comprehensive debt relief action.

- *Stabilization of real interest rates on outstanding international debt.* The impact of increases in real interest rates, as was the case in the early 1980s, would seriously threaten the viability of many adjustment programs by aggravating the burden of debt service.

- *Adjustment of indebted G-7 countries.* Correction of fiscal and current account balances in industrialized societies without inducing deeper recession is viewed as a requisite for global financial stability on which resumption of growth in the developing world depends.

■ *Expansion of trade opportunities through reduced tariffs and protectionism in the industrialized countries.* Faced with continued decline in terms of trade, developing countries can earn foreign exchange only through expanded access to industrial country markets. Reduction of many barriers impeding market access are seen as critical to the success of the adjustment process.

Protracted economic difficulties in many industrialized societies raise doubts among many critics about the prospect that developing societies can count on favorable external conditions to facilitate their respective adjustment processes.[37] Whether the design of adjustment programs will take continuing adverse conditions into account remains to be seen. If adverse external conditions prevail, critics ask if resource-poor, indebted countries can continue to be blamed for the failure of adjustment programs.

Failure to Create Conditions for Wealth Generation

A third major criticism of adjustment programs is that they have failed to give attention to creating favorable conditions under which generation of national wealth can take place on a long-term basis. Specifically, this criticism asserts that the narrow focus of orthodox adjustment programs on correcting balance of payment (BoP) lending and expanding the tradeable goods sector overlooks the needs of creating economic conditions under which medium-size and small enterprises can flourish and national economies can ensure a sustained recovery.

This failure is attributed to the cumulative results of adjustment programs' design problems. For example, draconian cutbacks in government expenditures have frequently led to dramatic and often extended reductions in public investment in infrastructure. Deteriorating and inadequate infrastructure, in turn, has become a major bottleneck to economic expansion and often in terms of developing domestic markets.

Second, the emphasis, oftentimes ideologically motivated, on reducing the role of the state has left an economic and social vacuum that has crippled expansion of private sector growth in many countries.

In the absence of resources and a vibrant entrepreneurial class, the state has been called upon to provide a range of important and often necessary economic functions. Critics point out that budgetary reallocations under adjustment have divested the state of many essential functions and created a void in services and productive activities that undermine economic stability and vitality of many countries.

Third, reduction in public expenditures particularly in health and education, has diminished the development of human capital necessary to respond to new economic opportunities.

Fourth, immediate and undifferentiated reduction in import tariffs has not provided adequate time to allow national industries to improve their competitiveness with foreign firms. Consequently, deindustrialization in many countries resulted from sudden trade liberalization and further eroded the industrial base of many fragile economies.

These and other negative impacts on local economies led one analyst of adjustment programs to conclude that although "it is likely that microeconomic efficiency has been improved, IMF and World Bank's insistence on increased exports of traditional commodities, rapid import liberalization and drastic cuts in public investment are retarding Africa's recovery, and pushing many African economies away from achieving the long-term objectives of greater food self-sufficiency, an efficient manufacturing sector, diversified export composition and markets, and increased export volume."[38] The scope of this criticism, and many others of similar genre, underscores the call to redesign adjustment packages so that they establish specific objectives, clarify priorities, assess in-country institutional and managerial capacity, and tailor all activities to the specific conditions of each country. For example, with more time and supportive policies, a number of import substitution industries could have been restructured to become more competitive internationally.

The Social Dimensions of Adjustment

The United Nations Children's Fund (UNICEF) study, *Adjustment with a Human Face*, provided the catalytic jolt that obligated international lending institutions to consider adjustment's social dimensions. The criticism highlighted the failure of the World Bank and the IMF to establish social objectives that would condition the reforms and restructuring carried out during the adjustment process. The UNICEF study documented the fact that, in the absence of social objectives in adjustment programs, the most vulnerable sectors of adjusting societies, particularly children and women, were bearing the brunt of economic contraction associated with adjustment programs. The political consequences of ignoring the social dimension, illustrated by riots and demonstrations in numerous adjusting countries, including Tunisia, Morocco, Zambia, Sri Lanka, and Venezuela, greatly enhanced the credibility of UNICEF's message.[39]

In the course of the decade, social mitigation programs and "social sector conditions" acquired a higher profile in Bank adjustment programs. Social mitigation components were incorporated into various adjustment programs, including activities that sought to foster income-generation through small-scale enterprises and to protect health and social services. Special compensatory programs, such as those in Ghana and Bolivia and more recently in Guinea, Haiti, and Madagascar, sought to reduce the adverse impacts on the poor.[40] By the end of the 1980s, one-third of all adjustment loans addressed social aspects of the adjustment process in one form or another.[41]

Although World Bank policy now calls explicitly for protection of the most vulnerable sectors as countries undergo the dislocations of adjustment, the demands for greater protection of the vulnerable still abound from governments and local groups alike. The continuing decline in the well-being of the poor sectors of many adjusting countries has generated a new round of questions about the real purpose of social mitigation programs. For example, critics question whether mitigation programs are designed to improve the structural status of the poor and vulnerable and to generate long-term economic benefits. Or are social mitigation components of SALs designed to co-opt the poor during the adjustment process while a new constellation of the country's elite establishes its control over the country's economic growth process? As UNICEF's study proposed in the mid-1980s, adjustment programs must be conditioned by clearly defined social objectives. The challenge remains largely unanswered in the eyes of many critics.[42]

Ownership of Adjustment Programs

Structural adjustment involves restructuring a country's political economy. Reforming institutions and changing policy invariably lead to shifting control of, and access to, a country's resources. The implicit purpose of adjustment is to diminish the influence of some social sectors or interest groups whose political and economic control has blocked efficient use of a country's resources. At the same time, adjustment programs stimulate the political and economic ascendance of other groups that can improve the country's competitiveness on international markets. In short, there will always be winners and losers in the adjustment process.

The experience of the 1980s demonstrates the fact that a requisite of smooth implementation of adjustment programs is the forging of a domestic power base, usually a coalition of social groups, that can displace the previous coalition of economic and social interests. In the 1980s, effective coalitions that facilitated the adjustment process were frequently formed among export-oriented sectors of national economies with a base in commercial agriculture and industry. This new coalition frequently replaced coalitions based on the "military, the public sector, organized labor, and urban, white-collar interests."[43]

Architects of adjustment programs early in the 1980s skirted the ownership issue because they preferred the relative ease of striking agreements with small groups of national planners in government agencies. Even working with a cross section of the economic and political elite, not to mention broad sectors of the population, seemed to complicate and slow down the implementation process. As the drastic social and economic consequences of adjustment programs began reverberating throughout adjusting societies, protest mounted immediately, often threatening political stability in many countries. At the heart of those protests was condemnation of the antidemocratic manner in which fundamental, long-term societal decisions had been made.

Failure to address adequately criticisms relating to lack of ownership is reflected in the recommendations articulated by the governments of Africa, the Caribbean, and the Pacific under the LOME IV Convention in 1992. The resolutions call for:

- the need to foster democratization processes, since the greater public involvement in decision-making processes [that] results is vital to the success of structural adjustment measures and [the governments urge], therefore, that the implementation of SAPs in individual states should not run counter to democratization processes;

- broad participation by the population as being of decisive importance; in this connection, [nongovernmental organizations], women's organizations and trade unions can play a key role.[44]

Little if any dissent is heard today about the need for broadening government ownership of adjustment programs supported by the World Bank. Critics claim that the underlying issue, though one not voiced publicly by the Bank, is not simply how to garner political commitment and ownership of adjustment programs. Instead what must be answered is: ownership by whom and for what ends? The World Bank's implicit answer has been to foster broader ownership by the government so it can reflect the interests of economic groups that can help rekindle economic growth in the country by strengthening its competitiveness in the global market. Although building new coalitions around elites favoring export-oriented policies may help alleviate short-term BoP problems and stimulate economic growth in the medium term, there is no certainty that the ascendancy of this new coalition will provide for long-term sustainable development in which people's basic needs will be met. Nor, the critics point out, is there certainty that political realignments flowing from this shift in economic power will engender a democratization of the political process on which long-term economic well-being is predicated.

THE SUSTAINABILITY OF ADJUSTMENT PROGRAMS

As the two summaries presented above indicate, the scope of disagreements about the impact of structural adjustment is broad, and the terms of the disagreements are equally sharp. That this major tool of development policy should be the focus of such intense and protracted debate is both encouraging and disturbing. It is encouraging that the failures of adjustment programs have spawned a closer examination of the operative assumptions and objectives that have guided development strategies during the past 40 years. Often a wide spectrum of social groups in developing countries has assessed development approaches and set forth proposals to reformulate national development priorities. It is disturbing that this policy instrument, applied so widely and with such serious consequences, remains enshrouded in such uncertainties and controversy. Economic restructuring, with long-term economic and social impacts, has been applied in scores of developing countries, often with little understanding of its long-term consequences.

It is important to signal that there is now little dissent about the fact that the scope of issues that must be examined to understand the impact of policy-based lending has broadened. The social dimensions of adjustment have been accepted, albeit reluctantly, by the architects of adjustment lending. For example, poverty alleviation has become a stated purpose of adjustment; restructuring government expenditures, particularly the need to reduce military spending to address social needs, has become more important; and distributional outcomes of adjustment are important criteria in assessing long-term impacts of economic restructuring.

Despite these reforms in the concept and practice of adjustment, this privileged tool of development policy has remained shielded from new issues shaping humankind's survival agenda. Architects and proponents of adjustment programs failed to consider the impact of profound economic reforms on the environment of adjusting countries. They failed to ask whether the policy and institutional reforms would help put adjusting countries on a sustainable development path.

This failing is particularly remarkable in light of the World Bank's public statements regarding the environment. In 1972, at the United Nations Environment Conference, Robert McNamara, then president of the Bank, made it clear that the Bank recognized the fact that a mutually supportive relationship had to be forged between its economic growth strategies and protection of the environment: "The question is not whether there should be continued economic growth. There must be. Nor is the question whether the impact on the environment must be respected. It has to be. Nor—least of all—is it a question of whether these two questions are interlocked. They are. The solution of the dilemma revolves clearly not about whether, but about how."[45] Twenty years later this perspective has still not found its way into the logic or design of economic reforms promoted in developing countries around the globe by the World Bank.

By 1987, the World Commission on Environment and Development, known as the Brundtland Commission, presented its compelling definition of sustainable development, arguing that "humanity has the ability to make development sustainable to ensure that it meets the needs of the present without compromising the ability of future generations to meet their own needs."[46] Particularly remarkable is that the seven "strategic imperatives" for sustainable development place reviving growth as the most pressing order of business, a priority consistent with adjustment programs. The Commission, again consonant with the stated purposes of adjustment, explicitly embraced the perspective that alleviating poverty was critical to reducing destructive pressure on a country's natural resource base. Despite the clear link of the Commission's recommendations and strategic imperatives with the purposes of structural adjustment, the architects of structural reform programs did not consider them relevant to the macroeconomic and sectoral restructuring being promoted through adjustment lending.

Growing public pressure, expressed largely through an international nongovernmental organization campaign launched in the early 1980s, prodded the World Bank to undertake meaningful institutional and policy reforms. In 1987, President Barber Conable announced the internal restructuring of the Bank, including creation of the Environmental Department, from which subsequent environmental reform efforts were developed.[47] President Conable's public statements, as exemplified by his address at the Tokyo Conference on the Global Environment and Human Response Toward Sustainable Development, reflected the growing commitment the Bank attached to addressing the environmental crisis:

> The World Bank and others in the development community have learned that protection of the environment warrants specific and discrete emphasis. We have also learned that environmental issues cut across all development sectors and are affected as much by domestic politics as by international trade practices.
>
> We know also that we cannot fulfill our responsibilities by merely passing around "unleavened loaves of empty words." Words must be subsumed by action, meticulously and rigorously assessed. That, in essence, is the World Bank's approach to environmental issues as they intersect with the imperatives of development.[48]

Despite the statements of public concern and commitment, and despite the efforts to improve the Bank's environmental record on project-level investments, at virtually no point during the 1980s was there a focused effort to understand the impact of World Bank macroeconomic lending on the natural resource sector. At no point was there an institutional commitment to understand the impact of macroeconomic adjustment on the sustainability of developing country strategies. The World Bank's dismissive attitude toward the potential impacts of adjustment on the environment was reflected in the following statement drawn from one of its recent assessments of adjustment lending: "Although adjustment programs have not focused on environmental issues, most of them included measures that, on balance, appear more likely to help than to hurt the environment."[49] This blanket statement of probable positive effects is not based on rigorous examination of the issue.

It is important to clarify what is at stake in failing to assume responsibility for the environmental impact of economic restructuring. In the most immediate sense, macroeconomic and sectoral reforms can have direct impacts, both positive and negative, on the environmental integrity of a country. Correction of economic distortions, removal of subsidies, and increased efficiency can generate immediate environmental improvements. By the same token, reallocating government expenditures, expanding production of agricultural tradeables, and expanding industrial or extractive industries can seriously aggravate environmental deterioration. In addition, restructuring national economies can contribute to or detract from the long-term sustainability of a national development strategy. For example, restructuring can promote consumption of natural resources at unsustainable rates, it can encourage changes in agricultural regimes that can disrupt microclimates, and it can promote industrial development whose emissions and pollution can exceed the sink functions or pose major threats to human health as well.

In this sense, economic restructuring has direct and long-term implications for human well-being and the viability of the planet. Macroeconomic planning can be used to ensure the rational use and management of natural resources. Or, if planners choose to disregard these issues, there is little doubt today that environmental degradation and resource limits will condition both economic development and social well-being. Involved here, then, is a basic challenge of ensuring that the pursuit of development, that is, a qualitative improvement in the human condition, is not compromised by the unconditioned quest for economic growth. These are the issues that the case studies presented in the following three chapters will discuss.

CHAPTER TWO ENDNOTES

1. The five studies are: *Structural Adjustment Lending: A First Review of Experience* (Washington, D.C.: 1986); *Adjustment Lending: An Evaluation of Ten Years of Experience* (1988); *Adjustment Lending Practices for Sustainable Growth* (1990); *Restructuring Economies in Distress* (1991); and *The Third Report on Adjustment Lending: Private and Public Resources for Growth* (1992).

2. World Bank, *Restructuring Economies in Distress,* op. cit., p. 544.

3. World Bank, *Adjustment Lending for Sustainable Growth,* op cit., p. 22.

4. World Bank, *The Third Report on Adjustment Lending: Private and Public Resources for Growth,* op cit., p. 2.

5. World Bank, *Restructuring Economies in Distress,* op. cit., p. 22.

6. World Bank, *The Third Report on Adjustment Lending: Private and Public Resources for Growth,* op. cit., p. 2.

7. World Bank, *Restructuring Economies in Distress,* op cit., p. 39.

8. World Bank, *The Third Report on Adjustment Lending: Private and Public Resources for Growth,* op. cit., p. 50.

9. World Bank, *Restructuring Economies in Distress,* op. cit., p. 67.

10. Ibid.

11. World Bank, *The Third Report on Adjustment Lending: Private and Public Resources for Growth,* op. cit., p. 18.

12. Ibid., p. 22.

13. World Bank, *Restructuring Economies in Distress,* op. cit., p. 59.

14. Ibid., p. 179.

15. Ibid., p. 164.

16. Ibid., p. 174.

17. Ibid., p. 136.

18. Ibid., p. 146.

19. Ibid., p. 124.

20. World Bank, *The Third Report on Adjustment Lending: Private*

and Public Resources for Growth, op. cit., pp. 30-48.

21. Ibid., p. 3.

22. Ibid., p. 19.

23. Paul Mosley, Jane Harrigan, and John Tage, *Aid and Power: The World Bank and Policy-based Lending* (London: Routledge, 1991).

24. Ibid., pp. 208-32.

25. Ibid., p. 229.

26. Ibid p. 230.

27. Ibid., p. 301.

28. United Nations, *Statistics and Policies: ECA Preliminary Observations on the World Bank Report: Africa Adjustment and Growth in the 1980s* (Addis Ababa, 1989).

29. Ibid., p. 11.

30. United Nations, Economic Commission for Africa, *African Alternative Framework to Structural Adjustment Programs for Socio-Economic Recovery and Transformation (AAF-SAP)*, New York, 1989.

31. Ibid., p. 33.

32. Africa, Caribbean, Pacific-European Economic Community, "Working Documents, ACP-EEC Joint Assembly, Report of the Working Party on Conditions for Implementing the Structural Adjustment Policy under Lome IV and the Effects Thereof on the Conditions for Implementing the Structural Adjustment Policy under Lome IV," Brussels, 1992, p. 7.

33. See, for example, Elliott Berg and Alan Batchelder, *Structural Adjustment Lending: A Critical View*, Washington, D.C., 1984, p. 32; World Bank, Structural Adjustment Lending: A First Review of Experience, op. cit., pp. 70-72.

34. United Nations Economic Commission for Africa, ibid, p. 1, and pp. 3-6.

35. *Beyond UNPAAERD: From Talk to Action* (New York, 1991), p. 9.

36. World Bank, *Sub-Saharan Africa: From Crisis to Sustainable Growth* (Washington, D.C., 1989), p. 15.

37. World Bank, *Global Economic Prospects and the Developing Countries* (Washington, D.C., 1992), chapts. 1 and 2.

38. Giovanni Andrea Cornia, "Is Adjustment Conducive to Long-term Development: The Case of Africa in the 1980s," in *From the Depth of Crisis to Sustainable Development*, G. Vaggi, ed. (New York: MacMillan, forthcoming), p. 33.

39. Examples of the link between stabilization-adjustment programs and social protest are abundant. Documentation of this relationship is found in news reports, for example: John Mukela, "The IMF Fallout," *Africa Report* (January-February 1987), pp. 65-67, and George Alagiah and Melvyn Westlake, "An Overdose of the IMF Medicine," *South* (February 1987), pp. 17-19, regarding riots in Zambia; in more extensive reporting, for example, Roger Plant, *Sugar and Modern Slavery* (London: Zed Books, 1987), pp. 140-49, regarding riots in Dominican Republic in 1984; and in more analytical efforts, for example, Christian H. Gladwin, ed., *Structural Adjustment and African Women Farmers* (Gainesville: University of Florida Press, 1991).

40. Elaine Zuckerman, "Compensatory Programs: Redressing Social Costs of Adjustment," World Bank, Washington, D.C., 1989; Elaine Zuckerman, "The Social Costs of Adjustment," in World Bank *Restructuring Economies in Distress*, op. cit., pp. 247-69; Lionel Demery and Tony Addison, *The Alleviation of Poverty under Structural Adjustment* (World Bank, Washington, D.C., 1987); Helena Ribe, ed., *How Adjustment Programs Can Help the Poor: The World Bank's Experience* (World Bank, Washington, D.C., 1990).

41. World Bank, *The Third Report on Adjustment Lending: Private and Public Resources for Growth*, op. cit., p. 5.

42. Gregory Fossedal, "IMF Conditionality, 1980-1991." Alexis de Tocqueville Institution, Arlington, Virginia, 1992. See, for example World Bank, *Structural Adjustment Lending for Sustainable Growth*, op cit., p. 8.

43. Joan Nelson, *Fragile Coalitions: The Policy of Economic Adjustment,* (Washington, D.C., Overseas Development Council, 1989) p. 27.

44. Africa, Caribbean, Pacific-European Economic Community Joint Assembly, op. cit., p. 6.

45. Robert McNamara, *The McNamara Years at the World Bank: Major Policy Addresses of Robert S. McNamara 1961-1981* (Washington, D.C., World Bank, 1981), p. 196.

46. World Commission on Environment and Development, *Our Common Future* (New York: Oxford University Press, 1987), p. 8.

47. Barber Conable, Address to the World Resources Institute, Washington, D.C., 1987.

48. Barber Conable, "Development and the Environment: A Global

Balance," Presented at Tokyo Conference on the Global Environment and Human Response Toward Sustainable Development, Tokyo, Japan, 11 September, 1989.

49. World Bank, *Adjustment Lending Policies for Sustainable Growth*, op. cit., p. 51.

CASE STUDY FOR CÔTE D'IVOIRE

*by the London Environmental and Economics Centre,
based on a study by the* Centre Ivoirien de Recherches
Economiques et Sociales *(CIRES)**

MACROECONOMIC HISTORY AND BROAD PATTERN OF DEVELOPMENT

Macroeconomic Setting Prior to Adjustment

During the first 15 years after political independence in 1960, Côte d'Ivoire was considered one of the outstanding economic success stories in sub-Saharan Africa. The country enjoyed rapid economic development, reflected in an average real gross domestic product (GDP) growth rate of over 7 percent per year from 1960 to 1975.[1] This exceptional record was based largely on exports of primary products, especially coffee, cocoa, and timber, and industrial growth.

In terms of total output and employment, agriculture dominates the economy of Côte d'Ivoire. In 1989, 46 percent of GDP came from cash and food crops, forestry, and fisheries.[2] More than one-half the labor force is directly employed in agricultural production. Throughout the early period of rapid economic growth, agriculture was heavily taxed. Agricultural surpluses were appropriated implicitly by means of administratively determined prices set below border (i.e., world) prices and explicitly through export taxes on specific cash crops and commodities. The revenues obtained from these policies financed the

---

**Joseph Yao, Kouadio Yao, Joseph Akomian, and Odil Angoran comprised the CIRES research team.

49

development of public services and of both public and private industry. Rural income was thus effectively redistributed to stimulate development of urban centers, especially the main port and economic center of Abidjan.[3]

Although initially successful, the strategy left Côte d'Ivoire highly vulnerable to external shocks. Industrial development focused largely on import substitution, leaving the country heavily reliant on coffee, cocoa, and timber exports. These three accounted for roughly 80 percent of total exports in 1965; by 1980, they still represented about 60 percent. Moreover, while heavy taxation of agriculture kept a lid on rural incomes, formal urban sector wages remained consistently high, putting upward pressure on the real exchange rate. Membership in the West African Monetary Union (WAMU), however, precluded devaluation of the nominal exchange rate as a means of maintaining export competitiveness.

The first major external shock was the oil price rise of 1973-1974. Côte d'Ivoire absorbed it with little apparent effect. Any negative repercussions were soon offset by a dramatic rise in world prices of coffee and cocoa in 1975-1977. Windfall revenues arising from this temporary commodity boom were not passed on to producers. Instead, they were used to finance a major expansion of public investment, which increased 250 percent in real terms from 1975 to 1980. Inevitably, many marginal projects were undertaken, with relatively low returns overall.

The subsequent fall in export crop prices, followed by the second oil price shock of 1979-1981, was not matched by adequate cutbacks in public spending. Domestic private savings could not fill the resulting fiscal gap, so the government turned to the international capital markets and WAMU's central bank.[4] A combination of foreign commercial debt and central bank credits maintained current expenditure and investment levels in the short term.

The massive inflow of foreign exchange, first from the commodity boom and then from foreign lending, combined with monetary expansion in the form of central bank credits, was reflected in a surge in inflation (the Dutch disease). Nominal prices rose at an average annual rate of 16 percent between 1974 and 1980 versus a mean rate of 5.7 percent before 1974. Because of the fixed nominal rate of exchange (CFA franc 1 = FF 50), domestic price inflation inevitably led to appreciation of the real exchange rate. In other words, rising domestic prices led to increased costs and reduced competitiveness of exports and import substitution industries. Imports increased and the trade balance deteriorated, further exacerbating a widening current account deficit and requiring more foreign loans. The government responded with additional restrictions on imports, but they only served to reduce the competitiveness of exports even further.

By 1981, Côte d'Ivoire experienced a massive fiscal gap, a current account deficit, and a foreign debt burden equal to 12 percent, 17 percent, and 35 percent of GDP, respectively. With the global credit crunch of the early 1980s, the inevitable consequence was a balance of payments (BoP) and fiscal crisis. As in so many other developing countries, the government was forced to appeal to the international financial institutions (i.e., the World Bank and the International Monetary Fund (IMF)) for emergency credits. Assistance took the form of short-term stabilization packages and medium-term structural adjustment loans (SALs), always conditional on government spending cuts and economic policy reform.

Stabilization and Adjustment Program in Côte d'Ivoire

The principal objective of short-term stabilization in Côte d'Ivoire, as elsewhere, was to reduce the current account deficit. According to the conventional diagnosis, a sustained external imbalance reflects excess demand, particularly for traded goods. The standard prescription usually includes some combination of expenditure reduction (cuts in domestic absorption) and expenditure switching (a shift of resources from nontraded to traded sectors). Devaluation of the nominal exchange rate can be a direct and immediate method of achieving the latter goal, but this instrument was unavailable to Côte d'Ivoire owing to membership in the WAMU. Stabilization therefore had to be achieved entirely through a reduction in aggregate demand, to be accomplished by means of fiscal and monetary policy. The government could reduce the public budget deficit through spending cuts and/or revenue enhancement and restrain expansion of the money supply through reduced central bank credits and higher interest rates.[5] In practice, stabilization in Côte d'Ivoire was achieved almost entirely through public spending cuts.

Medium-term structural adjustment in Côte d'Ivoire was also conventional, but again it was constrained by the fixed nominal exchange rate. Policy reforms were aimed to stimulate the supply of traded goods, especially industrial and agricultural exports. How did policy change? Major trade reforms included harmonization of import duties, conversion of nontariff barriers to tariffs, and an innovative attempt to simulate a devaluation using a combination of import tariffs and an export subsidy. Sectoral reforms included price liberalization, reduced producer and consumer subsidies, and restructured public sector enterprises.

Adjustment efforts in Côte d'Ivoire were supported by the World Bank under four sequential SALs from 1981 to 1990 and a multiyear arrangement under the Extended Fund Facility from 1981 to 1983. Additional support was obtained from IMF under two standby arrangements in 1984 and 1985. Some bilateral donors, notably the French government, provided adjustment loans.

The first SAL (1981-1983) was aimed to reduce the public sector and current account deficits and stabilize public foreign debt service. The loan agreement called for significant public expenditure cuts, monetary restraint, and liberalized interest rates. Sectoral measures included trade reform and restructured public sector enterprises, especially the large parastatal agricultural enterprises.

Macroeconomic reforms under SAL I were not initially effective. Though public capital expenditures were reduced from 18 percent of GDP in 1980 to 15 percent in 1982, current expenditures were not cut. Moreover, government revenue forecasts were not met, reflecting falling export commodity prices on world markets, low levels of agricultural production owing to drought, and disappointing results from offshore oil prospecting. The result was little improvement on the fiscal and external accounts, combined with declining real per capita income. On the other hand, there was some real improvement in incentives for tradeable agriculture, which was reflected in producer price increases of 33 percent for coffee, cocoa, and paddy rice from 1981 to 1984.

Under SAL II (1984-1986), continued efforts to reduce government expenditures and domestic absorption were combined with expanded sectoral reform in industry and agriculture. An explicit goal was to reduce the effective level of protection of industry to 40 percent in hopes of reviving export competitiveness. However, the centerpiece of trade reform was a simulated devaluation that combined the liberalization and harmonization of import tariffs with an export subsidy equal to 20 percent of value added. Some revisions were also made to the Investment Code.

Macroeconomic reforms under SAL II were effective this time. Government capital expenditures were reduced to 7.6 percent of GDP by 1986 and were matched by a diminished fiscal deficit. In retrospect, however, much of this success is attributed to favorable external factors, such as better weather for crops, higher world prices for coffee and cocoa, and depreciation of the real exchange rate owing to the brief rise of the U.S. dollar. Although there were significant improvements in macroeconomic balances and a real increase in GDP, the respite was temporary. World coffee and cocoa prices fell back, and the economic decline resumed from 1986.

Sectoral reforms planned under SAL II were largely ineffective. The proposed export subsidy was delayed and underfinanced, and numerous exemptions were granted from measures designed to reduce protection (i.e., relief from tariff increases on intermediate goods). A government study of the reforms revealed that the effective level of protection remained high, at about 65 percent. Import restrictions were further reinforced when the CFA franc resumed its appreciation against the U.S. dollar from 1985 and in response to the devaluation of currency in Ghana and Nigeria, two potential regional competitors. Import duties were increased 30 percent in 1987 and again 12 percent in 1989.

A third SAL covering 1986 to 1988 was never implemented. Planned sectoral measures included further real increases in producer prices of coffee and cocoa. The plan was thwarted by additional price declines on world markets, resulting in large deficits registered at the state commodity marketing board *(Caisse de Stabilisation)* equal to 1.7 percent of GDP in 1987. In response, the government suspended interest payments on its external debts in 1987 and suspended cocoa sales in 1988.

SAL IV (1989-1990) was only partly implemented. Planned cuts in public sector nominal wages were abandoned owing to political unrest. In addition, and contrary to proposals for increased agricultural output prices under SAL III, continued large deficits at the state commodity marketing board finally led the government to cut producer prices of coffee and cocoa 75 percent and 50 percent, respectively, in 1989. Other export crops were also affected by a reduction in the guaranteed floor price of oil palm, liberalization of cotton and rice trading and prices, reduced subsidies on inputs, and other measures. At the same time, forestry reforms included elimination of timber export quotas and fiscal reform. They are discussed in the following sections.

Côte d'Ivoire's most recent adjustment efforts essentially continue earlier measures to reduce domestic absorption through reduced public expenditures and improved tax collection. In the face of the current global recession, however, there are few prospects for a rapid renewal of growth in Côte d'Ivoire. The current depressed state of the economy is all too well-illustrated by deep discounts on the value of public sector foreign debt on secondary markets that averaged 3 percent of face value in March 1991. Foreign investment remains stagnant, and long-term commercial credit is virtually unobtainable. At the sectoral level, agriculture remains predominantly extensive, with low use rates for fertilizers and other modern inputs. Industry remains heavily protected and inward looking.

In a recent retrospective review of the adjustment experience in Côte d'Ivoire, Morrisson notes that the urban economy felt the impact of stabilization most heavily.[6] Urban poverty has increased, reflecting increased unemployment owing to layoffs in the public and formal sector and reduced demand in the informal sector. But despite rising urban unemployment and simultaneous cuts in subsidies for transport, rice, water, and electricity, real wages remained stable. Rural incomes have also been relatively stable. The rigidity of real wages has meant that any potential improvement in the terms of trade faced by rural producers was not realized. On the contrary, the rural sector has simply faced diminished demand for its products.

IMPACTS OF STRUCTURAL ADJUSTMENT ON THE ENVIRONMENT

Major environmental problems in Côte d'Ivoire include deforestation and soil degradation, affecting rural agriculture primarily, and domestic and industrial pollution, affecting urban centers and coastal fisheries. The principal cause of land degradation in rural areas is the lack of a consistent and secure land tenure system. Pollution problems may be attributed to inadequate regulation and a failure to compensate for negative external impacts. Environmental problems in Côte d'Ivoire are discussed in the following sections.[7]

Land Tenure

Excessive logging and land clearing for agriculture may be attributed in part to the failure of rural land tenure.[8] The problem derives from a gradual breakdown and growing inadequacy of indigenous common property management systems. It has been aggravated by the failure of government to develop effective land tenure institutions either to complement or to replace traditional systems.

Indigenous land tenure systems in Côte d'Ivoire vary according to culture and circumstances in different regions. Nevertheless, most traditions share certain fundamental features. At the risk of oversimplification, indigenous systems of land management in West Africa are based on the collective territorial claims of a family or clan. These claims are justified in terms of initial occupation and land clearing or outright conquest. Area size depends on local political history.

Under traditional management, all land is held in trust by the chief and elders of the ruling family or clan. Members of the family as well as any others must apply to the chief or elders for usufruct rights (i.e., the right to clear unoccupied land for cultivation, according to their needs and the availability of reserves). Use rights are traditionally granted free of charge, although a token gift may be expected, and some form of religious sacrifice is often required. In principle, use rights are valid only so long as land is under cultivation, but allowance may be made for occasional fallow. Use rights are also transferable, but only within the family or clan. The use of forested land for hunting and gathering, including removal of timber, is generally not regulated under traditional tenure systems.

Indigenous systems of common property management were adequate when population densities were relatively low and most exploitation was carried out to meet subsistence needs. Traditional land tenure systems have not adapted well to the pressures of rapid population growth, heavy immigration and high population mobility, and the resulting increased demand for arable land. They have also failed to deal effectively with the advent of commercial land use, particularly modern forestry.

The official government stance vis-à-vis indigenous land tenure systems has alternated between direct contradiction and benign neglect. During the early period of colonial rule, French authorities laid claim to all vacant and unoccupied land under the Decree of 20.07.1900. This act essentially denied any traditional claim to lands not then under cultivation. The motive was to establish a legal foundation for distributing unoccupied land to French colonists. This end was furthered by the Decree of 25.07.1932, which defined the legal procedure for obtaining individual freehold title to land. Under the latter decree, private claims and the acquisition of title could be based simply on evidence of active land use. A subsequent decree, dated 15.11.1935, recognized the additional authority of the state to claim any lands within 5 kilometers (km) of human settlement if they had been abandoned for more than 10 years. This decree was evidently intended to allow public authorities to control the growth of urban areas. But under the Decree of 17.05.1955, the colonial government reversed much of the previous legislation and renounced public claims to vacant, unoccupied, or unexploited land.

The policy reversal embodied in the 1955 decree may reflect a general trend of liberalization on the part of the colonial authorities. Or the colonial government may have wished to gain the favor of traditional rural elites in an attempt to stave off the growing political influence of nationalist African unions, which were dominated by educated urban elites. Whatever the real motive, the effect was the same. Freed from the constraints of central authority, the traditional chiefs gave way to long pent-up demands for unexploited land. The resulting explosion in rural land transactions led to the rapid constitution of vast private plantations and timber concessions held in the name of absentee African urban elites, managed by Europeans and employing mostly migrant labor from neighboring African countries.

With independence and the promulgation of the new constitution of 07.08.1960, the government reaffirmed the system of land tenure law inherited from the colonial power. More important than any legal text from this period, however, is a well-known presidential statement, albeit undocumented, to the effect that rural lands belonged to whoever puts them to productive use. Subsequent attempts to codify a comprehensive rural land law for Côte d'Ivoire have been largely ineffective. The government is unable to reconcile indigenous land tenure custom with the legal framework and pattern of land ownership left over from the colonial period. In particular, there remains a fundamental conflict between indigenous customs, which hold that land ownership (as opposed to usufruct) is inalienable, and the emphasis on private freehold maintained by European legal traditions. The experience of land tenure deregulation under the 1955 decree indicates considerable potential for abuse of weak and informal customary arrangements.

The unfortunate result of such prolonged ambiguity and inconsistency in rural land law is that secure tenure over land remains elusive. Many farmers resort to wholesale clearing of forest land simply to stake a claim and gain recognition from civil authorities.[9] Other farmers who have illegally occupied forest reserves have occasionally been granted permanent rights to remain. Perhaps not surprisingly, political elites benefited the most from the existing situation, using their wealth and influence to persuade traditional chiefs to part with vast tracts of communal forested land, obtaining the lion's share of any lands reallocated by government, and frequently circumventing administrative regulations designed to limit the size of private holdings.

At the other extreme, migrant farmers cultivating small plots are particularly disadvantaged under the current system. With little social or political influence and even less economic clout, they have little means of acquiring secure formal title to land. Access to land under indigenous systems may also be difficult to obtain, given the reluctance of traditional chiefs to allow land to pass permanently outside the clan. Migrant farmers are thus often reduced to itinerant tenant farming or wage labor on plantations. In both cases, they risk arbitrary eviction at a moment's notice. Under such circumstances, they can hardly be expected to concern themselves with land husbandry and conservation.

Deforestation

The natural forest ecology of Côte d'Ivoire can be divided into three distinct groups, corresponding to the dominant botanical associations: humid evergreen, semideciduous, and transitional. As recently as 1940, the forests of Côte d'Ivoire blanketed over 90 percent of the total land area of the country (318,000 km2). About one-half the original resource consisted of closed canopy, humid evergreen forest. More than three-quarters of the original expanse of natural forest has since been lost, with some recent estimates suggesting that little more than 20,000 km^2 of closed canopy forest remain in Côte d'Ivoire.

Deforestation in Côte d'Ivoire is remarkable not just for the total surface area affected but also for the high rate of land clearing.

Deforestation immediately following independence averaged more than 500,000 hectares per year, or about 5 percent. The rate of clearing was even higher in the closed forest zone, about 6.5 percent per year.[10] During the 1980s, despite growing international concern about the loss of tropical forests, annual deforestation in Côte d'Ivoire totaled at least 300,000 hectares.

What factors explain this vast land clearing? Deforestation has two principle causes: agricultural expansion and timber extraction. Their relative contribution to overall deforestation in Côte d'Ivoire is not well-known. As in many tropical countries, however, agricultural land clearing generally takes place on lands first opened up and made accessible by loggers.[11] Virtually all logged-over land in Côte d'Ivoire has subsequently been cleared for farming.[12]

Given the relatively low density of commercially valuable timber in the natural forests of Côte d'Ivoire, logging is carried out selectively. Only a handful of trunks is removed from each area (7 cubic meters per hectare on average for virgin forest). However, clearing logging trails and felling individual trees can destroy 50 percent of the surrounding natural vegetation. Land clearing for agriculture takes care of the rest.

It may be argued that massive deforestation was necessary for economic development. Indeed, the production and export of timber and agricultural commodities were and still are a major employer and the principal source of income and investment finance in Côte d'Ivoire. On the other hand, the virtual destruction of the original forest stock also entails considerable risk. Revenues from forestry and agriculture have been consumed, with little reinvestment to ensure future productivity and no new industry established to provide income. With the country's natural wealth depleted, its long term economic welfare remains in doubt. The technical term for this loss is user cost, the loss of potential future income from current consumption of a resource.

Additional costs of deforestation include a variety of so-called external impacts, such as the loss of plant and animal habitat, the loss of species diversity, and extinction. Other external impacts include disturbance of hydrological cycles, affecting ground and surface water supply; changes in local or global climate; and increased runoff, flooding, and soil erosion.

Excessive deforestation can be explained in economic terms, using the concepts of market imperfection and policy failure. The basic idea is that economic and institutional incentives are distorted in such a way that logging firms and farmers (as well as policy makers) will inevitably fail to account fully for the costs of deforestation in their land-use decisions.

The timber industry is subject to pricing and other policy distortions, for example, those that lead firms to cut and extract timber as quickly as possible, with little or no regard for future needs (user cost) or the negative external impacts of their activities. These distortions are described in more detail below, in the context of recent policy reforms.

Soil Degradation

Five types of soil degradation are recognized in Côte d'Ivoire: wind erosion, wave and tidal action, accelerated water erosion, and chemical and biological degradation.[13] None has attained a critical level on a national scale. Where the density of population and agriculture are relatively high, however, notably the central and eastern regions (the forest zone), continuous cultivation has caused some degradation of natural soil fertility.

The dominant farming system in the forest zone is based on permanent cultivation of cash crops combined with shifting cultivation of food crops. The major cash crops are coffee and cocoa, which are perennial and can be cultivated indefinitely with no significant soil degradation. Most food crops, on the other hand, are annuals. Because they are typically cultivated using little fertilizer or other inputs, they rapidly deplete natural soil fertility—hence the continual need for fertile virgin land. Rotation will not damage the land in the long run, provided that exhausted plots are abandoned long enough to recover their fertility under a natural bush fallow.

The system of long rotations was compromised in recent years by increased demands for land, leading to reduced fallow periods. Recent expansion of agriculture in the forest zone of central and eastern Côte d'Ivoire reflects massive migration and land clearing for production of coffee and cocoa. Technology has changed little. Although there are a few large, modern plantations, most farms remain small (about 2 hectares), and they continue to rely on traditional, extensive, low-input low-output production. Use of chemical fertilizers and other modern inputs remains low. Soil degradation has accelerated owing to the depletion of soil fertility under food crops and disease afflicting the major cash crops. The natural forest has been virtually eliminated outside the reserved areas, and is evidenced by the fallow land which exceeds the total cultivated surface by about 30 percent.[14]

Traditional extensive agriculture may have been sustainable at one time, but it is clearly not suited to the current high density of farming. Moreover, in addition to degrading soil fertility, agricultural expansion may have jeopardized productivity in other ways. There is some evidence that as agriculture expands and the natural forest area declines, local hydrological and climatic conditions may change, to the detriment of crop yields.[15] The ability of farmers to adapt to such changes by planting drought-resistant varieties may be severely limited in the short term. For example, the major cash crops—coffee and cocoa—require many years' tending before they bear fruit. In addition, these crops are heavily promoted in the forest zone by tied credit schemes, extension services, and crop marketing programs.

Whether the underlying cause is reduced precipitation or declining soil fertility, anecdotal evidence confirms that farmers have begun to abandon the denuded Cocoa Belt, migrating in search of higher crop yields in the relatively untouched western forest.

Pollution

Industrial and domestic pollution appears to be a negligible problem. Industrial activity and associated pollution are concentrated in and around Abidjan. Although there is little evidence of significant pollution, what problems do exist are attributed to an ineffective regulatory regime. Little information is available on rural or domestic pollution, except implicitly as a contributing factor in degradation of the lagoons near Abidjan.

The principal negative impact of pollution is the degradation of coastal and inland fisheries from domestic, industrial, and maritime sources. Some rural communities that previously relied heavily on fishing have vastly reduced catches. The problem is attributed to organic wastes and the lack of treatment facilities in industry and many residential areas. Petroleum tankers flushing their tanks near the port may also be a source. However, it is difficult to determine the significance of pollution relative to other factors, including increased fishing arising from population growth, improved fishing technology, and foreign fishing fleets offshore. Major changes in the ecology of the lagoons are due to the construction of canals that let in more sea water and raise salinity levels.

BROAD MACROECONOMIC POLICY AND ENVIRONMENTAL IMPACTS

The broad economic experience of Côte d'Ivoire over the past three decades may be characterized by an initial period of rapid economic growth, with high levels of public investment in industrial and urban infrastructure and public services. This investment was based at first on agricultural surpluses derived from the export of cash crops and timber. Following the increasing volatility of, and overall decline in, world commodity prices from the late 1970s, the government turned to external debt financing to sustain the investment boom. This phase ended prematurely in the early 1980s owing to the sudden scarcity of international commercial credit, continued declines in commodity prices, and deteriorating terms of trade.

The resulting recession was aggravated by the disappointing returns realized on previous investments in industry and the expansion of public services. It seems likely that Côte d'Ivoire could have made better use of the surplus obtained from export agriculture, much of which was effectively squandered on increased current consumption.

Macroeconomic stabilization and adjustment consisted largely of cuts in public spending combined with rather less effective supply-side reforms. With the failure to stimulate exports, external imbalances were reduced through a sustained decline in real income. Urban areas felt public sector layoffs and rising unemployment most heavily.

The following discussion of links between broad macroeconomic adjustment and the environment is largely confined to qualitative speculation owing to the lack of empirical data and appropriate analytical models.

Fiscal Policy

Stabilization and adjustment efforts significantly reduced current government expenditures, largely through cutbacks and public sector unemployment. One direct effect may have been cuts in current spending on environmental protection. More generally, the resulting recession and reduced aggregate demand might be expected to ease pressure on natural resources, assuming no change in underlying market and policy failures affecting use of these resources. Because the recession hit urban areas hardest, however, some who would otherwise have gone off to seek their fortunes may have been persuaded to remain in the country. Immigration from other African countries may also have slowed. More people staying on the farm may mean increased pressure for forest clearing and land degradation. Meanwhile, the rigidity of formal urban sector wages may have mitigated any potential benefits in real terms of trade between the rural and nonfarm sectors.

The environmental impacts of reduced public investment are also ambiguous. On the one hand, urgently required sanitation projects or antipollution measures may have been postponed. On the other, the reduced public investment in rural infrastructure (e.g., roads, bridges) and public services (e.g., agricultural extension, health, education) may have reduced the pace of forestry and agriculture expansion by increasing the effective cost of opening up virgin forest lands.

Monetary Policy

The links between monetary policy and environmental degradation in Côte d'Ivoire are entirely speculative. In general, nominal price inflation has been low relative to non-WAMU countries. This situation should have a neutral or benign effect on the use of natural resources. But because of chronic fiscal deficits, WAMU countries have been plagued by gradual appreciation of the real exchange rate. Considering timber exports, for example, the effective producer prices in Côte d'Ivoire are border prices. An appreciating local currency thus implies increasing nontraded input costs, which will reduce competitiveness and the profitability of timber exports, in turn creating an incentive to cut and sell standing timber sooner rather than later.[16]

Under a stabilization program, monetary restraint through reduced central bank credits to government has a deflationary effect. The result is reduced demand through cuts in public spending. This situation will relieve upward pressure on nontraded prices, hence also on the real exchange rate. Such restraint may thus reduce incentives to harvest and export standing timber.

CHAPTER THREE

Trade Policy

A major distortion of trade in Côte d'Ivoire was the appreciation of the real exchange rate and the loss of export competitiveness. Côte d'Ivoire was unable to use a devaluation to accommodate the inflationary fiscal profligacy and monetary expansion of the Seventies, owing to WAMU membership. The government has repeatedly tried to stem the rising flood of imports with high tariff and nontariff barriers, but these attempts have only dampened the competitiveness of export sectors further.

Attempts to reform trade policy and stimulate exports have included a simulated devaluation (i.e., export subsidy) combined with harmonization and reduction of import duties under SALs II and III. Additional sectoral incentives are described below. If these reforms had been effective, they might have resulted in increased industrial output—and pollution as well. For industries that rely on natural resource or agricultural inputs (e.g., wood, food processing), increased production may have exacerbated environmental degradation, given the underlying market and policy failures in rural land management. Note that if rural land rights were secure, a stimulation of agricultural exports could actually encourage conservation and investment by increasing rural producers' incomes. In any event, the planned trade reforms were largely ineffective, with little or no net effect on exports and the environment.

SECTORAL POLICY

Various attempts were made over the past decade to reduce supply-side distortions, structural and institutional inefficiencies that impede sectoral growth. Proposed reforms include liberalization of consumer and producer prices, reduction of subsidies, and privatization and restructuring of public sector enterprise.

The impact of these reforms on the environment and natural resources is often difficult to determine owing to multisectoral linkages. Effective supply-side reforms can aggravate environmental degradation by stimulating production whose processes are characterized by market failure and negative environmental impacts (e.g., excessive land degradation arising from tenure problems, pollution due to production externalities). And some supply-side reforms can further environmental objectives, as they do when cuts in subsidies (e.g., electricity, fertilizer) result in more efficient use of polluting inputs. In the following sections, potential linkages are discussed for three major economic sectors: agriculture, forestry, and industry.

Agriculture

Rain-fed cultivation of food and cash crops constitutes the main engine of development in Côte d'Ivoire. Coffee and cocoa together accounted for more than one-half the total value of commodity exports in 1987.[17] The relative importance of agriculture has decreased little since independence. Recent adjustment reforms probably had far less impact on agriculture than did the decline in world commodity prices, particularly for the main export crops, coffee and cocoa. Once again, the environmental impacts of these changes are ambiguous.

By depressing farm incomes, the historical pattern of heavy taxation on agriculture has certainly had negative environmental impacts. It discouraged investment and locked producers in traditional low-input low-output, extensive farming. It may also force rural populations to exploit any available open-access resources (e.g., forests) to supplement farm income. Yet heavy taxation may also have persuaded some of the rural population to leave for the city. Urban migration may have reduced pressures on the rural environment while creating new urban pressures in the form of congestion and pollution.

Subsidies on fertilizers, agricultural extension services, and other incentives encouraged export agriculture during the boom years of the 1970s. At the same time, cash crops were heavily taxed through low producer prices fixed by a monopsony public marketing board. The net incentive effects are ambiguous. The World Bank report found less than unity effective rates of protection for coffee and cocoa in 1985. But price stability under the state marketing system may have had some positive incentive effect by mitigating producers' price volatility risk, even though domestic prices were consistently below world levels.

Until 1989, the major objective of adjustment reforms in the agricultural sector was to promote increased cash crop exports through higher producer prices. This measure was offset by reduced public subsidies for modern imported inputs (fertilizers and pesticides, used mostly on cash crops) to promote their more efficient use. The net impact of these reforms, had they been implemented, remains uncertain. Higher producer prices may simply have affected the relative mix of crops selected by farmers. Reduced subsidies, on the other hand, could discourage the adoption of more intensive technologies and thus perpetuate high rates of deforestation under traditional systems of extensive agriculture.

In reality, producer prices for export crops were reduced in 1989, in line with falling world prices. Imported input prices increased owing to cuts in subsidies. The short-term effects will have been minimal because of supply rigidities. The major cash crops are perennial; hence farmers cannot respond immediately. If the price changes are maintained, however, one can expect reduced efforts and production from existing cash crop plantations and reduced conservation efforts.

One can also expect a slower expansion of cash crops onto remaining forest land, but the latter effect will be mitigated by the relative price inelasticity of aggregate agricultural output. Labor and other constraints limit the ability of smallholders to expand total output. Hence price changes for particular crops tend to favor a shift in the mix of crops grown rather than an expansion or retreat of total cultivated surface area (which tends to track rural population growth). There will also be little supply response to any changes in aggregate returns to agriculture owing to the absence of other economic opportunities for rural smallholders in the medium term.

A shift to food crops may have been further encouraged by recent price liberalization (e.g., increased rice prices) and the fact that food crop production generally involves less intensive use of imported inputs. The overall environmental impacts may be negative because annuals are more destructive of soil fertility and thus require large amounts of land under traditional shifting cultivation.

Forestry

Timber exports have historically come in third place, behind coffee and cocoa. From 1960 to 1983, timber products represented 13-32 percent of the total value of commodity exports, with a downward trend discernible from the early 1970s. Prospects for the timber industry in Côte d'Ivoire are not good. The best native forest was logged over in a short time; only relatively patchy reserves of inaccessible and less valuable stands remain. Most of the previously logged areas have since been cleared for agriculture, leaving little hope for natural regeneration of timber stocks on a large scale.

Forested land in Côte d'Ivoire is legally divided into two categories. The *Domaine Forestier Rural* consists of secondary logged forest and fallow land, mostly under traditional management, that is intended as a reserve for agriculture. The *Domaine Forestier Permanent* is comprised of public forest reserves, including logged and virgin forest, that are intended for sustainable timber production under concessions leased by the government to private firms.

Concessions are granted under 5- to 20-year leases in units of 2,500 hectares. Since 1967, only citizens of Côte d'Ivoire could obtain and hold concessions legally. By 1986, Ivoirian concessionaires outnumbered foreigners 10 to 1. However, although nominal ownership of forest concessions is now concentrated among Ivoirian nationals, capital ownership in the forest industry remains largely in foreign hands (70 percent by value in 1983).[18]

Five types of fees are charged to concession holders: (1) a one-time license fee and (2) communal property damage assessment, both payable at a flat rate per concession; (3) a license renewal fee and (4) ground rent, payable on an annual basis at a flat rate per concession; and (5) stumpage fees assessed on the volume of logs extracted. The latter vary by species to reflect relative quality and by destination (domestic processing or export).

At prevailing rates up to 1990, all concession and stumpage fees together amounted to about CFA francs 93 per cubic meter, or less than one-quarter of 1 percent of the average freight on board value of exported timber. Concession and stumpage pricing policies thus grossly understate the true scarcity value of timber (and of forests). Low concession fees have led to the growth of a lively secondary market in concession rights, and there is a strong likelihood that the allocation of forest concessions is subject to rent-seeking. Stumpage fees are intended to finance public reforestation efforts, but the level of fees is wholly inadequate. Total replanting from 1966 to 1985 covered just under 59,000 hectares, compared to approximately 6 million hectares of forest logged over the same period. And even this amount of planting required additional funds from foreign donors. Moreover, because stumpage fees are assessed on logs extracted instead of on marketable stocks, there is a strong incentive for high-grading, resulting in heavy collateral damage and further subverting any incentive to manage immature stocks or replant.

Logging firms and timber processors are also subject to income taxes as well as export duties on international sales. These taxes represented about 11 percent of gross revenue in the timber industry in 1985 and contributed about 6 percent of total government revenue.[19] Export taxes vary by species and type of product; the highest rates (up to 45 percent) are charged on exports of high-value raw logs, with preferential rates as low as 5 percent for processed timber products derived from secondary species. The aim of these differential tariffs is to promote the processing of more plentiful species and the conservation of the rarest species while increasing value-added on all timber exports.

In addition to these price incentives, domestic processing was further encouraged by export bans on certain species and by regulations requiring fixed proportions of total log production to be delivered to local mills. As a result of these policies, log exports fell from about 80 percent of total timber exports in the early 1960s to under 50 percent in the mid-1980s. Secondary species exports have grown from less than one-quarter of the total in 1960 to more than one-half in 1983, although this change may also reflect the growing scarcity of primary species.[20]

A common problem with increased domestic processing is that most processing operations in Côte d'Ivoire are extremely inefficient. Some firms maintain their processing operations simply to be eligible for participating in the far more lucrative log export trade.[21]

Recent policy reform in the forestry sector has focused on the augmentation of concession fees and stumpage taxes and the institution of an auction system for export licenses. Fiscal reforms planned under the forestry sector adjustment program sponsored by the World Bank would increase concession and stumpage fees significantly between 1990 and 1995. Concession fees will rise 250-1,000 percent and stumpage fees 300-1,000 percent. More information is required on planned increases in export duties and changes in concession policy (e.g., period and replanting covenants) under the adjustment program.

Reform of concession and stumpage fees will effectively double the average amount paid per cubic meter. This change will increase the proportion of economic rents from forestry activities that accrue to government, but fees will remain far too low to have any significant influence on concession management practices. None of the reforms is likely to have nearly so much impact on the rate of logging as the increasing scarcity of commercially valuable species.

Industry

Industry has assumed growing importance in the economy of Côte d'Ivoire, but progress has been slow. Accounting for 19 percent of total output and 7 percent of exports in 1965, industry had grown to 25 percent and 13 percent, respectively, by 1987.[22] Much of this growth was in import substitution manufacturing. Heavy public investment and direct government control have been a common theme, with a wall of trade barriers used to maintain high effective rates of protection from foreign competitors.

In theory, the promotion of industry through trade protection can impact the environment in several areas: the use of natural resource inputs, the rate of urban migration and the size of the residual rural population (thus the level of pressure on both urban and rural environments), the relative profitability of agriculture (with many knock-on effects, including the mean rate of investment and intensification), and, directly, the level of industrial pollution. Little evidence is available to determine the environmental impacts of industrial protection in Côte d'Ivoire, although the scale of industrial development suggests that environmental impacts have been relatively modest.

Recent reforms of industrial policy were aimed to promote the export of processed agricultural and forest products (e.g., processed foods, wood products, textiles). This effort would tend to stimulate demand for agricultural commodities used as raw material input, which could have negative environmental consequences in the context of underlying distortions in land use.

The capital-intensive nature of industrial development in Côte d'Ivoire has failed to attract much labor out of agriculture. Trade protection has also depressed relative returns to agriculture; hence it has reduced incentives for investment and intensification. Protection also resulted in high unit production costs and prices for manufactured consumer goods, depressing real farm wages and rural income further.

POLICY SCENARIOS (EMPIRICAL ANALYSIS AND SIMULATION)

From an economic perspective, the optimal forest stock in Côte d'Ivoire can be estimated from a comparison of relative returns to forestry (defined as sustainable timber production) and agriculture (gross margins to cash and food crops, net of purchased inputs). For this purpose, an optimal control model was adapted from Ehui and Hertel.[23]

The first step was to reestimate Fisher's aggregate agricultural yield index to include cash crops, which had been ignored in the original version of the model. The yield index was weighted by nominal world prices for cash crops and domestic prices for (nontraded) food crops.

A fundamental assumption of the model is that agricultural yields under the prevailing extensive production system are linked to deforestation. Deforestation in the current period is assumed to increase yields because crops benefit from more fertile newly cleared land. Conversely, yields are expected to fall with cumulative deforestation, reflecting a gradual decline in mean soil fertility.[24]

Using coefficients derived from the revised aggregate yield function to estimate returns to agriculture, one can recalculate the optimal forest stock for Côte d'Ivoire. The resulting estimates are considerably larger than Ehui and Hertel's. The only significant difference between the two models is the inclusion of cash crops. Intuitively, this change might be expected to increase aggregate yields and returns to agriculture, resulting in a smaller optimal forest stock. However, the econometric analysis produces smaller coefficients on all independent variables in the new aggregate yield function and lower calculated values of the yield index in all years. When the smaller coefficients are plugged into the equation used to calculate the optimal forest stock, a different result is obtained. It does not appear to reflect any meaningful difference in the data but simply mirrors the way that the equations are formulated.[25]

Despite slightly different results, both this case study and Ehui and Hertel estimate an optimal forest stock in excess of actual reserves, assuming modest rates of time preference. Both studies also note that the optimal forest stock would be much larger if the value of nontimber products and other environmental benefits were included in estimated returns to forestry.

One implication of the difference in the magnitude of the two estimates is a huge disparity in the discount rate required to bring the optimal stock into line with the actual stock (i.e., the rate of time preference required to justify the current small stock). In Ehui and Hertel's version, a relatively low rate of about 9 percent is required, whereas for this case study the rate of discount has to rise to 80 percent before the optimal and actual forest stocks converge (at 2.2 million hectares). In general, both studies note a significant impact on the optimal forest stock by varying the discount rate applied.

This focus on discounting highlights the fundamental reason for the discrepancy between the actual forest stock and the optimal estimate. Essentially, land tenure insecurity and distortions of timber concession policy may be expressed in terms of high rates of time preference. These influences lead producers to extract the maximum value in the minimum time and all but ignore any potential returns beyond the current year. Clarification of rural land tenure and reform of forest concession policy may help to attenuate private time preferences, thereby reducing incentives for rapid forest conversion.

High rates of private time preference may reflect not only the prevailing tenure situation and underlying institutional incentives for land clearing but also the relative poverty and lack of opportunities confronting farmers. For most rural households, sustainable management of natural forest for timber production is just not a viable option. From the perspective of farming populations, the relevant returns to forestry are limited to casual employment by timber firms at low prevailing wages and subsistence exploitation of nontimber products, such as wildlife and certain plants. These benefits do not compare to potential returns to farming.

Further simulations were carried out with a submodel that linked the relative prices of timber products and agricultural inputs to general population growth, the nominal exchange rate, and cash crop output prices.[26] The numeraire is aggregate agricultural output prices, which in turn are a function of traded (cash crop) and nontraded (food crop) prices.

The submodel is based on a positive statistical correlation of the nontraded price (PN) with population growth, which is interpreted as a reflection of increased demand for food crops in the context of supply constraints. This increase leads to decreasing real prices of forest products and fertilizer relative to aggregate agricultural output prices. The end result of population growth is thus increased conversion of forest land to agriculture and a smaller optimal forest stock.

Simulations carried out with the submodel yield the conclusion that a devaluation (if feasible) would have beneficial environmental effects. It would because real prices of tradeable forestry products and imported fertilizers would rise more than aggregate real prices of agricultural outputs. In other words, returns to forestry, which is presumed to encourage forest conservation, look better relative to agriculture. Increasing the producer prices of traded crops (i.e., coffee, cocoa) predictably results in a lower optimal forest stock owing to higher relative returns to agriculture.

The simulations are relevant to the adjustment experience of Côte d'Ivoire insofar as they shed light on the possible impact of reduced domestic absorption. The model suggests that cutting aggregate demand will effectively reduce relative returns to agriculture, thus reducing the pace of forest conversion.

On the other hand, although adjustment in Côte d'Ivoire has indeed dampened demand (to the extent that it has been effective at all), the resulting recession has been largely urban. Indeed, the rural economy may have enjoyed some improvement in relative terms of trade. This change could actually encourage agricultural production and accelerate unsustainable forest exploitation, particularly in light of stagnant employment opportunities in most Ivoirian cities. A possible mitigating influence might be the drop in coffee and cocoa prices since 1989, which would combine with urban recession to discourage immigration from neighboring countries. Thus the net impact of adjustment on the environment remains ambiguous.

CONCLUSIONS

This case study shows that there is no simple link between macroeconomic adjustment and the environment. Part of the reason is the conflicting nature of many adjustment reforms, which can have contradictory effects on the ways that natural resources and the environment are exploited. The empirical analysis suggests that certain macroeconomic policy reforms may have favorable environmental impacts, notably a devaluation of the CFA franc, if that were feasible. But in general, underlying institutional factors and market and policy failure at the sectoral level appear to have a far more significant impact on natural resource use than macroeconomic instruments.

Côte d'Ivoire is typical of many developing countries in the types of environmental market and policy failures that occur. Market failures run the gamut; they include externalities (e.g., the absence of markets for certain environmental services), public goods and open-access exploitation, imperfect information, lack of mechanisms to hedge risk and uncertainty, and lack of competition in markets for certain key goods and services. On the policy side, the use of natural resources in Côte d'Ivoire is plagued by macroeconomic and sectoral price distortions as well as institutional weakness.

Many relevant policy failures are described here, particularly in terms of the potential positive or negative environmental impacts of recent economic policy reforms. The analysis of underlying structural failures in resource markets is less developed; it is confined largely to qualitative discussion of rural land tenure system tensions. The problem of external impacts and the absence of markets for certain environmental services provided by forests is also suggested. Briefly, the major environmental market failures in Côte d'Ivoire include:

- *Externalities and the lack of markets for environmental goods and services.* Evidence suggests that significant external impacts may be associated with deforestation for timber extraction and agriculture. They include the loss of many nontraded secondary forest products and important environmental services, such as microclimate maintenance and watershed protection. The existence of such nonpriced external impacts implies that traded forestry products are underpriced while agricultural outputs may be overpriced in an open market.

- *Public goods and open-access exploitation.* Forest conservation for microclimate regulation may be a public good insofar as no individual can conserve enough natural forest to maintain a hospitable climate regime for sustainable crop production. But perhaps the government can (the net benefits are uncertain). There are also clear indications of tenure insecurity and open-access problems in the exploitation of natural forests, for both timber (owing to excessively short concessions and the lack of replanting requirements) and agriculture (owing to the notion of appropriation by land clearing and the ambiguity and conflict between indigenous and formal tenure systems). The case study highlights the need for rural land tenure reform, but not at the expense of traditional communal property rights.

- *Imperfect information and the lack of mechanisms to hedge risk and uncertainty.* These factors can elevate private time preference rates and thus discourage prudent resource conservation. Potential contributing factors include the poverty of rural producers, volatility of prices (especially prevalent of late), and ignorance of new technology.

The major policy failures affecting use of natural resources and the environment in Côte d'Ivoire (some of them partly or wholly corrected under recent adjustment reforms) include:

- *Agriculture.* Monopsonistic pricing of agricultural outputs, especially export crops, can potentially depress cash crop production, but it may be offset by various input subsidies. The ambiguous legal system governing rural land tenure is an example of institutional policy failure.
- *Forestry.* Inappropriate pricing and tenure policy for forest concessions and insufficient incentives for domestic processing. Heavier taxation and more restrictions on the forestry industry are needed to achieve a sustainable production level, in addition to more vigorous protection of forest reserves.
- *Industry.* Ineffective regulation of polluting enterprises, consumer subsidies for electricity, and trade protection of inefficient polluting operations.

The analysis described here is a new field of research in Côte d'Ivoire. These results and conclusions inevitably reflect the partial nature of the information available, the paucity of previous work, and the almost total lack of relevant statistical data. Different conclusions might be obtained with more complete information and more sophisticated analytical tools. Nevertheless, this study makes a substantial contribution to the analysis of environmental issues in Côte d'Ivoire by helping identify the relative importance, underlying causes, and social and economic consequences of environmental degradation. It also highlights the urgent need for additional research on links between economic conditions and the environment in tropical countries and for the collection of more systematic and comprehensive environmental data.

1. J. Yao, Y. Kouadio, J. Akomian, and O. Angoran, "Structural Adjustment and the Environment: The Case of Côte d'Ivoire," report to World Wide Fund for Nature, Washington, D.C., 1992.

2. World Bank, *World Development Report 1991: The Challenge of Development* (Washington, D.C., 1991).

3. Heavy taxation of agriculture may have kept average wages down by depressing rural incomes, but this effect has not been exploited, given a policy of maintaining relatively high wages in the urban formal sector and a capital-intensive approach to industrial development.

4. Central bank credits to the member governments of WAMU are normally limited. However, as the *Centre Ivoirien de Recherches Economiques et Sociales* points out, Côte d'Ivoire has consistently breached the nominal ceiling, reflecting the country's political influence in the union.

5. In countries with well-developed capital markets, monetary policy is an important tool for demand management. But Côte d'Ivoire's financial sector is relatively undeveloped, reducing the impact of changes in interest rates and reserve requirements.

6. C. Morrisson, "Balancing Adjustment and Equity," *OECD Observer* 172(1991):13-16.

7. CIRES had considerable difficulty finding background information on the nature and extent of environmental degradation in Côte d'Ivoire. This situation is partly due to the scarcity of previous studies and the lack of basic empirical data. Some of the difficulty appears to result from reluctance or perhaps excessive tardiness on the part of government agencies approached for information. A direct appeal by the London Environmental Economics Centre was required to obtain draft copies of reports on the state of the environment, recently prepared by the Environment Department (under the Ministry for the Environment and Construction) and the Remote Sensing and Geographic Information Unit of the Department of Public Works (*Grands Travaux*).

8. J. Yao *et al., op. cit;* J.E. Akomian, "Etude sur le Regime Foncier Rural Ivoirien et les Problèmes Environnementaux Majeurs Qui en Découlent" (Mimeographed, 1991).

9. Other factors that push rural populations onto remaining forested

lands include chronic rural poverty, population pressure and the lack of appropriate technologies for intensification of agriculture, and the lack of alternative employment opportunities.

10. This figure may reflect a greater demand for land situated in dense forest, which is highly regarded by coffee and cocoa producers, as well as the pressure of timber exploitation.

11. T. Amelung, "Tropical Deforestation as an International Economic Problem" (Paper delivered at the Egon-Sohmen Foundation Conference on Economic Evolution and Environmental Concerns, Linz, Austria, 30-31 August 1991).

12. E.B. Barbier, S. Rietbergen, and D.W. Pearce, "Economics of Tropical Forest Policy," in J.B. Thornes, ed., *Deforestation: Environmental and Social Impacts* (Chapman and Hall, 1991).

13. This section draws on information provided by soil scientists at the International Institute for Scientific Research for Development in Africa (IIRSDA). This recently created organization inherited the facilities and many staff of a previous French overseas research center (ORSTOM) located at Adiopodoume, Côte d'Ivoire.

14. A.O. Ayemou, "Analysis of Forest Management Strategies in Côte d'Ivoire: An Economic Model" (Ph.D. diss., University of Illinois, Urbana, 1989).

15. Yoro, personal communication, *Institut International de Recherche Scientifique pour le Developpement en Afrique*, Adiopodoume, Côte d'Ivoire, 1991, S.H. Schneider, "Tropical Forests and Climate," *Climate Change* (Kleuver Publishers, London), special issue 19(1-2) (1991).

16. An appreciating currency also implies declining costs for traded inputs, such as imported machinery. Important questions are the relative value of traded inputs in total costs and the extent to which their real cost has changed owing to tariff reform.

17. World Bank, *From Crisis to Sustainable Growth* (Washington, D.C., 1989).

18. Ayemou, op. cit.

19. Ibid.

20. Ibid.

21. Ibid.

22. World Bank, *From Crisis to Sustainable Growth*, op. cit.

23. S.K. Ehui, and T.W. Hertel, "Deforestation and Agricultural Productivity in the Côte d'Ivoire," *Amer. J. Agr. Econ.* 71(1989):3, 703-11.

24. The observed decline of yields with cumulative deforestation could alternatively be interpreted in light of the views of an IIRSDA soil scientist who claims that physical degradation of soil fertility under agriculture in the forest zone has not been a significant problem. Instead, the major environmental problem arising from agricultural expansion in the forest zone is a long-term and apparently permanent decline in mean annual precipitation. Hence the negative effect on yields of cumulative deforestation would reflect the progressive loss of the climatic benefits of natural forest (Yoro, op. cit.).

25. Recall that the second term in CIRES's equation (4) compares relative returns to agriculture and forestry. In Ehui and Hertel's version, agricultural returns exceed forestry returns. The effect is to reduce the optimal stock (owing to a negative sign on μ). In CIRES's version, the difference between agricultural and forestry returns in the base case is essentially zero; hence the second term in equation (4) drops out (i.e., there is no offsetting deduction), and the resulting optimal forest stock is larger than Ehui and Hertel's.

26. Simulations with the submodel yield only small changes in the size of the optimal forest stock owing to the way the latter is calculated.

CASE STUDY FOR MEXICO

by the London Environmental and Economics Centre,
based on a study directed by Juan Carlos Belausteguigoitia*

MACROECONOMIC HISTORY AND BROAD PATTERN OF DEVELOPMENT

Overview

In terms of macroeconomic policy, Mexico has experienced the full range from *dirigiste* import substitution policies to the current laissez-faire, privatization-oriented, export-led policies to those that respond to times of overabundant foreign income and to foreign exchange crises. It is difficult to say categorically and unequivocally that one policy was better or worse for the environment than another. What does emerge from this case study is that economic instability is not good for the environment. When the economy is badly managed, resources devoted to environmental protection decline and pressures on industry and agriculture to "keep its environmental house in order" are much diminished.

Because Mexico's experience shows that private sector policies are largely more successful than those of the public sector in keeping the macroeconomic forces in equilibrium, there is reason for preferring them on environmental grounds. In general, this study demonstrates the best

*José María Rivera, Norma Alvarez, Pola Strauss, Magdalena Fernandez, Cecilia Kuthy, Jose Carlos Fernandez, Olga Elena Perez, and Carlos Muñoz Peña comprised the research team from the *Instituto Tecnologico Autonomo de Mexico* (ITAM).

balance for sustainable development: government environmental controls with careful macroeconomic management and extensive use of the private sector whenever the latter has a comparative advantage.

Macroeconomic History: From the 1940s to the 1960s

At the beginning of World War II, Mexico was predominantly a rural economy, with about 75 percent of its population living off the land (the same proportion is now urban). Yet it was beginning to raise living standards through large government investments in irrigation (for agriculture) and the industrial production boost provoked by the war. Although the government subsidized agricultural prices, a policy that has since caused fiscal and environmental problems, it prudently managed its public finances over the 1940s, 1950s, and 1960s to an extent that has not been matched until recently. Inflation was in line with international trends, the exchange rate was relatively stable (from 1955 to 1970, it remained at 12.5 pesos to the dollar), and the fiscal deficit and foreign debt remained small and manageable. At the same time, national income grew slowly but steadily.

The economy looked stable, perhaps even sustainable, but it was not. The growth was being achieved increasingly through subsidies to industry and protectionism, and government pricing policies and neglect of the environment were paving the way for chronic environmental difficulties. The use of subsidies meant that the government's fiscal prudence could not continue to be maintained because industry, which was featherbedded through protection, was becoming increasingly inefficient. The policy of low prices for key agricultural products to urban workers and a favored industrial sector encouraged an already rapid rate of urbanization. At the same time, subsidies to agricultural inputs led to inefficient fertilizer use. Overall, this period of economic development paid scant attention to the environmental consequences of the structural changes being made in the economy.

Experiences in the 1970s and Early 1980s

The 1970s began, for Mexico, with an expansionist economic policy in which public investment played a leading role. To finance this expansion, the fiscal deficit rose from 1.8 percent of gross domestic product (GDP) in 1971 to 7.6 percent in 1976. The consequences were predictable. Inflation rose and imports were sucked in rapidly; confidence in the currency dropped, causing a capital flight. This combination of events necessitated a devaluation in 1976, the year President Echeverria's administration ended and President Lopez Portillo's began. The following year, the government announced a considerable increase in oil reserves. The possibility of increasing oil exports to alleviate the fiscal imbalances was taken up with vigor. Oil exports increased steadily during the late 1970s and early 1980s, amounting to about $14 billion by 1984. But from a macroeconomic point of view, this rapid expansion created more problems than it solved. The substantial increases in demand generated by the increased revenues meant that domestic prices of nontradeable goods rose sharply. Further, these revenues, which should have been converted into other forms of productive capital if the economy was to pursue a sustainable development path, were too frequently used to finance both current expenditures and investment projects of doubtful value. In sum, this was a period of unsustainable and poor economic growth in both quantitative and qualitative terms.

In years when oil prices were high, government revenues were high, but in other years they fell sharply. In 1981, when the oil market was weak, Mexico faced a huge current account deficit. Private investors lost confidence in the handling of the economy and capital started to move out on a large scale. This situation necessitated a devaluation of 57 percent in February 1982 and a suspension of payments to foreign creditors the following August.

The Oil Boom and the Environment

The bias in the economy toward oil not only reduced the attractiveness of investments in other sectors but, with subsidized domestic oil prices, also encouraged excessive and indiscriminate use of petroleum products at home. This state of affairs, combined with exploration and oil production, had several adverse environmental consequences. Petroleum exploitation opened up regions that had hitherto been inaccessible. The ecological consequences of the new settlements have not been fully analyzed, but it is clear that some areas suffered considerably. The ocean environment has been substantially damaged by the petroleum residues and associated waste matter, and inland and coastal waters have suffered as well. Further, cheap gasoline and kerosene resulted in levels of use that are at least partly responsible for the air pollution problems facing Mexico's large cities. Petroleum pricing and air pollution are discussed in more detail below.

Economic Policy from 1983 to 1989

By 1983, the oil boom had run its course, and the government was forced to make difficult macroeconomic decisions. These were embodied in a structural adjustment package called the *Plan Integral de Recuperaciòn Económica*. The instruments used in this program were entirely orthodox and in accordance with International Monetary Fund (IMF) guidelines. They involved reducing public expenditures, cutting the fiscal deficit, raising real interest rates, depressing real wages, and shifting resources to the export sector. In addition, the government began to shift its economic philosophy from protectionism and state control to liberalization and privatization. In 1986, Mexico finally joined the General Agreement on Tariffs and Trade, thus committing to less restrictive trade practices. In terms of privatization, the government began divestiture of state-owned hotels, automobile factories, and textile companies and liquidated some that could not be sold. These changes represented a major shift in economic policy. Their immediate impact in economic terms was favorable. Inflation was reduced (although it still remained at 60 percent per annum), and the external imbalances were brought down in the two years from 1983 to 1985. Then the country experienced an earthquake and another sharp drop in the international price of oil, necessitating a further adjustment in its macroeconomic position. This was carried out in 1986 with the assistance of the IMF, and, in fiscal terms, it was again successful. The public sector deficit was turned into a small surplus. But there was a cost in terms of the decline in economic output—it fell 3.6 percent during 1986.

In 1987, economic activity and employment showed some recovery, but the economy remained in the grip of a high inflation rate and nervous expectations about the government's handling of the economy. The high inflation rate was beginning to be institutionalized in the wage and price determination mechanisms to such an extent that it was spiraling out of control. This situation is not uncommon, and the authorities were rightly convinced that it was impossible to maintain a stable high rate of inflation. In December 1987, the Economic Solidarity Pact was announced.

The pact focused on reducing the inflation rate, and in doing so, it combined orthodox measures of tightening credit and reducing public expenditures with less orthodox policies whereby the exchange rate was allowed to float and prices were subject to negotiation. In terms of controlling inflation, the pact was successful. Inflation dropped from 159 percent in 1987 to 50 percent in 1988. At the same time, private investment began to respond to the buoyancy of non-oil exports, resulting from the flexible exchange rate and the greater freedom to import capital and intermediate goods.

The Economy from 1989 to Date

In 1989, Mexico sought to make further structural adjustments by renegotiating its foreign commercial debt. The justification for this effort was the fact that the economy was being hampered in its attempt to move to a higher growth path by the size of its debt and the demand it made on its foreign exchange earnings. At the same time, there was a need to change the term structure of the debt so that more long-term funds could be used to replace some of the shorter-term borrowing. Because the government moved to a more liberal economic policy regime and fiscal management grew more effective, confidence in Mexico increased abroad. The benefits of these policies are beginning to be realized now, with added impetus from establishment of the North American Free Trade Area.

The next section looks at how macroeconomic policy and macroeconomic management have affected the environment. At the same time, it asks how these impacts could have been more favorable.

MACROECONOMIC POLICY AND THE ENVIRONMENT

General Observations

Although there is no simple relationship between the level of public expenditures and environmental degradation, there appears to be a tendency to cut the environmental budget when expenditures are cut and to increase it when expenditures increase. Thus changes in public expenditures are related to the resources devoted to the environment. In many respects, this situation is not surprising. With pressure to cut expenditures, the less important items go first, and the environment is not as high a priority as health or education for most governments. In Mexico, the government recognized the importance of environmental issues explicitly when it established the Bureau of Urban Development and Environment (SEDUE) in 1983. But this ministry has generally had a derisory budget, and in periods of fiscal cuts, the environment-related budget, which includes national parks, has fallen faster than that of government spending in general.

The relationship between government spending in general and the environment is more complex than it may appear. Periods of high spending in the Forties, Fifties, and Sixties resulted in a distorted agricultural sector and a pro-urban bias, with harmful environmental consequences. The cause was less the level of spending than its composition. A similar observation applies to the periods of retrenchment, when spending was cut. With some cuts, less was available for public waste disposal and public investment programs, but in other cases (e.g., the sale of public enterprises), the pressure for subsidies was reduced and more was available for pressing environmental and other needs.

Another aspect of the fiscal policy-environment link implicit in the discussion of Mexico's economy is whether the government was less attentive to the need for sustainable development in periods of macroeconomic crises. In terms of exploiting its oil reserves, the government has tended to draw more out of the ground when the economy was in difficulty. What changed radically during the economic crisis was investment in the oil sector including exploration and development of new fields and renovation and safety measures at existing sites. This practice need not be inconsistent with a policy of sustainable development so long as an amount equal to that wealth is invested to ensure the country's economic well-being. Unfortunately, no evidence exists to suggest that it has been. On the other hand, Mexico also has additional mineral sources of wealth as well as renewable sources, such as its tropical forests. No evidence exists to suggest that the government has used these sources more intensively in hard times. If anything, the rate of extraction was lower during recessions.

Taxes, Domestic Price Policy, and the Environment

The environment, of course, is affected not only by fiscal spending in general. It can be influenced much more by indirect policy measures, such as taxes and subsidies. Mention has been made of the problems Mexico created by subsidizing agricultural products to urban workers and the environmental impacts of subsidies for fertilizers and pesticides. Subsidies to petroleum products have resulted in levels of their use that exacerbate an already serious air pollution problem in cities. Many of these policies have encouraged an urban bias that is partly responsible for the large urban population in the country, although to what extent they are responsible is not known.

In recent years, the cost of public services, such as water and energy, have increased. Yet the prices charged are still much too low to cover even the nonenvironmental costs of providing them. The environmental costs have yet to enter the calculations. One argument used extensively to counter the use of higher prices to protect the environment is that it hurts the poorest and most vulnerable groups. For this reason, macroeconomic policy should seek to allocate resources in other ways, perhaps rationing the availability of key environmental factors. This reasoning has been influential in restricting auto use in Mexico City to combat air pollution. But the policy is not all that successful, and the use of charges would not be as regressive as is often claimed.

Trade Policy and the Environment

Mexico is well aware that strict U.S. environmental controls will be an incentive for industry to set up in Mexico if it can avoid those controls. There is evidence to suggest that the Maquiladora program reveals some environmental damage as a price for creating employment and output. The subject is discussed in greater detail in a later section, but it is worth pointing out here that the occurrence of damage is not reason enough to argue against the program or to demand the same standards for the two countries. Because the costs of environmental damage are not necessarily the same, there may well be a rationale for Mexico's having different environmental standards in some noncritical areas than those of the United States. Conversely, it would not make sense for Mexico to require the same air emissions standards as those in the United States simply because the costs of the latter would be prohibitively high for a country with one-fifth the living standard of its northern neighbor. This is a difficult position for politicians to state publicly although many might agree with it in private.

The other link between the environment and trade is protectionism. Where industry can successfully argue for protection against foreign competition, the level of that protection will be higher if the industry is subject to the polluter pays principle. This situation is not peculiar to Mexico, and the pressures on government not to raise industry's costs are present even when there is no official protection. But often Mexico's industry has successfully resisted imposition of the principle. Because government has limited resources for environmental protection, this opposition meant that little is done about several environmental problems caused by industry.

The next section looks at some specific sectoral issues and asks how macroeconomic policy has affected them. They include soil erosion, deforestation, and water management. It is followed by an examination of the Maquiladora program, energy subsidies, and their environmental impacts. The review of Mexico's experience discusses some general themes that emerge. They include the development-environment trade-off, the relationship between debt and the environment, and the role of poverty in the environment-macroeconomic policy trade-off. The last section sets forth the conclusions.

KEY ENVIRONMENTAL ISSUES IN MEXICO

Soil Erosion

As is true of many environmental problems in Mexico, data on the extent of soil erosion are sketchy and, more important, are seriously deficient for analyzing the problem and implementing an appropriate response. Acknowledging that estimates are inconsistent, studies indicate that the problem is significant and is growing. In 1945, an estimated 45 percent of the country's land area suffered from accelerated erosion; more recent estimates are 80 percent for the mid-1970s and 71-98 percent in the 1980s. It has been argued that Mexico has one of the most severe erosion problems in Latin America, with 150,000-2,000,000 hectares of arable land lost through erosion annually.[1]

Erosion results from many complex factors, including natural phenomena, which can be as important as human activities. What follows is a discussion of the impacts of the government's policies toward agriculture as well as its direct investment in protecting the landscape and preventing erosion.

Government Policies That Influence Erosion

Two factors are important in linking government policy and topsoil loss. First, annual crops can be environmentally damaging when grown on unsuitable soils and at unsuitable elevations. Consequently, any instruments of policy (e.g., taxes, exchange rates) that favor the excessive growth of such crops will indirectly impact soil loss. Second, deforestation is a major contributor to soil loss, and any policies that encourage loss of forest cover encourage the loss of topsoil.

Policies Contributing to Soil Loss Through the Planting of Inappropriate Crops

What subsidies are responsible for Mexico's producing large quantities of corn? At the margin, this crop is environmentally damaging, especially when it is grown on unsuitable soils or sloping lands. Government policy encourages the growing of corn by keeping its domestic price much higher than the world price. It is estimated that the soil damage from planting corn will lead to the loss of 1 million tons of soil, whose value is the equivalent of 12 percent of the harvest, by the year 2000.

These subsidies are reinforced by others that encourage excessive cultivation of the crops; subsidies on water, pesticides, and fertilizers are all indirectly responsible. In addition, excessive fertilizer use is a cause of poor soil conservation practices.

An overvalued exchange rate also encourages production of annual, as opposed to perennial, crops (e.g., coffee, fruit) because perennials respond more directly to export markets.

Policies Contributing to Soil Loss Through Deforestation

As the next section points out, Mexico has also suffered from extensive loss of forest cover. Because this loss effects soil erosion, it is important to look at policies that cause deforestation. It is argued later that some deforestation can be traced to the lack of properly defined property rights. In some areas, which community or group of communities has the right to use the land has not been settled. Moreover, it is not in the government's interest to try to settle them. Another hypothesis is that the system of land-use rights incorporated in the *ejido* system favors clearing the land for pasture and livestock instead of maintaining a sustainable forestry. Unfortunately, because of lack of data, these ideas remain hypotheses, but with a strong possibility of their being at least partially correct.

The Direct Role of the State

Considerable responsibility for misuse of land must be borne by the Federal Agricultural Reform Law, which states that all land that is "unused" may be subject to forced cultivation "regardless of whether it belongs to the nation or a private party." There is no doubt of the need to provide land to those who do not have it. Mexico has a grave problem of poverty and income inequality that needs to be addressed. The problem is to define the rights to use of this land in a way that is environmentally less damaging. Fragile lands and steep slopes are not suitable for the uses to which they are put once the land has been reallocated.

Through the General Law on Ecological Equilibrium and Environmental Protection, the government attempts to define ecological standards for using the land and carrying out certain processes. These guidelines indicate acceptable practices, but offenders cannot be fined or jailed because the government has not allocated the resources needed for effective enforcement.

In terms of budgetary allocations, the government devotes little to soil conservation. For example, the Agricultural Secretariat spent only 0.6 percent of its 1987 budget on soil conservation. The main reason appears to be the lack of a long-term view of ecosystem protection that a soil conservation program requires. Much of the concern is focused on level ground, and slope and mountainside farming is not given much attention.

Conclusions on Soil Erosion

It is remarkable how little is known at the quantitative level about this problem, which is certainly important for Mexico. Several hypotheses have been advanced for the rate of soil loss, and most are likely to be correct. But how important are they? What impact would changes in the fiscal and other economic variables have on corn production in different areas, and how would soil erosion rates change? What impacts would changes in input subsidies have? And what should be the priority areas for government action? To answer these questions, data are needed on a consistent basis, and they are urgently needed.

Deforestation

Forests are an important resource for Mexico, not only for the timber products and fuelwood that they provide but also for the biodiversity that they support. Many mammal and bird species that they harbor are endemic; 53 percent of the reptile species and 14 percent of plant families can be found nowhere else in the world. The country is also important for its tropical ecosystems. On a global scale, it ranks seventh in terms of tropical forest extension.

But Mexico has been losing its forests at a rapid rate. The Food and Agriculture Organization of the United Nations estimates a loss rate of 1.3 percent per annum. Other more detailed regional estimates show that in the last 10 years, about one-half the forest cover has been lost. As is true with soil erosion, data are confused, irregularly collected, and not current. In fact, deforestation rates for most of the country's states are not known with accuracy. Most trustworthy are the regional studies using satellite information.One researcher, Cuarón, concluded that in the Southeast (Chiapas, Oaxaca, Veracruz, and Tabasco), the rain forests shrank at an annual rate of 7.7 percent between 1976 and 1986.[2] Dirzo carried out a similar study in Sierra de los Tuxtlas and found a deforestation rate of 4.6 percent per annum between 1967 and 1988.[3] Although the picture is incomplete, conditions are undoubtedly serious in terms of forest loss.

Reasons for Deforestation in Mexico

Three broad explanations are given for forest loss: the structure of land ownership and land use restrictions, failure to consider the many forest benefits, and the role of poverty in creating a demand for forest resources.

The Structure of Land Ownership

The types of land ownership in Mexico are private property, social property (*ejidos* and *comunidades*), and state property. An individual's private ownership of agricultural land is limited (e.g., 100 hectares for irrigated land, 800 hectares for forest land). Further, all such land must be in permanent exploitation or it may be expropriated.

For social property, the rules are even more complex. Ownership is collective for a group of farmers, *comunidades* have no private ownership, and *ejidos* allow part of the land to be individually "owned." Ownership in this context is ringed with restrictions. The land may not be sold, rented, mortgaged, or taxed. In addition, no outsiders may work there either as hired hands or as partners. Recently, a restricted partnership was permitted in which outsiders could form a contract to participate in the use of the land for up to 3 years. With regard to forests, outsiders may be involved in exploiting timber only with the express approval of the State Regulatory Authority. Contracts are limited to 3 years; then individuals must give all their assets to the community unit. Prices to be paid or received are renegotiated annually.

Government property is allocated for use increasingly often, with occupation followed by some form of transfer of ownership.

The pattern of ownership and use has profound implications for the way in which land is used. As previously noted, some difficulties arise because the title to community land is unclear. When two groups have competing claims, the tendency is to exploit the land on a much shorter-term basis than would otherwise be the case. Mexico's government has not been able to resolve this common problem. Sometimes deforestation results from conflicting land claims. Although forest regulations state that disputed property is to be treated as a protected area, enforcement capacity is lacking.

A main hypothesis about community land ownership and use is that the restrictions identified above result in less profitability for forestry investment and sustainable use and more for agriculture and cattle raising. Hence they increase forest clearance for these purposes. It is not possible to quantify these impacts, but several factors favor the thesis. First, forestry requires more than the 800 hectares that are permitted under the regulations. On the other hand, for livestock and crop farming, the permitted scale has less impact on unit costs. Second, forestry contract restrictions on outsiders have limited such external involvement; the contract period is too short and the bureaucratic restrictions too demanding. Third, the mortgage restrictions have a greater impact on forestry, whose need to raise capital is greater than that of agriculture. Fourth, the costs of coordinating members of a community to exploit a complex resource using borrowed capital and so on are high. For all these reasons, forestry is not attractive. But what is not clear is whether any forestry would be sustainable if these sociolegal conditions were to be changed. Would it suffer from the problems faced in Indonesia and the Philippines, where efficiency of scale often means efficient destruction of forest resources. Any changes in this area will have to be accompanied by others that ensure sustainable forestry.

Unaccounted Public Benefits from Forestry

Forests are being lost partly because those who control their use do not consider their benefits to the many who have no control over their exploitation. Drainage stabilization and other forest services are not given due weight. And although the government has taken the responsibility for protecting the drainage areas, it does not have the resources to do so. Perhaps these services could be paid for by using private funds more effectively. Mexico has 13 Protected Forestry Zones, covering 18.9 million hectares, where restrictions on land use and felling apply. But resources of the *Secretaria de Agricultura y Recursos Hidraulicos (SARH)* are inadequate for enforcing the regulations. For damage to one such area, see the discussion on the Upper Lerma Basin in the section on water resources.

Other important benefits of forests—to maintain biodiversity, for example—are also clearly undervalued. Because the benefits of biodiversity are global, they cannot be realized without some channeling of international funds into protection efforts. This is beginning to happen. A recent World Bank loan for environmental protection is partly for this purpose. Use of the Global Environmental Facility is another conduit for support. Debt-for-nature exchanges are beginning to be carried out in Mexico. The first such exchange was completed in 1991, and SEDUE has exchanged public debt for funds to be used in scientific stations in the Lacandonian Forest.

Poverty and Deforestation

Often cited is the argument that poverty is a cause of deforestation.

The existence of poverty in Mexico is not in question. In 1977, 73 percent of rural residents, 15.6 million people, were living in poverty (with daily earnings of less than 84 U.S. cents). By 1984, the poorest 73 percent of rural residents had increased to 17.6 million.

Conclusions

Deforestation in Mexico is a serious issue even though how much forest has been lost and how fast it is disappearing are not clear. In terms of its links with macroeconomic policy, the relationship is less clear than it is for other environmental concerns. The focus here has been on the structure of land ownership and restrictions on land use. Also discussed was government's limited ability to deal with land claims and the pressure it is under to provide land in the face of a serious poverty problem.

More resources are needed to deal with this problem. Some may come from the government, but it is not likely to meet the need. Instead, the private sector and the international community must be major providers. There may be a role here for innovative macroeconomic instruments, such as debt-for-nature swaps, special international funds, and so on.

Water Resources

The management of water in Mexico is one of the clearest cases of a pricing policy's adverse environmental consequences. Water is diverted from the countryside to the cities, where it is supplied to the relatively well-off community at highly subsidized rates. Some 20 percent of urban dwellers, most of them poor, pay high prices for poor-quality water delivered by road. Further, about one-third of urban households do not have sewerage connections.

Water for most of the cities is lifted from low-lying areas to large human settlements that are usually situated more than 500 meters above sea level. The large cost is borne almost entirely by the taxpayer. Further, this deviation of water leaves less for the farmers, whose livelihood is badly affected. When superficial sources like the Lerma dry out, the farmers have no water and no compensation. Then pressure to migrate to the cities clearly increases.

If water were priced at the cost of its delivery and the authorities responsible for it were made financially accountable in terms of earning a certain rate of return on their capital, they would be motivated to use cheaper sources of water, including rain water, which is currently added to the drainage system, where it combines with the sewage and flows out. Second, they would be motivated to maintain the system. Much of the water being delivered by the high-cost hydraulic schemes is lost through leaks, filtration, and unregistered connections. According to one calculation, losses from the system supplying Mexico City alone (about 28 percent of the total) are enough to supply Madrid or Rome. Third, authorities would improve the policy affecting use of subterranean reservoirs, which are being mined. And fourth, the additional income would make it possible to extend the supply system to more users without adding to the fiscal burden of the government. Funds for urgently needed treatment plants could be raised in this way. Present treatment plants handle only 10 percent of the municipal sewage volume. Only 35 percent of these plants are in use, and even they are not run efficiently. Of the total municipal and industrial waste water, only 15 percent receives treatment. There is little incentive to treat industrial waste water when the cost of fresh water is so low.

The government is beginning to take action to correct these problems. The National Water Commission approved a diversified financial structure that reduces dependence on fiscal income and looks to tariffs and private sector credits instead. This change will enlarge the private sector's role in managing the country's water supply. Some water treatment schemes have been introduced using funds from the World Bank, the Interamerican Development Bank, and other international agencies. The impact of these measures has not yet been assessed.

An example of improvement efforts are those in the basin of the Lerma-Santiago River. The largest in Mexico, it supplies the cities of Toluca, Queretaro, Celaya, Irapuato, Guadalajara, and Tepic, with an overall population of more than 10 million. The upper Lerma basin has been severely degraded owing to the extinction of its spring (a result of excessive pumping), the return of highly polluted water, and severe deforestation in the higher parts of the basin. Measurements show that the basin has lost one-third of its production potential because of topsoil loss. Population and industrial growth are blamed. But as has been demonstrated, it is the economic structure of incentives that allows such growth in the first place and then encourages misuse of the water.

Quantitative information on the economy-environment links is limited in this area, as in many others. Lack of data on key environmental issues is a real problem in the country. In some cases, the cause is a lack of funds. But in others, such as operating costs, the authorities are reluctant to supply information that may be used against them.

KEY AREAS OF ECONOMIC POLICY AND THEIR ENVIRONMENTAL IMPLICATIONS

This section discusses three areas of policy: the Maquiladora program, energy pricing, and privatization.

The Maquiladora Program

The Maquiladora program, which began in the 1960s, was an attempt to stimulate industrialization of the border areas with multinational (primarily U.S.) companies' capital. The effort was generally a success in this regard. From 12 plants in 1966, the number grew to 1963 by 1991. Nearly 500,000 are employed, and annual foreign exchange earnings are expected to be in the range of $5 billion.

The strongest advantage for U.S. companies to locate in Mexico is the cost of labor. Not only is labor much cheaper, but either the required skills are available or workers can be readily trained. In addition, the 1970s was a period when the United States began to impose environmental regulations that raised manufacturing costs. Did companies locate in Mexico to avoid U.S. environmental regulations? Further, did their presence in Mexico cause significant environmental difficulties? A Conservation Foundation study[4] concluded that the number of firms that came because of environmental considerations was not significant. Labor costs were by far the most important factor. The study also concluded that a slackening of environmental regulation in Mexico from the official position adopted by then would not result in these companies' becoming more profitable.

Whether the environmentally lax situation was important in attracting industry is not clear. Certainly it was a factor. But relative exchange rates were also important, as shown by the number of new firms in 1982, when the peso was devalued relative to the dollar.

Mexico's official position has been that environmental regulation should be the same in the two countries, so that it does not influence location. But implementation of environmental legislation in Mexico has been much weaker than in the United States, making it easier to operate there. In 1982-1988, legislation on environmental issues took a major turn in Mexico: both the Federal Environmental Law and the Environmental Protection and Equilibrium Law were promulgated. The Federal Environmental Law involved regulations on emissions and the construction of new plants with possible deleterious environmental impacts. It also established a framework for cooperation between the U.S. Environmental Protection Agency and SEDUE, the environment agency established in 1983, to eliminate double standards and exchange experience and information. The Environmental Equilibrium Law was designed to fine companies that exceeded emissions norms specified in the legislation. Again, enforcement was virtually impossible. SEDUE, which has this responsibility, was hampered by a lack of funds and human resources as well as by a lack of baseline data on which plants were emitting what. In addition, firms that may have wanted to comply with some requirements were limited in doing so by the government's limited capacity for collecting waste and recycling it. When the Environmental Protection and Equilibrium Law came into force in 1988, only four recycling plants and one commercial incinerator existed in the entire country.

It is likely that some undesirable plants were attracted to Mexico, but it is not possible to say which ones or how many there were. More important, perhaps, is the fact that the environment did deteriorate as a result of the program. This statement does not mean that the program was not worthwhile. Environmental standards are not an absolute, but they have to be set against economic benefits. There is some evidence to suggest environmental deterioration in plant areas. It is also clear that more effective enforcement could reverse some of this damage. In addition, as economic growth proceeds, it may be possible to devote more resources to cleaning up. Without a more detailed analysis of impacts, it is not possible to say whether the price was too high. This issue will become all the more important when the environmental implications of the free trade zone are analyzed.

Energy Pricing

One policy present throughout the post-World War II period in Mexico is pricing energy well below international prices. This has proved costly in both economic and environmental terms. As pointed out earlier, energy subsidies were responsible for a significant part of the budget deficit. Calculations show that internal pricing of petroleum by PEMEX (the national petroleum company of Mexico) was responsible for about 15 percent of the public deficit in 1982. Insofar as this deficit meant that resources for the environment were limited or reduced, energy pricing has indirectly impacted the environment. Another indirect impact is through the relationship between energy pricing and the demand for labor. Low energy prices led industrial firms to substitute energy for labor, thus increasing unemployment with all its social and environmental consequences. Sterner has quantified the impact of energy prices on labor demand in Mexico.[5]

It is the impact of energy prices on atmospheric pollution that is of greatest concern here. Air pollution from industry and transport is a serious problem in most cities. In the Mexico City Metropolitan area, about 5 million tons of contaminants are released annually, 85 percent from vehicles and the remainder from the 35,000 industrial establishments. The health impacts of air quality in the federal district are only too well-known.

Ideally, pricing should include environmental costs. If not, prices could be raised to eliminate implicit subsidies. How effective would a policy of higher energy prices be in terms of reducing environmental pollution in Mexico's cities? Although there is no detailed quantitative answer, there are indications that raising prices would reduce the demand for fossil fuels. Sterner's study shows that fuel use would have been 20 percent lower in the 1970s and 1980s if the consumer price of petroleum products had been allowed to fall.[6] Undoubtedly, emissions would have been reduced.

Yet other considerations enter into formulating a policy to limit emissions. First, would it be reliable? In this regard, prices would be superior to controls, which need a complex structure of inspections that are not feasible. Second, is the policy flexible enough to deal with sudden changes? Should thermal conditions require a sudden reduction in emissions, pricing works too slowly. But then voluntary controls, which can work well in emergencies, could be added. Third, are continued efforts to reduce emissions the incentive provided for in the policy? Charges are more effective than they would be under a system of "command and control" so long as the charges are maintained at their real levels in the face of inflation. Last and most important are the measures politically acceptable? Higher prices run into difficulties here. It is argued that everyone should have to make sacrifices to reduce pollution. If fuel prices are raised, people with the money may not have to cut their travel but others would. In addition, the measure would hit the poor hardest. This argument has to be taken seriously.

Data on fuel expenditures by income group shows that the differences among income groups is not that large—ranging from about 3.6 percent of household income in the lowest quintile to about 5 percent for the highest quintile. With an input-output framework and a household demand model, the impact of a 20 percent increase in fuel prices on the lowest quintile is estimated at about 0.25 percent of its income, allowing for all adjustments. This is not a major impact, and it could be corrected by other fiscal adjustments. Similarly, the impact of a 20 percent increase in fuel prices and total production costs is less than 0.5 percent.

The case for such price increases as a measure to protect the environment is strong. Equally important are the drawbacks of other measures. Restricting vehicle access to roads does not seem to work. Retrofitting or introducing lower-pollution vehicles would take a long time. And it would be necessary to provide adequate public transport, which itself would require institutional changes.

Privatization

Privatization has become a major instrument of government policy since the mid-1980s. Growth in the state sector in the 1960s and 1970s was partly due to the increased number of state enterprises; by 1980, they accounted for one-fifth the industrial investment and total output. The government has been particularly active in finance, mining, industry and transport, and communications. Disillusionment with the performance of these enterprises grew in the 1980s as their subsidy demands began to be felt and their economic efficiency began to be questioned.

Reducing government involvement in industrial activity is a complex process, entailing liquidation, merger, decentralization, and privatization. Many companies were divested. Of more than 1,155 such enterprises, 139 either had been or were being sold to the private sector by August 1990.

Unfortunately, there is no study to show how these companies affected the environment. One can logically argue for a less damaging impact on the environment or for a more damaging impact. When the government is both the polluter and the regulator, regulation can be weakened. This situation is especially likely when funds are not available to meet targets or when pollution charges will be passed on through government subsidies anyway. On the other hand, a privatized industry is also likely to be given easy passage, at least in its early years. No government agency would want to take responsibility for stifling a newly privatized industry by imposing environmental regulations. Similarly, an industry being prepared for privatization is less likely to be encumbered with controls that would reduce its profitability. Experience in Western Europe with privatization has encountered this tension between profitability and environmental concerns.

To link the privatization program with changes in the environment, the only statement that can be made with some certainty is that insofar as the program is reducing pressures on the deficit, it is also releasing resources for environmental purposes.

CONCLUSIONS

Although no clear conclusions on links between macroeconomic policy and the environment can be drawn, some themes emerge. First, "bad economics" was detrimental to Mexico's environment. This statement applies at the macroeconomic level, at which the protectionist import substitution phase laid the foundation for the country's present economic problems. It also applies at the micro-level, at which inappropriate subsidies caused water and energy management problems, with adverse environmental consequences. In this regard, the structure of pricing and subsidies to urban dwellers is partly responsible for Mexico's high urbanization rate. Second, from a sustainable development point of view, Mexico has not managed its natural resources well. It tended to overuse them and then tended not to invest the surplus or to invest it inefficiently. However, there is no evidence that it responded to short-term debt crises by increased mining of its natural resource base. Third, poverty is an issue that influences the environment in a complex way. It is not through the poor's degrading the resource base more but through the pressure on government to provide fiscal subsidies and to provide land for agriculture, land that is often fragile and not suitable for the use to which it is put.

With regard to specific economic policies, Mexico may have suffered from pollution imported from the United States as some companies set up in border areas. But the country has benefited and the balance probably favors the industrialization program. The country's energy pricing policy has resulted in higher levels of pollution than necessary, and the arguments for not tackling this issue (i.e., impacts on the poor) are not as valid as they are made out to be. Further, the direct impacts of the privatization program remain unclear, but its indirect impacts, through budget deficit reductions, are most likely good.

CHAPTER FOUR ENDNOTES

1. J.M. Maass and S. García Oliva, "La conservacion de suelos en zonas tropicales," *Ciencia y desarrollo* 15(90) (1990).

2. Alfredo Cuarón "Ecosistemas Tropicales y Primatas," (Ph.D. diss., University of Costa Rica, 1989).

3. J. Dirzo "Rescate y restauración ecológica de la Selva de los Tuxtlas," *Ciencia y Desarroll,* no. 97, (1991).

4. H.J. Leonard "Are Environmental Regulations Driving U.S. Industry Overseas?" (Washington, D.C.: The Conservation Foundation, 1984).

5. T. Sterner "Factor Demand and Substitution in a Developing Country: Energy Use in Mexican Manufacturing," in *Scandinavian Journal of Economics,* 91(4)1989, pp. 723-39.

6. Ibid.

CASE STUDY FOR THAILAND

by the London Environmental and Economics Centre,
based on a study by the Thailand Development
Research Institute (TDRI)*

MACROECONOMIC HISTORY

Overview

Over the past 30 years, Thailand has achieved impressive growth rates, averaging over 7 percent per annum from 1960 to 1980 and more recently soaring to over 12 percent. The country is now referred to as the leader of the next wave of the newly industrialized countries (NICs). This pace of economic development was achieved in spite of several major shocks in the world economy and significant trade and current account deficits that threatened the stability of the Thai economy. Like many developing countries in the 1970s, Thailand financed its economic development by foreign borrowing, accumulating a significant external debt between 1975 and 1985. As a result of oil price shocks, the world recession, and declining agricultural commodity prices, the ratio of debt to gross domestic product (GDP) increased rapidly in the early 1980s, reaching 39 percent of GDP in 1985. This situation prompted adoption of various structural adjustment policies to control the external imbalance and associated foreign debt problems. Some reforms were carried out through government initiatives, and others were part of the World Bank's two structural adjustment loans (SALs) in 1982 and 1983.

---

*Theodore Panayotou and Chalongphob Sussengkarn conducted the research.

Structural Adjustment Programs

The ability of the Thai economy to respond to the adverse external environment in the 1980s was undermined by serious weaknesses in domestic policies and structural imbalances. By the late 1970s, Thailand was suffering from declining land availability, exhaustion of the domestic market (limiting further industrialization), domestic price distortions, and excessive liquidity creation. There was a "need to shift the pattern of growth from one based on the extension of land under cultivation and on import substitution industries to one based on increasingly intensive use of land and on industries producing for domestic and export markets under competitive conditions."[1]

The World Bank identified five areas in which policy measures should be implemented as part of a comprehensive restructuring program:[2]

- resource mobilization, particularly in the public sectors;
- monetary policy, including measures to maintain high rates of private saving and to manage external debt and the capital account;
- energy policy and conservation, with particular attention to pricing;
- industrial policy and measures to promote industrial exports;
- agricultural policy and measures to maintain high rates of growth of agricultural production and exports.

These policy recommendations (except those on monetary policy) were partly used in forming specific measures of the first and second SALs. The first, SAL I, aimed at gradually reducing the current account deficit as a percentage of GDP through improved incentives, increased efficiency, and reduced fiscal imbalances. Some additional measures were taken in agriculture, industry, and energy and in fiscal policy and institutional development. Originally, the Thai government had hoped to rely on exports to alleviate the external deficits and provide the main driving force in the manufacturing and agricultural sectors. However, adverse movements in the world economy prompted the government to shift its focus from relying on exports to relying more on the use of prudent fiscal and monetary policy and measures to keep the external deficit at a sustainable level without seriously hurting growth in income and employment.

SAL II, negotiated in 1983, reflected this change in focus and involved medium-term reforms in fiscal policy, tax administration, and state enterprises. New SAL II elements that should be mentioned were: in the industrial sector, a measure to explore the feasibility of export credit and guarantee schemes; in the energy sector, a reduction in the price differential among different types of fuel, energy conservation measures, and establishment of the National Energy Conservation Center; and in the agricultural sector, the land bank study and water resource development and management.

Success of Structural Adjustment from a Macroeconomic Perspective

Since 1986, the economy has experienced unprecedented growth driven by exports of manufactured goods. It is hard to quantify the extent to which the SAL program contributed to this success, but the adoption of generally prudent monetary and fiscal policies reflecting a structural adjustment-like prescription enabled Thailand to take advantage of favorable improvements in the world economy without any serious debt overhangs from the past.

The Thai study identifies six crucial factors that brought about the recent economic success in Thailand. First, there were favorable changes in the external environment, including sharp declines in oil prices and interest rates and major exchange rate realignments with the U.S. dollar. Second, the transition of the Asian NICs toward commodities other than traditional labor-intensive manufactured exports, such as textiles and garments, left a gap in the market that Thailand was able to fill. Third, prudent fiscal management kept the external balance situation under control. Fourth, successive exchange rate adjustments meant that Thailand managed to maintain a fairly realistic exchange rate and remained competitive in international markets. Fifth, Thailand enjoyed political and social stability over the period. And last, there were both a good entrepreneurial base and supplies of low-wage labor with good basic education from which to draw.

But the accelerated growth was not achieved without serious costs to the environment. Environmental problems abound, particularly as the infrastructure and institutions needed to deal with them lagged behind the development process.

THE IMPACT OF STRUCTURAL ADJUSTMENT ON THE ENVIRONMENT

Development in Thailand has transformed rural environmental problems into urban ones. The main rural environmental problems include deforestation, forest encroachment, cultivation of marginal and fragile lands, soil erosion, flooding and water shortages, and other natural resource-related problems. Urban environmental problems include crowding, slums, traffic congestion, solid waste and water and air pollution from both households and industries, lead in gasoline, sulphur in diesel fuel, and hazardous waste from industries.

Macroeconomic Policies

Monetary, fiscal, and foreign exchange seem far removed from natural resources and the environment. Yet they will affect resource allocation and use.

Interest Rates

The rate of interest is the price linking the present with the future. The higher the interest rate, the higher is the cost of waiting and therefore the faster the rate of resource depletion and the lower the investment in resource conservation. This effect may be mitigated or reversed by the fact that a higher interest rate will slow the general pace of development, tending to reduce resource depletion and environmental degradation.

Interest rate ceilings and implicit interest rate subsidies for promoted industries have been the main interest rate distortion affecting the agricultural sector and the rural sector in general. Credit policy relies on mandates, quotas, interest rate ceilings, and constrained use of loan proceeds, all of which resulted in fewer than 40 percent of the farmers' having access to institutional credit. To address this problem, a central bank provision requires that a certain percentage (13 percent in recent years) of commercial bank deposits be directed to agriculture. But most farmers prefer more flexible terms and increased credit availability even if they have to pay higher interest rates. The shortage of credit in rural areas has had a negative impact on agricultural investment, thus discouraging more intensive farming on existing lands and promoting the movement toward further land clearance for agriculture.

Exchange Rate

The exchange rate is the price linking domestic tradeable goods with foreign goods. An overvalued exchange rate means that exports are discouraged and imports encouraged. This state of affairs will reduce pressure on the natural resource stock to the extent that exported commodities use natural resources as inputs. In the specific context of Thailand, most of the resource-based commodities are internationally tradeable (e.g., tin, fish, rice, cassava, rubber, logs) or are substitutes for tradeable commodities (e.g., natural gas, lignite, hydropower). Hence an overvalued exchange rate reduces their depletion by reducing their price relative to nontradeable goods.

Thailand maintained a fixed exchange rate from 1960 to 1984, but the rising strength of the U.S. dollar in the early 1980s and the 1980-1981 inflation caused the exchange rate to be overvalued. In November 1984, the baht was devalued and the fixed exchange rate system abandoned, with the baht pegged to a basket of currencies. Through a combination of a strong economy, low inflation, and successive exchange rate adjustments, Thailand has managed to maintain a fairly realistic exchange rate. Consequently, damage to its export performance from overvalued exchange rates has been minimized, with the exchange rate policy affecting the natural resource sector fairly neutrally.

Minimum Wages

Minimum wage laws in Thailand tended to increase capital intensity in the manufacturing industry and reduce the growth of formal wage employment. This situation has had implications for the rural sector that, under Thailand's conditions of labor abundance, lead to increased use of low-cost labor in depleting natural resources and encroachment of resource sectors by underemployed labor. But because of the low general compliance and the fact that minimum wage adjustments have barely kept pace with inflation, any minimum wage effects are likely to be small.

Trade Policies

Trade policies have changed the terms of trade between agriculture and industry, thereby influencing the relative profitability of the two sectors. Although trade liberalization has been a central component in the process of structural change in Thailand, there still remains considerable effective protection for industry (the overall rate of 40 percent in 1982 rose to 82 percent in 1971), compared with the negative effective rates of protection of agriculture, which for 1981 averaged -65 percent for rice, -22 percent for maize and cassava, and -12 percent for sugar cane.

The promotion of industry at the expense of agriculture determines the types of environmental problems that are likely. At first glance, one might expect an increased demand in natural resource inputs for industry, increased industrial pollution and urban congestion, and decreased pressure on rural land and water resources. Unfortunately, the outcomes in Thailand have not been so simplistic because they depend largely on Thailand's institutional and policy context. The implications for each sector are considered separately below.

Conclusions on Macroeconomic Policies

In the 1970s and most of the 1980s, environmental considerations played no explicit role in the formulation and implementation of macroeconomic and trade policies in Thailand. It would be unrealistic and undesirable to tailor these instruments to meet environmental objectives because of the many other overriding considerations, such as industrialization and economic stability, that determine these policies. Yet environmental implications should somehow be taken into account when these policies are being formulated. Consideration of the resource and environmental implications of macroeconomic policies could be implemented in the following ways: (a) environmental costs may tip the scale against marginal policies by raising their social costs above their social benefits; the reverse may occur with policies that have positive environmental effects; (b) macroeconomic and trade policy interventions might be scaled up or down on account of their environmental implications; and (c) provisions might be made for cushioning the negative environmental effects of policies when such policies cannot be scaled down sufficiently to reduce their environmental costs to acceptable levels.

Forestry

Forests that covered over 50 percent of Thailand's total land area only 30 years ago covered just 25 percent in 1988, even less if forest degradation is also taken into account. Land clearing for farming and uncontrolled logging have been the two forces driving deforestation in Thailand. Logging is now officially banned but it goes on illegally. Land clearing for agriculture continues, but at a reduced rate because most forest land suitable for agriculture has already been encroached upon. Destruction of watersheds and loss of biological diversity are becoming increasingly more important than the shortage of timber resources and fuelwood because the latter two are both tradeable and substitutable; the former two are not. Forest clearing caused catastrophic landslides and floods in southern Thailand in 1988, precipitating the nationwide logging ban.

Consider the two main causes of deforestation in turn. First, forest clearance for agriculture was promoted as a result of distorted economic incentives in the agricultural sector, population pressure, rural poverty, and the failure to address the open access nature of the forest resource. Between 1950 and 1988, 108 million rai of forest land was cleared, 90 percent of which was converted to agriculture. Consequently, the amount of crop land tripled between 1950 and 1988, from 52 million rai to 148 million rai (2.53 rai = 1 acre; 6.25 rai = 1 hectare).

Agricultural policies, although not intended (and not perceived) to affect the utilization of resources in the forestry sector, have in fact had powerful indirect impacts. In particular, the export tax on rice and rubber has by implication encouraged cassava production. Agricultural taxation, especially of crops like rice and rubber that are cultivated mainly on titled land, depresses the returns to investment in land development and conservation relative to other investments, such as clearing new forest land to plant maize, cassava, and other nontaxed crops. In addition, the fertilizer tax had a negative environmental impact in the special context of Thailand with its open access land frontier. The taxation of fertilizer turned the relative costs of agricultural production against intensification of existing agricultural lands and in favor of expansion onto new forest lands.

With assistance from the World Bank, the government is currently carrying out a major land titling program to improve farmers' security of land ownership and to halt further forest encroachment. Unfortunately, squatters in reserved forest lands are given only 5- to 25-year rights to farm, and the rights are not transferable. It is feared that this policy will do little to halt further forest encroachment because such a half measure will not provide sufficient incentive for increased investment on existing lands.

A logging ban was introduced in 1989 to address the deforestation problem directly. It is largely ineffective because the underlying incentives for agricultural land clearing remain firmly in place. A fast-growing population, leading to increased rural poverty, the lack of alternative employment opportunities, and other social pressures has further compounded the problem. According to the Ministry of Agriculture, the logging violations have been committed almost entirely by villagers as a way to supplement income. To alleviate rural poverty, the government has turned a blind eye to illegal squatting on forest lands. In some cases, government support has been more overt. For example, 1.2 million landless families have been resettled on "deteriorated" forest land in the last decade.[3] An increase in rural real income by 1,000 baht (1972 prices) would result in a reduction of deforestation by 100,000 rai; hence the annual forest loss could be cut in half by raising rural incomes 50 percent.

Second, Thailand is a classic example of rapid loss of tropical forests as a result of concessions, taxation, and pricing policies in the forestry sector. A concession or timber license grants the rights to timber on the site. Although such rights are of considerable value, concession fees have been extremely low and largely invariable with respect to the area and value of the timber onsite. To top up the concession fee, the government also levied stumpage fees per tree based on the number of trees that the concessionaire planned to fell each year. The fees varied by species but were too low and were based on timber harvested, not on the timber value onsite. As an overall consequence, the scheme encouraged a few large logging firms to accumulate large concessions, which they were unable to police or harvest efficiently, and the stumpage fee encouraged high grading and considerable damage to the remaining stand. These trends were further compounded by timber royalties levied on timber cut both inside and outside the reserve forests. Again, the royalties were largely invariant with respect to log size, providing additional incentives for high grading and wasteful harvesting.

This combination of concessionaire pricing distorted investment incentives against reforestation by understating the true scarcity of both timber and standing forest and encouraged logging in marginal and fragile lands, with significant social costs in terms of soil erosion and loss of biological diversity.

Agriculture

The importance of the agricultural sector in the Thai economy has been on a long downward trend, with the percentage share of agriculture in GNP falling from 33 percent in 1969 to 23 percent in 1985.[4] The thrust of Thai agricultural policy in the process of development was the extraction of surplus from agriculture in the form of savings, foreign exchange, cheap food, and cheap labor for the promotion of industrialization. The main policy instruments toward this end were export taxes and quotas, consumption subsidies, and industrial protection. More recently, farm price supports and input subsidies were introduced to promote agricultural production and improve the farmers' welfare.

Agricultural policies in Thailand have had profound effects on soil and water quality and deforestation trends both by affecting the farmers' choice of crops and use of inputs, such as fertilizers, pesticides, and irrigation water, and by reducing incentives for land investments. Further expansion of the sector is now seriously constrained by a binding scarcity of arable land resources. The structural adjustment loans in the 1980s focused on the need to shift the pattern of growth from one based on the extension of land under cultivation to one based increasingly on intensive use of land. The policy interventions in the agricultural sector are considered here in terms of their implications for the environment and sustained development.

Export Taxes on Rice and Rubber

As part of the trade liberalization strategy, export taxes on rice and rubber were reduced. Successive past governments consistently taxed rice and rubber even though, in the specific context of Thailand, both these crops are environmentally superior to the cassava and maize that were planted as alternative crops. This differential tax policy, combined with free access to forest land and a loophole in the European Community's common agricultural policy, led to an increase of over 100 percent in the area planted with cassava over a 7-year period, at considerable cost to forest cover and soil quality. Had the government included these environmental costs in the export price of cassava through an appropriate tax and issued titles to forest land, the cassava boom may never have occurred, but a more sustainable form of agriculture may have evolved.

The reduction in export taxes on rice and rubber corrects the production distortion created by such a policy of differential taxation. At first sight, this change would appear to have environmentally benign effects as more land is planted to rice and rubber, which tend to be more protective of the soil. But the overall effect is ambiguous because of the tendency to replace natural forest with rubber plantations. And as rubber moves onto higher and higher slopes and more marginal lands, it also becomes less protective of the soil. Still, reductions in agricultural taxes should have environmentally benign effects as both the agricultural surplus and returns to land improvement investments increase. Yet in the presence of an open forest frontier, more extensive farming may be encouraged instead. These complex links are understood more easily with use of a computer general equilibrium (CGE) macroeconomic model in a policy simulation exercise that eliminates export taxes on rice and rubber. The results are discussed in the section on environmental impacts of specific policy scenarios, below.

Taxation of Fertilizer Inputs

Unlike most developing countries, Thailand has taxed rather than subsidized fertilizers and other chemical inputs. On the face of it, a fertilizer tax should benefit the environment by encouraging more traditional and sustainable soil conservation practices and reducing the environmental costs of chemical runoff and water pollution. But with Thailand's open access land frontier, the fertilizer tax turned the relative costs of agricultural production against intensification of existing agricultural lands and in favor of expansion into new forest lands. Moreover, the heavy taxation of urea (a 17 percent import duty) biased fertilizer use in favor of nonnitrogen-based compound fertilizers that are less suitable for Thai soils.

The increasing need for intensification of agriculture has prompted the government to distribute subsidized fertilizer through the Marketing Organization of Farmers. But the subsidy failed to increase fertilizer use and crop yields because government sales simply replaced private sales, the less appropriate mixed fertilizers are still being promoted, and the underlying problems of insecure land ownership remain to be tackled.

An Implicit Subsidy on Irrigation Water

The supply of water from publicly funded irrigation facilities free of charge is an important subsidy to the agricultural sector. Betrand has estimated the implicit irrigation subsidy at 200-700 baht per hectare for paddy, at 400 baht per hectare for sugar cane, 300 for tobacco, and 150 for maize.[5] This subsidy has both positive and negative efficiency, environmental, and distributional implications. On the positive side, the implicit irrigation subsidy offsets part of the price distortion and disincentive to agriculture in general, and rice in particular, owing to export taxes. On the negative side, it results in inefficient and inequitable use of water and to varying degrees may be held responsible for water logging, salinization, and flooding.

Indirect Pesticide Subsidies

The government indirectly supports pesticide use through its extension service and assistance in outbreaks. Heavy pesticide use has indisputable negative environmental effects and doubtful economic benefits in the long run as pest resistance builds. Pesticide subsidies, however indirect, should be resisted because they distort farmers' incentives in favor of chemical pesticides and against integrated pest management, which encompasses changes in cropping patterns and planting times and the choice of pest-resistant varieties, all of which are environmentally less damaging.

Availability of Free Public Forest Land

Over the past 40 years, 96 million rai of forest land have been converted to agricultural land to farm cassava, maize, sugar cane, rubber, and other cash crops; the remainder was converted for rice production. In the same way that free water has benefited farmers in irrigated areas, free land benefited farmers in the rain-fed areas. Agricultural growth was achieved largely by clearing new land for cultivation. For upland crops, the contribution of land area was almost 100 percent. The failure to account for the social opportunity cost of land and forests and related externalities and the underinvestment resulting from insecure ownership imply considerable efficiency losses and costs to the environment. The present stagnation in agricultural yields is the result of falling productivity on lands that were opened up in the 1970s. Owing to poor infrastructure, insecure land titling, and inadequate investment, yields can be sustained only so long as the original productivity of the land lasts. According to a study by Feder and others, land titling in itself would increase agricultural productivity 10-30 percent and consequently was included in Thailand's structural adjustment program.

In recent years, the supply price of converting forest land to agriculture rose on two counts. National disasters linked to deforestation and the public's growing environmental awareness are creating pressures for more effective protection and expansion of protection forests to cover most of the remaining natural forest land. And as good land is exhausted, increasingly less accessible and more marginal land has been opened up for cultivation.

In sum, agricultural policies intended to increase agricultural production or squeeze surplus out of agriculture for industrialization have resulted in distorted incentives that are detrimental to both the economy and the environment. Export taxes on rice and rubber distort the farmers' choice against these two crops and in favor of other crops such as maize, sugar cane, and cassava, which are less protective of the soil. Fertilizer taxes in the presence of open frontier distort the farmers' choice between intensification on existing farms and extension into new forest lands. Chemical fertilizer subsidies distort the farmers' incentives in favor of chemical fertilizers and against organic fertilizers and soil conservation, which are environmentally more benign than chemical fertilizers. Pesticide subsidies distort the farmers' choice between pesticides and integrated pest management, which is less environmentally damaging. The supply of free irrigation water deprives the farmer of any incentive to conserve water and encourages overuse and waste, resulting in inefficiency and environmental (waterlogging and salinization) and distributional problems (the worse-off rain-fed farmers subsidize the better-off irrigated farmers).

Fisheries

Input subsidies (e.g., credit, tax exemptions for fishing machinery) and output price supports have been used in the fishing industry to raise incomes and alleviate hardship. But these policies are self-defeating in the long term and have put considerable stress on the natural resource base. To the extent that price supports raise fishing incomes, new entrants are attracted to the industry; as a result, the resource base deteriorates, incomes fall, and additional support is required.

Intervention in international trade, such as promotion of exports and tariffs on fish imports, may temporarily raise fishing incomes, improve the balance of payments, and protect the local industry, but these benefits cannot be sustained under the present open access status and depleted state of the resource. At present, fishery exports can be increased only through unsustainable exploitation of the open access resource.

Industry

Trade protection through the promotion of industry has been critical to the use of natural resources by influencing their industrial input, affecting the rate of migration and size of the residual rural population that exerts pressure on the natural resource base, affecting the relative profitability of agriculture, and directly determining industrial pollution levels.

Agriculture's terms of trade have deteriorated over the years because industry was heavily protected through import tariffs and investment incentives. Structural adjustment in the 1980s began to reverse this trend as the import tariff structure was reformed and trade distortions reduced through lower and more uniform tariff levels. But industry still benefits from a considerable capital subsidy in the form of investment and export incentives. Overall, the supported investments have been less profitable, more centralized, more capital intensive, and not more export oriented than the average new investments in the sector as a whole.[6] In addition, the promoted investments have generally failed to meet the environmental protection requirements of the Investment Promotion Act (IPA) 1977. According to a recent Thailand Development Research Institute study covering 1986-1989, the Board of Investment has promoted industries classified as potential hazardous waste generators—chemical products, electronics, metal transformation, textiles and machinery, and engines—without adequate provision for, and enforcement of, the environmental protection measures provided under section 19 of the IPA. The proportion of promoted investment for hazardous waste-generating industries increased from 25 percent in 1987 to 55 percent in 1989, the majority located in the Bangkok metropolitan area and posing a major health risk because of the high population density.[7]

Industrial promotion for export also had important effects on how natural resources are used in other sectors, especially agriculture. The reduced profitability of agriculture that results from industrial protection would at first hand appear to be conducive to conservation because the less profitable agriculture is, the less intensively and extensively land and water resources are used. In the specific context of development in Thailand, however, population pressures in rural areas are not being alleviated as much as was hoped because the capital-intensive nature of the promoted industries failed to attract much labor out of agriculture. Despite the remarkable structural change in the economy, Thailand continues to be one of the most rural and agricultural economies in the world, with over 65 percent of the labor force engaged primarily in agriculture. This trend may be reversed as industries begin to relocate to rural areas after being driven out of the high-cost urban areas by overburdened infrastructure, congestion, and pollution problems. In addition, the declining profitability of agriculture as a result of industrial protection has lessened incentives for farm land development and soil conservation because of both reduced incentives for investment and reduced savings. Further, as a result of higher production costs and higher prices for industrial consumer goods caused by industrial protection, the farmers' welfare is jeopardized and the rural-urban income distribution worsens.

As well as impacting agriculture, Thailand's industrial development also increased pressure on the natural resource base in other sectors. Many of the promoted industries are indirectly resource based (e.g., agroprocessing, furniture production, mineral processing, fertilizer, gas separation). In addition, industrial demands for energy inputs have increased along with industrial waste outputs. The capital-intensive industries promoted by industrial and trade policies are certainly more environment intensive (generally producing more air, water, and noise pollution) at the margin than the low-input agriculture being displaced.

Industry has changed structurally in recent years. In 1979, nonhazardous waste-generating industry represented 71 percent of industrial GDP, but by 1989, the figure was 42 percent. At the same time, hazardous waste-generating industries doubled, from 29 percent to 58 percent.[8] Given Thailand's relatively large size and the considerable assimilative capacity of its environment, the current level of industrialization and implied pollution loads would not be a serious problem if it were distributed throughout the country. But industry is concentrated in the Bangkok metropolitan region, whose air and water bodies are receiving pollutants far in excess of their assimilative capacity.

During the past five years, Thailand's industrial development made a major leap forward, with the manufacturing value added growing at an average 12 percent per year and industrial exports over 30 percent per year. Investment scarcity and slow export growth are no longer problems. If anything, Bangkok, Chaingmai, and several coastal tourist centers are experiencing the stress of rapid growth of investment and overdevelopment without corresponding expansion of infrastructure, public services, and protection of the environment.

Energy

Thailand, with its dependence on fuel imports, suffered heavily from the second oil price shock. The rapid growth of energy demand, coupled with the oil price hike, resulted in a fuel import bill on the order of $3 billion in 1980. The government was reticent to raise domestic energy prices but, by the 1980s, had resolved to confront the problem with adjustments to domestic prices, development of alternative energy sources, and conservation measures. Some of these initiatives had already been undertaken as part of the Fifth Development Plan and later were fully integrated into SALs I and II.

Energy prices have been raised in recent years to reflect the world price of imported oil. But the structure of petroleum product prices has been distorted to reflect distributional and regional policy considerations instead of true costs. Gasoline products are heavily taxed (85.5-105 percent), fuel oil and diesel products are hardly taxed (1-10 percent), and liquid petroleum gas (LPG) and kerosene are subsidized (6-13 percent).[9]

The distributional benefits from such cross-subsidization must be balanced against the efficiency losses from relative price distortions. For example, LPG subsidization had the unintended effect of encouraging the conversion of automobile engines from gasoline to LPG.

Overall, reforms in the energy sector have undoubtedly had some positive environmental implications. Since the establishment of the National Energy Conservation Center, considerable progress has been made in identifying priority areas for energy conservation. In addition, there have been significant cuts in the energy investment program and energy-intensive industry projects. Price distortions were reduced in the past two years, although sufficient distortion still remains to encourage inefficient interfuel substitution.

ENVIRONMENTAL IMPACTS OF SPECIFIC POLICY SCENARIOS

A 90-sector CGE macroeconomic model was used to run several policy scenarios to explore economy-environment link in an intersectoral framework. The simulations covered some of the basic policy and structural changes that took place in Thailand during the structural adjustment period:

- reduction of export taxes on rice and rubber;
- increase in domestic oil prices;
- increase in labor-intensive manufactured exports;
- increase in tourism growth; and
- reduction in real public sector investment.

Each simulation led to changes in resource use and the pattern of production. Environmental outcomes were linked to structural changes in the economy when possible through environmental coefficients. The environmental coefficients were derived from existing information or independent studies. For example, hazardous waste coefficients were easily derived from information on the amount of hazardous waste per unit of output in various sectors. Owing to the lack of data, it was not possible to feed the environmental impacts back into the simulation model to obtain their effects on the economy. The economic and environmental impacts of the five policy simulations are described below.

Reduction of Export Taxes on Rice and Rubber

Important policy measures initiated under Thailand's structural and sectoral adjustment program are the abolition of export quotas and licensing on maize and rice exports and the reduction of export taxes for rice and rubber. In the simulation, these export taxes were reduced to zero from a base value of 2.95 percent for rice and 9.75 percent for rubber.

The result is a 0.82 percent increase in the value added of the agricultural sector and a 0.38 percent and 0.27 percent output reduction in the industrial and service sectors, respectively. At this level of aggregation, it is concluded that industrial pollution is reduced, as are transport-related emissions and environmental degradation by tourism. However, the environmental impacts in the agricultural sector are ambiguous.

The increase in agricultural production that results from the reduced export taxes generates environmental impacts that: (a) intensify rice production and hence increase use of agrochemicals, switch land from upland crops to rice, and increase investment in land improvement and soil conservation and (b) extend rubber cultivation into higher slopes, with consequent deforestation and soil erosion.

The total land in agriculture increases an estimated 1.18 percent as a result of the increased profitability of agriculture, and for every 100 rai of land that is added to the cultivated area, an estimated 140 rai of forest is cleared.[10] Hence the expansion of agricultural land as a result of reduced export taxes results in 40 percent more land deforested. Most of it is for rubber cultivation, reflecting the relative ease of forest encroachment in the upland areas compared to intensification, given the fact that rubber is perennial. Maize, cassava, and other upland crops also shift to rubber.

The environmental impact of this shift is likely to be positive because rubber as a tree crop is more protective of soil and water. The environmental impact of forest clearance is negative because natural forest is replaced by rubber plantations, and as rubber plantations move into higher slopes and more marginal land, they become less protective of the soil. Indeed, the catastrophic landslides and floods in southern Thailand in November 1988 took place mostly in upland areas covered with young rubber trees. These events have been attributed to inadequate soil cover.[11]

In contrast, little expansion of the land under rice is attributable to deforestation. Most comes from switching from other more damaging crops (e.g., maize, sugar cane); hence the effect is environmentally benign. But the increased use of agrochemicals accompanying the rice expansion will reduce the overall environmental benefits. On balance, the net effect of a rice export tax reduction is likely to be positive.

Increase in Domestic Oil Prices

Following both the first and second oil price shocks, Thailand adjusted its oil prices upwards but not to world levels, thus continuing the oil price subsidy. In this policy scenario, a 10 percent increase in oil and gas prices was simulated.

Overall, the effect is deflationary, with GDP declining in all sectors. But industry is affected more than agriculture, with the exception of fishing, which is oil intensive. An obvious positive environmental impact is the reduction of energy-related emissions owing to more efficient energy use and conservation and to the shift at the margin from more energy-intensive to less energy-intensive activities. In terms of specific sectors, transport is reduced 0.9 percent and industry 0.41 percent, and power generation increases 0.54 percent, suggesting greater reductions in hydrocarbons (HC), volatile organic compound (VOC), nitrogen oxides (NO_x), and carbon monoxide (CO) than in sulfur dioxide (SO_2) and suspended particulate matter.

Increase in Labor-Intensive Manufactured Exports

This simulation was designed to examine the impacts of more rapid manufactured export growth, as occurred in Thailand in the last half of the 1980s. The overall environmental impacts are likely to be mixed. Labor-intensive industries are thought to be less polluting than capital-intensive industries because they tend to use less energy. But labor-intensive industries (e.g., slaughterhouses, tanneries, breweries) are major sources of water pollution. Major sources of hazardous waste are the fabricated product, electrical machinery, pulp and paper, and textile industries. On balance, when all types of pollutants are taken into account, it remains true that the heavy industries (i.e., cement, steel, petrochemicals) are more polluting than light industries.

Increase in Tourism Growth

In this scenario, the trend growth parameter was increased 10 percent to reflect recent structural changes in the Thai economy. Overall, a shift in this parameter increases service sector output 0.14 percent, reduces agricultural production 0.15 percent, and impacts the industrial sector minimally. Further disaggregation reveals trends in the energy, transport, and construction sectors, with significant environmental implications. Within the transport sector, jet fuel, low-speed diesel fuel, bus service, and ocean transport receive a major boost; consequently, HC, NOx, CO, and carbon dioxide emissions increase. In the energy sector, the increased energy consumption by tourism increases in SO_2 emissions. Construction of new hotels and supporting infrastructure in coastal areas has significant environmental implications in terms of destruction of mangrove forests and coastal erosion. The additional waste generated by hotels and restaurants further degrades the coastal zone and causes marine pollution in the absence of treatment facilities.

The change in land use along the coastal strip also has environmental spin-offs. The model predicts a 0.23 percent increase in land used for growing fruits and vegetables (partly to serve the tourist demand) and a reduction of 0.21 percent in paddies, 0.43 percent in cassava, and 1.01 percent in maize.[12] "The shift from upland crops that are associated with deforestation and soil erosion to high value crops such as fruits and vegetables that are land-saving and soil-protecting is an environmental improvement. The increase in the use of agro-chemicals, on the other hand, has negative environmental impacts unless properly managed."[13] Again, the net impacts are mixed and are difficult to assess without further research.

Reduction in Real Public Sector Investment

Most structural adjustment programs prescribe reductions in public expenditures. In this simulation, real public sector investment is reduced 10 percent. Overall, the impacts are deflationary, with a fall in aggregate demand, reducing GDP and domestic prices. But a boost in agricultural GDP is based on an assumed elastic export demand for agricultural goods. Hence natural resource depletion, forest encroachment, and agricultural pollution increase, but urban and industrial pollution decreases on the order of 1-2 percent as production in these sectors falls.

Consider also the type of public sector investment that is subject to cutbacks. If it causes a reduction in investments in environmental infrastructure (e.g., sewage systems, waste treatment plants) and pollution abatement expenditures, the environmental impact will certainly be negative.

GENERAL THEMES OF ENVIRONMENTAL IMPORTANCE

This section provides a framework for analyzing the results of the Thailand case study. The macroeconomic and structural adjustment policies and environmental impacts for each sector (i.e., agriculture, forestry, energy and transport, industry, water and waste disposal) for Thailand are summarized in matrix form in Annex B.

Pattern of Development

Thailand's choice of a development path that favored accelerated export-led industrial growth achieved considerable success as measured by the traditional economic indicators. The adoption of generally prudent monetary, fiscal, and exchange-rate policies largely reflected the general International Monetary Fund (IMF) prescription and certainly contributed to economic growth importantly. But ignoring the value of the environment in the process of development and structural change has its price; the environment is the ultimate constraint to further economic development. Thailand no longer suffers from domestic investment or foreign exchange bottlenecks; instead, environmental constraints are becoming increasingly binding and a source of discontent. Of particular and immediate concern are the lack of public infrastructure to alleviate air and water pollution and the costs of traffic congestion and pollution in urban areas. In the rural sectors, shortages of fertile land constrain further agriculture growth, and the environmental costs of deforestation became apparent in the 1989 catastrophic landslides. Coastal areas are not exempt; coastal pollution, inadequate infrastructure, and water shortages increasingly threaten the return from tourism. Mismanagement and degradation of the natural resource base are associated with both poverty and growth in the context of the institutional shortcomings that encourage open access to resources and negative externalities. Pressures on the environment were further exacerbated by government policies that subsidized wasteful resource use and environmental degradation.

Perhaps it is fair to say that the environmental sacrifices made were part of an overt trade-off in return for improvements as measured by economic and social indicators. But the trade-offs were neither efficient nor sustainable because the full costs of environmental deterioration were often unforeseen or were ignored in economic decision-making.

Transformation of a predominantly agriculture-based economy to an export-oriented industrial economy also has implications for the terms of trade between agriculture and industry, in particular for use of the natural resource base and protection of environmental quality. The overall aim of structural adjustment in Thailand was to shift the pattern of growth from one based on the extension of land under cultivation and on import substitution industries (both are economically inefficient and environmentally destructive) to one based on increasingly intensive use of land and on industries producing for domestic and export markets under competitive conditions. Such a shift promises certain environmental benefits: containment of forest encroachment and cultivation of fragile lands, reduction of watershed destruction and soil erosion, and increased investment in soil conservation. For industry, the shift in the sources of growth from protection and subsidy to efficiency and competitiveness means reduced use of resources and reduced generation of industrial wastes per unit of output. Yet these strategies have their own environmental costs. Agricultural intensification may result in excessive use of chemical fertilizers and pesticides and in overirrigation and waterlogging. Competitive industrial production, however efficient, results in air pollution, water pollution, and solid waste, some of it highly toxic. Although waste per unit of output might be lower under a liberalized market and trade regime, the total waste generated may be larger because of a larger output.

An important consideration is the relationship of agriculture and industry to the transformation of environmental problems over time. In Thailand, the policy of industry-led growth and export promotion resulted in industrial protection at the expense of the agricultural sector. The declining profitability of agriculture reduced both incentives and resources available for investment; hence attempts to shift toward more intensive farming practices were thwarted. Further, not only are the capital-intensive promoted industries more environment intensive (generally producing more air, water, and noise pollution) at the margin than the low-input agriculture that is being displaced, but they failed to attract sufficient labor out of agriculture, thus leaving a large pool of labor reliant on the natural resource base in rural areas. Needless to say, population problems further compound the problem. There is also concern that promoted industries will increase toxic wastes, posing hazards to health and environmental quality.

Overall, Thailand pursued sound macroeconomic policies in a conventional neoclassical sense but witnessed a major destruction of its natural resource base in the transition from an agricultural to an industrial economy. It confirms the assertion that good economics is a necessary, but not sufficient, condition to achieve sustained natural resource management. Although natural resource stocks and environmental quality were sacrificed as part of an overt trade-off for progress as measured by economic and social indicators, the route chosen was neither socially efficient nor sustainable. In the coming years, Thailand will need to make considerable investments in the environmental sector, both to release bottlenecks and to satisfy the demands of an increasingly affluent population for recreational parks and improvements in environmental quality. Some damage is irreversible, thus limiting options for future development. But what would have happened to the natural resource base without successful structural adjustment? The absence of growth would have meant persistent poverty, which may have been equally destructive to the resource base and the environment.

Population Pressure, Poverty, and Income Distribution

The economic outcomes and environmental impacts of structural adjustment programs and the development path in general are not evenly distributed throughout the population. Some sectors enjoy disproportional benefits and others bear disproportional costs. In this section, the relationship of growth to absolute and relative poverty and the environment is examined.

The rapid change in economic conditions over the past 30 years has had considerable impacts on income distribution and the overall welfare of the Thai people. Since the 1950s, an ongoing change in the economic structure was driven mainly by the production and export of manufactured goods. The share of agriculture in GDP fell continuously. From 1970 to 1987, for example, agricultural output fell from 27.02 percent of GDP to 17.5 percent. At the same time, manufacturing rose from 16 percent to 22.17 percent. The rapid change in exports and the production structure prompted labor migration to the higher-wage urban areas and concomitant rapid changes in lifestyle and income distribution both between social classes and among regional areas.

In addition to its remarkable economic development over the past 20-30 years, Thailand has also shown considerable improvement in most social indicators. Advances have been made in the provision of health care services and basic education, and there is a movement to lower fertility and mortality rates.[14] Consequently, Thailand rapidly reduced its population growth rate from over 3 percent in the early 1960s to 1.5 percent in the late 1980s, although absolute population pressure still remains a problem, particularly in rural areas.

The percentage of people living below the poverty line fell from 30 percent in 1976 to 25 percent in 1988. Socioeconomic development has been positive over a broad spectrum of indicators, and average per capita incomes have grown considerably. But 14 million people live in absolute poverty, 80 percent of them in rural areas. Equally significant is the widening income inequality between the rural-agricultural and urban-industrial groups. The national income share of the top 20 percent of the population increased from 49 percent in 1976 to 56 percent in 1988. By contrast, the share held by the bottom 20 percent dropped from 6.1 percent to 4.5 percent.[15] Widening income inequality accompanying growth characterizes Thailand's current economic development stage; it is expected to be reversed at a later stage. But the magnitude of the income gap and its predominantly rural character are particularly worrisome.

Trends in Per Capita Income Growth 1975-1985

The total per capita household income grew at an annual rate of 16.3 percent in 1975-1980, slowing to 9.1 percent per annum in 1980-1985. Absolute per capita incomes increased for all groups, but growth was not evenly distributed over socioeconomic groups, and in some years, the poorest quintiles suffered negative growth. Classification by production sector reveals that rural workers benefited least.

Trends in Income Distribution 1975-1988

Although absolute incomes increased for all groups over the period, the ongoing trend was toward widening income inequality, as reflected in the Gini coefficient ratio. The top 20 percent of the population increased its income share from 49 percent in 1975 to 56 percent in 1988. In contrast, all other lower-income groups continually shared less total income.

Overall, income growth structure indicates an imbalance between the agricultural and other sectors, with agricultural incomes only one-sixth of the others'. This condition was due to agriculture's relatively slow growth and the fact that employment transfers did not keep pace with the change in output structure. However, the situation has improved somewhat since 1986, when prices for the major crops began to rise. In a simulation exercise, it was found that a crop price increase will stem the trend toward growing income inequality and will alleviate rural poverty by reducing the percentage of the population living under the poverty line from 29.5 percent in 1986 to 25.2 percent in 1988.[16]

Trends in Regional Distribution of Poverty and Inequality

Poverty and inequality also have a definite geographical character. Incomes in the Northeast and the North are substantially lower than in other regions, and almost 90 percent of the poor live in rural villages. In 1988-1989, nearly 30 percent of village populations fell below the poverty line, compared to 13 percent in sanitary districts and under 7 percent in urban areas. Although the largest pockets of rural poverty are in the Northeast and the North, the poorest regions, the highest percentage of urban poverty is found in the Bangkok metropolitan region. There poverty is both prevalent and persistent and is much the result of rural-urban migration. In this sense, rural poverty and urban poverty are connected, although it is not usually the poorest of the poor who migrate to urban areas.

Rural Poverty and Environmental Link

Much rural poverty has been alleviated by expansion of agricultural land into the national forest reserves. Between 1950 and 1988, 108 million rai of forest land was cleared, 90 percent of it for agriculture. The open frontier forest land meant that landlessness remained low despite the fact that the population more than doubled, and agricultural profitability remained high despite a virtual stagnation in crop yields. Sacrificing the forest land to alleviate rural poverty and reduce urban-rural income differentials is effectively the trade-off Thailand has made in the development process. The strategy is clearly unsustainable on two accounts. First, the land frontier is not infinite, and little land is left for agricultural expansion. Second, national disasters linked to deforestation are the high damage costs that Thailand will continue to pay unless the deforestation trend is sufficiently reversed. Growing public awareness is already creating pressure for both more effective protection and expansion of protection forests to cover most or all remaining natural forests. But unless the underlying trend toward further encroachment is addressed, such policies are bound to fail. Measures to increase nonagricultural rural incomes, increase agricultural productivity on existing plots, and introduce effective land-titling schemes will be needed.

Can the current trend toward slower agricultural growth, continued forest encroachment, and persistent rural poverty be reversed? There is evidence to suggest that it can. First, population growth has dropped over the past decade. Second, industrialization will continue to attract migrants to urban areas, alleviating pressure on rural resources. (It should be noted that the scale of rural-urban migration is relatively modest, owing to the government's subsidizing highly capital-intensive industry.) And third, rural industry is expected to increase vastly its contribution to rural nonfarm employment, further alleviating pressure on rural natural resources. Relocating industry to rural areas largely avoids the substantial costs associated with the overburdened infrastructure, congestion, and pollution problems in Bangkok and its satellite cities.

Urban Poverty and Environmental Link

Recent economic growth in Thailand is associated with widening urban-urban inequality. The urban poverty trend reveals an increase both in the percentage of the poor living below the poverty line and in the severity of urban poverty. These trends reflect the definition of the poverty line. The decline in the level of urban services and the increasing costs of health care and transportation suggest that the poverty line might be too low; if so, the incidence of urban poverty is underestimated. Poverty among slum dwellers, squatters, and workers in the informal sector is a major source of congestion, water pollution, uncollected solid waste, and other environmental problems in Bangkok.

Structural Adjustment Policies and Their Impacts on Income Distribution, Poverty, and the Environment

Establishing the links between structural adjustment policies on the one hand and poverty and environmental impacts on the other requires examination of the growth and distributional impacts of adjustment and analysis of the poverty/inequality-environmental link. Attempting to separate these intermediate steps, five policy simulations of structural adjustment policies were used to assess their distributional impacts and environmental implications.

Reduction of Export Taxes on Rice and Rubber

Export tax reduction is expected to have a positive distributional impact because it affects the tax burden on agriculture and the rural sector, therefore reducing the high incidence of poverty in rural areas. It also improves the rural-urban terms of trade. Moreover, because the export tax on rice tends to be regressive, it should improve income distribution overall, but it may widen rural-rural and urban-urban income distribution.

Rice

The urban-rural income distribution will narrow because the reduction of export taxes will halt the regressive transfer of resources from agriculture (rural) to industry (urban) and will generally improve the terms of trade for agriculture. The rural-rural income distribution will widen because the increased price of rice will mainly benefit large commercial farmers (the top three deciles of rural households), whose total production is marketed; on the other hand, the bottom three deciles will receive only minimal gains because small paddy farmers market under 10 percent of their rice production and many are net purchasers of rice. The urban-urban distribution will widen because removing the export tax on rice raises the price of the staple food. Because the urban population purchases all its rice and the urban poor spend a large percentage of their income on food and a larger percentage of their food expenditure on rice, a higher rice price means lower real income for the urban poor compared to the nonpoor urban population.

Rubber

The distributional impact of removing the rubber export tax is more clearly positive because rubber is a cash crop that is cultivated by poor small holders in the South. Nonetheless, the beneficial impact on the environment from improved income distribution and poverty alleviation may be offset by the increased profitability of rubber cultivation, encouraging further forest encroachment and rubber planting on steep and fragile slopes.

Overall, the effect of the removal of export taxes on rice and rubber on income distribution and poverty is thought to be positive. These conclusions support the earlier studies by Trairatvorakul and the World Bank; they estimated the direct income impact on farmers of rice taxation at 8.4-14.5 billion baht annually and of rubber taxation 3.3 billion baht respectively.[17] The Bank concluded that "these indirect income effects of the pricing policies alone take out as much or more from the rural areas as the combined rural development expenditures for agriculture and non-farm activities."[18]

Increases in Energy Prices

The effect of increasing energy prices to world market levels on income distribution is more ambiguous. On the one hand, low energy prices tend to favor the urban and industrial sectors, which are more energy intensive than the rural and agricultural sectors; higher energy prices should improve income distribution. On the other hand, higher oil prices reduce energy-intensive nonagricultural employment, thereby reducing the opportunity both for supplementing nonfarm employment in the rural area and for migration to urban areas to work in industry. On balance, the impact of higher oil prices on the rural-urban income distribution will be positive. So too is the impact on rural-rural and urban-urban income distribution likely to be positive. Rural income distribution will improve because poor farmers use fewer modern inputs (including oil and agrochemicals) and market a smaller percentage of what they produce. Similarly, urban-urban income distribution is likely to improve because the urban poor use a less energy-intensive means of transport (mass transport).

Structural adjustment policies that raise the price of oil and gas to world price levels tend to reduce poverty in relative terms and increase it in absolute terms. The impact on the environment is thus ambiguous.

Promotion of Exports of Labor-Intensive Manufactures

Policies that help expand the exports of labor-intensive manufactures have positive impacts on both absolute and relative poverty because they create more employment opportunities and raise wages.

Promotion of Tourism

Tourism is a labor-intensive industry; hence its promotion is likely to have positive impacts on absolute and relative poverty. But some potentially positive impacts are offset by the Board of Investment's deliberate promotion of capital-intensive tourism and the increasing orientation toward low-quality mass tourism that is neither labor intensive nor environmentally benign. The recent reduction of promotional privileges to all industries as an integral part of structural adjustment will improve both the distributional and environmental implications of tourism growth.

Reduction of Public Sector Expenditures

Reduced government expenditures will feed through to reduced domestic demand and a fall in domestic prices. This change will boost agricultural exports because demand is relatively elastic and therefore will improve the rural-urban income distribution. Absolute poverty is also likely to be reduced with higher agricultural incomes.

Yet the overall impact on different sectors of society will much depend on the types of expenditures that are curtailed. For example, reduced public expenditures on water supply and sanitation, public transport, health, and education will undoubtedly have regressive distributional impacts. Reductions in environmental expenditures in the control of air and water pollution will also be regressive because it is the urban poor who are usually exposed to water and air pollution. On the other hand, if expenditures on investment promotion, industrial protection, and capital subsidies are reduced, then the distributional impact clearly will be positive.

Land Titling

According to Feder and others, the insecurity of land tenure in Thailand has been a serious impediment to investment, productivity growth, and diversification. Based on their study's finding that land titling would result in a 10-30 percent increase in agricultural productivity, the decision was made to include land reclassification and titling in Thailand's structural adjustment program.

The distributional and environmental benefits of such a policy are clear, but their value may be undermined by the decision to opt for issuing nontransferable 5- to 25-year land certificates rather than full land titles. This half measure is likely to reduce the incentives, dynamism, and resources (access to credit based on secure collateral and reduced risk of eviction) necessary to increase investment productivity and incomes.

In sum, land titling as part of structural adjustment programs makes good economic, distributional, and environmental sense, provided that land titles are made secure and transferable and the remaining forests are effectively protected from further encroachment.

Conclusions

The negative impacts of poverty on the environment are well-established: (a) poor people tend to have a stronger time preference (because of threatened survival) and thus discount the future more heavily, (b) there is little demand for environmental amenities at subsistence levels, and any environmental expenditures are ill-afforded luxuries, (c) poor people lack the technology to exploit and use natural resources efficiently, (d) poor people lack access to institutional credit to invest in land improvements, perennial crops, and soil conservation, and (e) poor people's opportunities to save, educate their children, and obtain alternative employment are severely limited.

Widening income differentials may also have detrimental environmental consequences, or they may prompt government intervention that has spin-off effects on the natural resource sector. For example, rising expectations fueled by general economic growth, the mass media, and changing consumption patterns in urban areas may encourage exploitation of the resource base. This behavior may manifest itself in shortened fallow cycles, premature tree harvest, and diverted expenditures from conservation to acquisition of consumer durables such as vehicles and modern housing. Widening income disparity also accelerates migration, which may overwhelm the urban infrastructure.

Government response to widening income differentials may have unintended environmental impacts. Thailand's failure to address rural poverty and widening income distribution resulted in the tacit encouragement of squatting and land clearance for agriculture without conference of long-term land security. Yet direct government intervention to alleviate hardship, such as the recent introduction of farm price supports, input subsidies, subsidized credit, and tax exemption schemes for fishing machinery, have unintended and mixed environmental impacts. Sometimes government intervention to achieve social equity objectives will complement environmental objectives; this will certainly be true of programs to alleviate extreme poverty. At times, intervention may create perverse incentives with unintended and harmful consequences for the sustainable use of natural resources. For example, subsidizing credit for fishing machinery and equipment is certain to deepen capital intensity at the expense of labor employment. It will also encourage new entry into the industry to the destruction of fish resources and the eventual nullification of any temporary gains to the fishermen. The point is that government interventions for equity objectives will not necessarily complement environmental objectives, except when extreme poverty is alleviated. Government must be aware of any possible spin-off effects on the environment, to be sure that any trade-off is explicit and intended. In other words, distributional and environmental objectives cannot necessarily be achieved simultaneously. These two objectives require two instruments. In some cases, the goals are complementary but in others, a conflict arises.

The structural adjustment policy scenarios provide valuable insights into the implications for poverty and income distribution of structural adjustment. But, unfortunately, the results are neither unidirectional nor unambiguous. For example, the promotion of labor-intensive activities has generally positive impacts on both absolute and relative poverty and consequently is likely to yield environmental benefits. On the other hand, reduced public sector expenditures may have positive or negative impacts on income distribution, depending on which public expenditures are curtailed. Here the environmental impact is also ambiguous.

Overall, the structural adjustment policies in Thailand increased per capita incomes for all groups and helped alleviate poverty. In this sense, a direct positive relationship can be established between economic development in Thailand and environmental impacts. But there are three important caveats. First, it may take time for structural adjustment policies to produce favorable distributional impacts; in the interim, short-term negative distributional impacts may lead to irreversible environmental degradation, such as the loss of tropical forests to encroachment by rural dwellers whose livelihood is affected by these policies. Second, when structural adjustment has negative effects on poverty and inequality, the impact on the environment is ambiguous. Further, government attempts to address social equity objectives may have unintended and unforeseen consequences on the use of natural resources.

MARKET AND GOVERNMENT POLICY FAILURES (INCLUDING INSTITUTIONAL AND INFRASTRUCTURE CONSTRAINTS)

Good macroeconomic management is a necessary but not sufficient condition for sustainable development. Macroeconomic mismanagement, on the other hand, is likely to damage the environment and may nullify the impact of good underlying sectoral and environmental policies. "Mounting foreign debt, widening balance of trade deficits, hyperinflation, rising interest rates, low savings, negative growth of investments, and growing budget deficits work their way through economic stagnation, increased poverty and shortening of the planning horizon to encourage environmental degradation."[19]

"Good macroeconomic management," as prescribed by the World Bank, the IMF, and other international development agencies, amounts to macroeconomic stabilization, demand management, trade and industrial policy reforms to promote exports, liberalization of imports, and encouragement of foreign investment. This definition of the goal can be met by reducing absolute and differential protection and the promotion of competition through institutional reform. The pursuit of such policies in Thailand has reaped rewards by generating economic growth, creating additional employment, alleviating poverty, and enabling long-term economic planning free from a debt overhang.

Hence the structural adjustment prescription stressed the need to reduce government policy failures that contributed to market distortions and economic stagnation, but it omitted an important factor. Inherent market failures in the natural resource sector, such as the public-good nature of many natural resources, the presence of externalities or spillover effects, and the absence of markets for environmental goods and services, were not explicitly or systematically addressed in the economic reform process. Moving toward a sustainable development path requires correction of both government policy failure and inherent market failure. It is here that the structural adjustment policies in Thailand may be faulted. The program addressed distortionary economic policies but not environmentally damaging market failures.

In the Thai case, there are many examples of inherent market failures in the natural resource sector that have remained uncorrected during the process of structural adjustment. There are also examples of government intervention to achieve other objectives, such as macroeconomic stability and poverty alleviation, that had unintended and negative consequences for the environment. Some examples are cited here.

Policy Failures

Government policy failure refers to inappropriate interventions in otherwise well-functioning markets to achieve broader objectives, such as macroeconomic stability or social equity, but without regard to their possible environmental spin-offs. It can also refer to the lack of, or inappropriate, government action to intervene to correct underlying market failures in the natural resource sector when benefits clearly outweigh the costs.

Industrial Promotion

Industrial promotion has increased the proportion of industries that are potential hazardous waste generators without adequate provision for and enforcement of the environmental protection measures of section 19 of the Investment Promotion Act 1977. Encouragement of export-oriented industries has seriously threatened environmental quality in Thailand and effectively undermined protective environmental legislation in this area. To promote export expansion without further threat to the environment would require the level of pollutants or amounts of hazardous waste per unit of value added to be used as a selection criterion for targeted industries in the same way that the export content has been used in the Thai industrial promotion policy.

Interest Rate Ceilings and Subsidies

Promoted industries benefited from reduced capital costs, but interest rate ceilings and subsidies caused credit shortages in rural areas and discouraged agricultural investment. The lack of agricultural investment threatens environmental quality in rural areas by encouraging more extensive farming and land clearance, or in the absence of an open frontier, by increasing land mining. Freeing up the credit market would be consistent with slowing down the pace of industrial development (thus allowing investments in infrastructure to catch up). It is also consistent with encouraging a movement toward more intensive farming because increased agricultural investment allows productivity increases on existing lands, thereby averting further land clearance.

Logging Ban

To halt the alarming deforestation rate, a logging ban was introduced, but it was ineffective because the underlying incentives for land clearance for agriculture remain firmly in place. For example, fertilizer taxes distorted the farmers' choice between intensification on existing farms and extension into an open frontier forest. In addition, government has often ignored illegal squatting on forest lands when a land-titling scheme would cost more than introducing such an initiative.

Development of Public Infrastructure

Urban and industrial growth has outpaced public infrastructure development. Consequently, the BMR is experiencing one of the world's worst problems of infrastructure bottlenecks—crowding, congestion, and urban pollution. The inadequacy of public infrastructure relative to demand is an example of government failure to make sufficient and timely public investments in public transport systems and household and industrial waste disposal facilities. The private sector cannot be relied upon to make adequate investments in these areas owing to the public-good nature of the services being provided. Now infrastructure bottlenecks are so severe that they are constraining further economic development, particularly in and around Bangkok. The government response has been to promote efforts to decentralize industry into the rural areas, reduce congestion, and spread the benefits of industrialization. But such efforts must clearly take environmental pros and cons into account.

The failure to make adequate investments in public infrastructure to reduce environmental stress is an inherent weakness of short-term stabilization programs that focus on reducing public sector commitments to reduce the internal deficit.

Taxation of Fertilizer Inputs

On the face of it, a fertilizer tax should benefit the environment by encouraging more traditional and sustainable soil conservation practices and reducing the environmental costs of chemical runoff and water pollution. In this sense, the fertilizer tax could be regarded as a quasi-environmental tax in which the externalities or runoff effects have been internalized by the producer. But in Thailand, the system of fertilizer taxes does not work that way because of the high taxation of organic fertilizers relative to chemical fertilizer and the presence of an open access forest frontier. In fact, the differential system of fertilizer taxes has biased fertilizer use in favor of nonnitrogen-based compound fertilizers that are less suitable for Thai soils. The traditional structural adjustment prescription would be to remove such distorting input taxes, but Thailand has not done so. Removing them would not be the best option for the environment because it would not help internalize the negative consequences of fertilizer use. But certainly the taxes should reflect the relative damage of chemical and organic fertilizers. Given the negative environmental externalities of the former and the positive environmental externalities of the latter, a case can be made for taxing agrochemicals and subsidizing organic fertilizers and integrated pest management.

Implicit Subsidy on Irrigation Water

The supply of water from publicly funded irrigation facilities free of charge is an important implicit agricultural subsidy. This policy led to inefficient use of water and is responsible for waterlogging, salinization, and flooding. Some countries have dismantled irrigation subsidies as part of their structural reform; in this sense, they show how structural adjustment reforms can reinforce environmental aims. In Thailand, the subsidy remains, providing a good example of market failure that has led to the inefficient use of a valuable natural resource. It therefore makes good economic, distributional, and environmental sense to introduce irrigation water pricing (perhaps in conjunction with granting tradeable water rights to farmers) to reduce wasteful water use, put scarce water to the best possible use, and control irrigation-related environmental problems. Revenues could then be used to maintain the system, expand its distribution network, and protect its watershed area.

Energy Pricing Policies

The real scarcity value of natural resource inputs in energy production and any external costs of polluting emissions should be reflected in energy prices. Thailand has kept the price of energy artificially low to subsidize industrial promotion. But in the early 1980s, the Thai government confronted the growing fuel import bill by raising energy prices to reflect the opportunity cost (international price) of imported oil. In addition, plans were made to develop alternative energy sources and adopt energy conservation measures. Consequently, the National Energy Conservation Center was established, and an action plan for energy conservation in transport and industry was developed. These initiatives were an integral part of the Fifth Development Plan and SALs I and II. Thailand's energy policy reforms are a good example of structural adjustment policies that complement environmental objectives. Correcting the failure of market prices to reflect the real costs of energy was also consistent with moves to reduce pressure on the external account by reducing the fuel import bill.

There is still room for improvement. No provision was made in the structural adjustment policies for differential pricing (and taxation) of leaded versus unleaded gasoline. Increased oil prices helped control the growth of oil consumption, but unleaded gasoline was not available and diesel oil was priced too low relative to its environmental damage. The Thai government is now working on the problem and recently introduced unleaded gasoline, pricing it below leaded gasoline to encourage a switch.

Market Failures

Much of the mismanagement of natural resources can be traced to malfunctioning, distorted, and often totally absent markets for environmental goods and services. Market failure can be interpreted broadly to include the institutional structure and property rights that determine the capacity of markets to function efficiently. With this broader definition (developed by Panayatou[20]), the following sources of market failure were identified:

- ill-defined property;
- nonpriced resources and absent or thin markets;
- spillover effects or externalities;
- high transaction costs, including information, negotiation, monitoring, and enforcement costs;
- public-good characteristics of many environmental goods and services;
- market imperfections, including monopolies, oligopolies, and segmented markets;
- myopic planning owing to "too short" planning horizons or "too high" discount rates arising from poverty, impatience, risk, or uncertainty; and
- market decisions made without adequate information that lead to irreversible results.

In Thailand, there are many examples of market failures that led to suboptimal environmental degradation and were not explicitly corrected in the structural adjustment process. Sometimes the structural adjustment policy instruments adjusted prices or reformed institutions in the same way that a policy intervention to correct the inherent market failures would also prescribe. In this sense, the structural adjustment policies complemented environmental objectives. But sometimes structural adjustment policies intensified existing incentives for natural resource degradation. The following examples illustrate the mixed effects of structural adjustment policies on Thailand's environmental sector.

Industrial Pollution Externalities

Industrial pollution externalities have not been internalized in production decisions in accordance with the polluter pays principle. Effluent charges, pollution permits, performance bonds, or another market-based instrument could have been used to internalize the environmental and health costs of industrial air and water pollution. There is no evidence to suggest that domestic or foreign investment would have been affected and growth slowed. In fact, the contrary is true. Foreign companies find it increasingly costly to operate in Thailand because they have to offer their executives higher salaries and bonuses to induce them to move to a polluted environment.

A recent study by TDRI estimated the internalization of environmental costs to industry at about 1 percent of the industrial GDP, or 5 percent of profits.[21] This cost will be reduced as industry directs investments increasingly toward less polluting processes and products to avoid pollution charges.

Externalities Related to Deforestation

Deforestation externalities are seen in downstream flooding and landslides, causing considerable damage to crops and infrastructure and loss of life and livelihoods. It may have micro- and global-climatic effects, with considerable external costs to both the domestic and global economy. Deforestation also reduces the supply of secondary forest products, on which rural communities particularly depend. Because they are not traded, these secondary products effectively have a zero price. They include fuelwood, forest fruits and medicinal plants, food, and clothing products from wildlife.

Insecure Land Tenure

A classic case of market failure related to the underlying institutional and legal framework governing land use is insecure land tenure. The presence of an open access land frontier effectively distorts the farmers' choice between agricultural intensification on existing lands and extension into forest or marginal lands. The government, in conjunction with World Bank support, has attempted to correct this market failure by introducing a land-titling scheme. Unfortunately, it limits land rights to squatters for 5-25 years, a half measure that may not provide sufficient incentives for increasing investments to raise productivity and incomes from existing lands.

International Trade and Comparative Advantage

Measures to internalize the environmental costs of production may affect the overall competitiveness of certain types of industry in international markets. They may affect domestic and foreign investment in these industries and reduce growth at least in the short term. Thailand evidences no negative consequences on the economy as a result of environmental policy. On the contrary, as foreign firms find it increasingly costly to operate in Thailand owing to additional costs associated with pollution and congestion, measures to reduce these externalities will have positive feedback on industrial investment, growth, and exports.

CONCLUSIONS

In Thailand, the ratio of debt to GDP increased rapidly in the early 1980s, reaching 39 percent of GDP in 1985 owing largely to the oil price shocks, the world recession, and declining agricultural prices. It did not run into the same financial difficulties as many other developing countries, particularly those in Africa and Latin America, because the Thai government took immediate corrective action. Some reforms were government initiatives, and others were part of the World Bank's two SALs in 1982 and 1983. Adoption of generally prudent monetary and fiscal policies at the time enabled Thailand to take full advantage of favorable improvements in the world economy without any serious overhangs from the past. But did these corrective policies in the form of structural adjustment improve or worsen the environment? Evidence suggests that structural adjustment policies reduced resource depletion and environmental degradation per unit of output, but because overall output increased, overall environmental quality declined. Is this trade-off economically efficient and environmentally sustainable? The current design of structural adjustment packages emphasizes the correction of government policy failures, but the underlying market failures related to the natural resource sector have not been systematically addressed. Consequently, the trade-off between economic growth and environmental quality was neither economically efficient nor sustainable. Only when the full social and environmental costs are internalized in the output decision is such a trade-off defensible. Even then, it is important to take precautionary action when the environmental costs are uncertain and potential irreversible environmental damage could severely limit future development options.

In the Thai case, there is little evidence to suggest that had market failures been corrected or mitigated, economic growth would have been slowed. There are at least as strong reasons to believe that growth could have been reinforced if traffic flowed more freely, the air and water were cleaner, and infrastructure were less of a bottleneck. New industries in waste reduction and management, waste treatment, recycling, environmental engineering, environmental auditing, resource rehabilitation, and reforestation would have filled any slack created by reduced investment in heavily polluting industries.

CHAPTER FIVE ENDNOTES

1. World Bank, "Program Performance and Audit Report Thailand—First and Second Structural Adjustment Loans (Loans 2097-TH and 2256-TH)," Report no. 6085, Washington, D.C. 1986, p. 67.

2. Ibid., p. 2.

3. T. Panayotou, "The Economics of Environmental Degradation: Problems, Causes and Responses," Development Discussion Paper no. 335, Harvard Institute for International Development, 1990, p. 108.

4. S. Chunanuntathem, S. Tambunlertchai, and A. Watlananukit, "Trade and Financing Strategies for Thailand in the 1980s," Overseas Development Institute Working Paper no. 22, London, 1987.

5. T. Betrand, "Thailand: Case Study of Agricultural Input and Output Pricing," World Bank Staff Working Paper no. 385, Washington, D.C., 1980.

6. World Bank, "Thailand: Managing Public Resources for Structural Adjustment." World Bank Country Case Study, Washington, D.C., 1984.

7. T. Panayotou, P. Kritiporn, and K. Charnpratheep, "Industrialization and Environment in Thailand: A NIC at What Price?" *TDRI Quart. Rev.*, 5(3)(1990).

8. Ibid.

9. World Bank, "Thailand: Pricing and Marketing Policy for Intensification of Rice Agriculture," World Bank Country Study, Washington, D.C., 1985.

10. T. Panayotou and C. Parasak, "Land and Forest: Projecting Demand and Managing Encroachment," Thailand Development Research Institute, Bangkok, 1990.

11. T. Panayotou, "Thailand: The Experience of a Food Exporter," in T. Sicular, ed., *Food Price Policy in Asia* (Ithaca, N.Y.: Cornell University Press, 1989).

12. T. Panayotou and C. Sussangkarn, *The Debt Crisis, Structural*

Adjustment and the Environment: The Case of Thailand (WWF-International, Washington, D.C., 1991), p. 4.15.

13. Ibid.

14. S. Hutaserani and S. Jitsuchon, "Thailand's Income Distribution and Poverty Profile and Their Current Situations" (Paper delivered at the Thailand Development Research Institute, End of Year Conference on Income Distribution and Long Term Development, December 1988).

15. Panayotou and Sussangkarn, op. cit., p. 5.2.

16. Hutaserani and Jitsuchon, op. cit.

17. P. Trairatvorakul, "The Effects on Income Distribution and Nutrition of Alternative Rice Price Policy in Thailand," Food Policy Research Institute Research Report no. 45, Washington, D.C., 1984; World Bank, "Thailand: Rural Growth and Employment," Washington, D.C., 1983.

18. World Bank, ibid.

19. Panayotou, 1990, op. cit., p. 63.

20. Ibid., p. 19.

21. Panayotou, Kritiporn, and Charnpratheep, op. cit.

CHAPTER SIX

CONCLUSIONS

*by the London Environmental and Economics Centre
and David Reed*

None of the adjustment programs studied in this research
project, whether developed by the individual countries or with
assistance from the World Bank and the International
Monetary Fund (IMF), gave explicit consideration to the impact of the
economic restructuring process on the countries' natural resource base.
Without explicit environmental objectives and natural resource sector
targets, it is difficult to make comparisons and draw specific correlations
with their environmental consequences. Further, reaching definitive
conclusions about environmental impacts is complicated by the
difficulty of separating a link caused exclusively by adjustment
interventions from relationships originating in previous states of
economic growth, in the structure of the economies themselves, or in the
impact of exogenous factors. In addition, identifying common
environmental impacts of the adjustment experience is complicated by
the fact that the three countries studied occupy different places in the
international economy, their economic structures differ, and the causes
of macroeconomic imbalances during the 1980s vary, as do the specific
objectives of the adjustment programs.

These factors influenced the focus of the conclusions derived from
the case studies. To give context to the specific conclusions about the
adjustment-environmental sector link, the first section examines the
sustainability of the development path pursued by each country. This
summary is followed by a discussion on two themes, the relation

139

between debt and environmental degradation and a hypothetical "environmental Kuznets curve," which purports links between macroeconomic performance and environmental degradation. The chapter then discusses more extensively the specific links between the impact of adjustment programs and the natural resource sector. A more detailed matrix linking economic instruments of adjustment programs to environmental impacts is included as Annex A.

THE DEVELOPMENT PROCESS OVER TIME: HAS A PATH OF SUSTAINABLE DEVELOPMENT BEEN FOLLOWED?

The development strategies pursued by Côte d'Ivoire, Mexico, and Thailand in recent decades vary significantly in accordance with their respective economic opportunities and advantages and in keeping with their respective political arrangements. Despite the structural and political differences, at various times in recent economic history, each country has extracted a surplus from the rural economy to finance increased public services and rapid industrialization. This strategy rapidly depleted natural assets, especially timber, soil fertility, and other renewable resources. Evidence suggests that extraction of natural capital was both inefficient and excessive in all three countries. The drawing down of natural assets is due in part to price distortions linked to shortcomings in government policy that failed to establish long-term policy for the natural resource sector. Excessive consumption of natural resources is also attributable to structural and institutional problems, including inadequate land tenure arrangements, lack of access to credit for farmers, and chronic poverty. In addition, in two of the three countries, success in drawing labor from the agricultural sector was often limited, owing to the capital-intensive nature of industries being promoted in those countries. Thus, although pressure on the environment in rural areas has continued or worsened, development of industry has created new environmental problems, often in the form of pollution and congestion.

It may be argued that environmental degradation was a necessary price to pay for economic development—that is, that countries traded their natural capital for improved human welfare. Although a trade-off between economic growth and environmental deterioration exists, that argument says nothing about whether the pace and scale of resource depletion were optimal from an economic and social perspective. All three studies reveal the fact that prevailing patterns of resource use entail considerable waste and loss of national wealth. Moveover, arguments about necessary trade-offs are hardly credible unless the revenues derived from resource depletion are invested in ways that ensure long-term sustainable improvements in human welfare.

The case studies provide evidence that the economic surplus extracted from the rural sector was not always wisely or equitably invested, particularly in Côte d'Ivoire and Mexico. This statement also applies to the surplus derived from exploitation of petroleum deposits in Mexico. In Thailand, the returns to industrial investment were considerable, and the economy has enjoyed considerable industrial expansion, but not without serious environmental deterioration in both rural and urban areas.

Even where the rural surplus was prudently invested, there is a growing awareness that assets of human origin are no substitute for natural capital. The environment provides many unique and essential services that protect and maintain a wide range of economic and life support activities in each of the countries. Hence excessive environmental degradation can undermine long-term prospects for economic growth and human welfare. Although in different ways, the three case studies indicate that each of the countries faces and will continue to face serious economic constraints owing to mismanagement of their natural resource endowment.

One striking feature of the three countries' development experience is that they provide classic examples of how market forces, in the absence of appropriate government policy, failed to protect the environment. To illustrate, sustainable development was not pursued owing to the following factors:

- *The public-good nature of the environmental sector.* Many environmental problems common to the three countries (e.g., deforestation) influence environmental quality on microregional, national, and global levels. The fact that rampant destruction of the forests disrupts the microclimate of a region and deprives the country and the world of the carbon sink function was not taken into account in decisions affecting the rate of conversion of natural resources to support industrialization in any of the three countries. Only international opinion and pressure, which increased significantly during the 1980s, introduced this concern to national policymakers. Even then it remained a marginal issue.

- *Unpriced services.* Environmental services, such as watershed maintenance and protection against erosion, provided by forests acquired value only after extensive flooding in Thailand threatened the viability of agricultural production and human settlements. Only when accelerated deforestation began influencing precipitation levels and hence productivity of coffee and cocoa trees in Côte d'Ivoire did environmental issues begin receiving more than passing attention. Given that these environmental services were provided apparently free of charge, they were not integrated into the economic planning on either a macroeconomic or sectoral level through most of the 1980s.

- *Externalization of environmental costs.* The drive to industrialize, particularly in Mexico and Thailand, excluded consideration of the collective side effects (i.e., the negative externalities of industrial production). Not until the externalities began constraining growth through increased urban congestion and pollution in Thailand and widespread health problems in Mexico did the need to internalize environmental costs in production and consumption occupy the attention of policy makers.

- *Short planning horizons.* On both national and individual levels, planning horizons in all three countries frequently gave preference to short-term rewards rather than longer-term social well-being through environmental stability. High rates of discount were applied to conversion of forests in all three countries; concomitantly, high discounting, whether prompted by impatience, poverty, or uncertainty, led individual farmers to employ management and cultivation patterns of agricultural lands and neighboring forests in which short-term benefits may have been significant. But the long-term social costs were also significant, and they were ignored.

- *Irreversibility of policy decisions.* Despite glaring uncertainties about future environmental impacts, all three countries made major policy decisions during the past decades that had irreversible environmental consequences. Drawing water from aquifers under Mexico City and from the Lerma valley created irreversible environmental problems whose impacts are not fully determined but that already threaten the ecological viability of both the Mexico City basin and the Lerma valley. In summary, the three countries did not pursue a sustainable development path. In varying degrees, they failed to consume renewable resources at a sustainable rate, invest wealth derived from converting stocks of natural resources in activities creating long-term productive value, and prevent excessive urban pollution and congestion in the course of industrialization. These and other shortcomings in managing the natural patrimony now constrain further economic growth and social well-being. Further, there is every reason to believe that these environmental constraints will deepen and spread unless major investment programs are undertaken to restore degraded natural resources and to prevent further deterioration.

THE RELATIONSHIP OF DEBT AND ENVIRONMENTAL DEGRADATION

In recent years, the idea of a direct link between the rate of environmental degradation and the level of foreign debt has gained some currency. Given that structural adjustment programs have been an important part of the institutionalized response to extended balance-of-payments (BoP) problems typical of countries with debt problems, these policy-based lending programs are part of the equation linking debt to environmental degradation. Specifically, structural adjustment programs are charged with deepening environmental degradation because, allegedly, their primary purpose was to guarantee compliance of highly indebted nations with their international financial obligations.

The most specific charge of this thesis is that international debt accelerated the rate of extraction and conversion of natural resources to enable the country to meet its external financial obligations. On the face of it, the arguments sound persuasive, and adherents to this school of thought point to the statistical relationship between indebtedness and environmental degradation in many developing countries. For example, econometric studies of the relationship between debt and deforestation suggest that a strong positive relationship exists.[1]

The evidence provided in the three case studies demonstrates that the relationship between debt and the environment is not simple, and there are dangers of interpreting any statistical relationship that may exist as a causal link. The first point to be clarified in accurately interpreting the debt-environmental degradation link is that the basic relationship between government policy makers and a country's natural resources was established long before high debt levels were contracted in the 1970s and 1980s. Two important dimensions to the relationship warrant attention. First, during the 1970s, many countries embarked on ambitious development programs in which the government was considered the driving force of economic growth. Often relying on heavy external borrowing, the government assumed a central economic function by creating a wide range of public enterprises, marketing boards, and financial institutions and by providing subsidies and incentives of many kinds. Côte d'Ivoire is a classic example. There the preponderant government role during the postcolonial period grew out of the desire to assert economic and political independence vis-à-vis industrialized societies and compensate for the absence of a well-established entrepreneurial class. The government, instead of exercising sound management over its natural resources, quite often drew on stocks of natural capital to finance ambitious development plans established during the 1970s. Second, as the discussion on political economy presented later in this chapter points out, elites permitted or encouraged exploitation of natural resource assets to assuage social discontent among the poor, often as a way of avoiding redistribution of assets and income that might threaten their positions of relative privilege. Hence, by using natural resource assets, governments were able, for a while, to finance investment programs, maintain high levels of consumption, sustain imports, and deflect political challenges stemming from growing social inequities. Extensive foreign borrowing, when it was available, was another means for many countries to maintain consumption levels and investment programs beyond levels their own resources could sustain.

It should not be surprising that, when the gross domestic product (GDP) was growing slowly or falling, those in charge of the government used whatever means were at their disposal to sustain investment and consumption levels and protect their positions, even when doing so was to the detriment of the more vulnerable social groups and the natural resource sector. Indeed, in some situations, growing debt service burdens have sharply exacerbated the pressures to protect consumption levels. Does use of natural assets for short-term purposes jeopardize the long-term economic and environmental viability of the country? This study shows that it has done so to varying degrees in the three countries, thus continuing a pattern of natural resource consumption established prior to the debt crisis of the 1980s.

The second main contribution to the debt-environmental degradation link discussion is the experience offered through the three case studies. In the case of Côte d'Ivoire, a major problem identified by the research team was the lack of objective data collected consistently over an extended period. Despite the fact that Côte d'Ivoire has the highest deforestation rate in the world, the research team there was unable to establish any evidence that debt directly aggravated or eased environmental degradation in general or in the forestry sector in particular.

A provocative discussion within the country, and one cited by the research team, points out that efforts to promote agricultural exports as a means of reducing the external imbalance could contribute to deforestation. The argument continues that if government plans to increase producer prices of principal cash crops had not been forestalled, and then reversed by dramatic price drops on international markets, they would have stimulated further deforestation through land clearing for tree crop plantations. Although this thesis warrants serious attention, it is not clear that the proposed price changes would have accelerated land clearing given other constraints on expansion of agricultural production. Moreover, any incentive effect of raising producer prices might be negligible compared to the underlying tenurial and institutional bias in favor of deforestation.

The Mexican case study did not produce any evidence in support of the debt-environmental degradation thesis, pointing out that response to macroeconomic crises in the form of increases in natural resource output requires quite a number of years and often additional capital as well. Thus drawing down stocks of natural capital could not provide foreign exchange in the short-term. The main point made in the Mexican study was that macroeconomic mismanagement was responsible for the increase in debt, the mismanagement due partly to an over-interventionist public sector outlook and partly to the misapplication of oil surpluses.

In Thailand, the ratio of debt to GDP increased rapidly in the early 1980s, reaching 39 percent of GDP in 1985 owing largely to the oil price shocks, world recession, and declining agricultural prices. Yet it did not run into the same financial difficulties as many other developing countries, particularly in Africa and Latin America. The Thai government took immediate corrective action to address the debt situation. Some of the reforms were taken through the government's own initiatives, and others were part of the World Bank's two structural adjustment loans in 1982 and 1983. According to the Thai study, the adoption of generally prudent monetary and fiscal policies at the time enabled Thailand to take full advantage of favorable improvements in the world economy without serious debt overhang from the past. Although rampant deforestation occurred during the mid-1980s, modeling analysis did not suggest that this problem was triggered or accelerated in any direct way by national debt obligations.

The thesis that there is a link between debt and environmental degradation warrants further analysis. Additional research needs to examine whether external debt aggravated or accelerated the nonsustainable dimensions of development strategies, particularly in countries with a narrow productive base. The case studies in this research effort were unable to prove or disprove a general causal relationship that is sometimes inferred from statistical analysis.[2] The experiences of the three countries indicate that debt and environmental degradation both stem from efforts to raise living standards by using assets, both natural and foreign, in ways that could not be sustained by economies or the environment over an extended period.

IS THERE AN ENVIRONMENTAL KUZNETS CURVE?

Another thesis that has recently acquired currency, particularly within some elements of the international financial institutions, is that environmental degradation is a necessary side effect of development during early stages of economic growth. Until the per capita GDP reaches a given level, it is held, the country cannot afford to address its environmental problems. This discussion has direct bearing on the relation between structural adjustment and the environment because the demand-depressing impact of stabilization efforts causes incomes to decline, certainly in the short term. Thus, if this thesis is valid, structural adjustment would simply prolong the time the country had to absorb environmentally damaging development.

The notion that there may be an "environmental Kuznets curve" is derived from the work of Simon Kuznets, who examined the relationship between income levels and distribution. He argued that during the early phases of industrialization, there is a tendency toward growing distributional disparities, particularly as the "modern" sector of the economy begins rapid expansion. Only after reaching a certain level of GDP per capita, he asserted, will the distributional inequities begin falling as the benefits of economic growth reach other sectors of society. This same notion is then applied to the environment, to wit, that environmental quality will initially decline from a "pristine" level as economic development proceeds and will subsequently improve as incomes rise. As their basic needs are filled through higher incomes, people will also begin to demand, and afford, higher levels of environmental protection and amenities. This statement becomes increasingly true as environmental problems begin to place greater constraints on economic growth.

The notion of the Kuznets curve is an interesting proposal, but it is misleading if environmental damage at a given rate is thought to be essential for economic development. It is a dangerous concept if this notion is used to assert that incomes have to reach a certain level before environmental degradation can be addressed in policy dialogue, let alone halted and reversed. The basic question is: Where is environmental damage acceptable and where is it not? With these policy determinations, policies can be designed to minimize damage at a particular level of economic growth. It should be recognized, for example, that the restoration option will not be available if prior damage is irreversible and substitution possibilities are severely limited or nonexistent, as is characteristic of much environmental capital.

The country studies offer important insights into the viability of this thesis. In Côte d'Ivoire, incomes have been stagnant for more than a decade, and domestic demand for environmental protection seems negligible. Most recent initiatives for environmental conservation there are due largely to foreign pressures in the form of diplomatic prodding and financial incentives. At the same time, environmental constraints are clearly starting to bind, particularly in the agricultural sector. Certainly the analysis presented here would support the proposition that Côte d'Ivoire could have achieved better economic growth at less cost to its environment. In that sense, it was not an irreducible Kuznets environmental curve. Can the country enjoy a higher level of development and income without compromising the environment? The answer depends partly on whether the environmental degradation that has already taken place is reversible. But again some of the suggestions made in the report indicate that the future development of the country depends on protecting its environmental resources and not on allowing them to deteriorate. That too is suggestive of a non-Kuznets curve philosophy for the country.

In Thailand, however, some such relationship may well be relevant. As economic growth takes place, resources are being channeled into environmental protection to address emerging environmental problems as well as into the internationally recognized problems of deforestation and loss of biodiversity. Was this environmental damage an essential price of the economic growth? The country study makes it clear that had appropriate environmental policies been established earlier on, the economic growth could have proceeded on target with significantly lower levels of contamination and degradation. The Thai case also demonstrates that there is no automatic trickle-down effect from economic growth that will be translated into improved environmental performance.

In the case of Mexico, there is no evidence that the GDP per capita "turning point," if there is one, has been reached. Environmental degradation continues, and until 1988, resources to tackle it were in short supply. New political pressures and alliances based largely in urban centers have forced the ruling party to begin broadening the resources for environmental protection. Nonetheless, the economy is at a juncture at which future economic expansion is indispensable to pull the country out of its structural problems. That needed growth, however, can no longer be bought at the expense of the environment. Thus one cannot think of economic growth "leading" and providing resources for the environment, as the Kuznets notion would suggest. Instead, economic growth and sound environmental management must be addressed at the same time.

In all three cases, it is clear that the economic growth that has been achieved could have been realized with less environmental damage had better environmental and economic policies been followed. This statement applies particularly to Côte d'Ivoire and Mexico.

THE IMPACTS OF STRUCTURAL ADJUSTMENT PROGRAMS ON THE ENVIRONMENT

The three preceding sections highlight the nonsustainability of the three countries' development strategies. The development paths they pursued created high levels of environmental degradation and generated unnecessary waste and loss of national wealth. The short-sighted premise that environmental issues could be addressed upon achieving a higher level of economic performance created environmental problems that now seriously constrain economic growth. Further, development policies encouraged standards of living that were maintained only at the cost of using resources, natural and foreign, that the countries could not support over an extended period. These general conclusions set the context for reviewing specific impacts of structural adjustment programs.

Over the past decade, the three countries underwent economic policy reform necessitated by acute fiscal and current account deficits in the late 1970s and early 1980s. All three adopted orthodox prescriptions for structural adjustment as defined and promoted by IMF and the World Bank, although they were applied with differing degrees of consistency and have met with differing degrees of success. Specific adjustment policies were designed to achieve rapid BoP stabilization and increase medium-term macroeconomic stability through correction of supply-side constraints and inefficiency. These packages were intended to change the whole set of relative prices facing producers and consumers, reform underlying institutional arrangements, affect overall levels of public sector investment in infrastructure, and promote productive private sector activities leading to more jobs and incomes. Given the breadth of these structural changes, it is beyond doubt that the adjustment programs would affect the ways and rates for natural resource use and would generate new levels and forms of environmental impacts. The studies clearly illustrate that the present design of structural adjustment programs failed to move the economies onto a sustainable development path on a number of accounts. These shortcomings are presented below in some detail.

The Interaction Between Inherent Market Failure and Government Policy Failure

Other studies of structural adjustment and the environment speculated on the probable impacts of specific instruments, considered individually and separately.[3] Hence these synchronic studies generally concluded that the impacts on the environmental sector are likely to be random and therefore mixed, that is, sometimes structural adjustment policies complement environmental goals; in other cases, they conflict and environmentally damaging effects can be observed. The three case studies support this view.

The reason for this somewhat ambiguous conclusion becomes obvious when it is recalled that environmental targets and policies have not been systematically integrated into the macroeconomic and sectoral reforms. No effort has been made to address either inherent market failures in the natural resource sector or failure of government policy as it pertains to that sector. Hence it is hardly surprising that the consequences of the reform process do not reveal a systematic trend linking policies of structural adjustment to developments in the environmental sector.

In some cases, correction of government policy failure corrects an inherent environmental market failure. For example, energy price subsidies to promote industrial development led to excessive energy use that, in turn, contributed to domestic and global pollution and wasteful use of energy resources. This is a good example of government intervention that fails to take into account the side effects on the environment. Here, reducing the policy distortion reduces energy demand and consequently the environmental costs related to pollution. Thus correction of the government policy failure as an integral part of structural adjustment also helps to correct the inherent environmental market failure, yielding positive environmental externalities. On the face of it, then, this structural adjustment policy would be expected to have observable environmentally benign effects.

But in other cases, correction of government policy failure exacerbates the underlying market failure in the natural resource sector. For example, reductions on export taxes on agricultural goods increase the export of these goods. The increased supply comes from either increased land clearance or increased investments on existing lands to secure higher yields. The latter option is not taken when the system of land tenure does not encourage investment and there is open access to uncultivated forest lands. Hence the reduction in agricultural export taxes under structural adjustment has environmentally damaging effects in the presence of open access resources and ill-defined property rights. The correction of government policy failure exacerbates the underlying market failure.

All three case studies amply illustrate the interaction between market and government policy failures in the context of structural adjustment. In some countries, the net environmental impact is damaging, in others benign. But in no case is it optimal. The net result depends on the specific mix of policies effected and the underlying economic, institutional, political, and social framework of the country undertaking adjustment. Although the side effects are mixed, some broad generalizations emerge from the case studies.

First, the fiscal constraint and consequent reduction in public expenditure programs adversely affected the environment through cutbacks in resources devoted to the environment. These reductions occurred in two main areas: (1) the reduction of environmental infrastructure activities, such as water supply, waste disposal facilities, public transport, and public parks and recreational areas and (2) project-level investments such as agricultural extension services. In some cases, evidence suggests, expenditures on public environmental projects were reduced by a higher percentage than were overall public expenditures. For example, during periods of fiscal reductions, the budget of environmental programs in Mexico's Bureau of Urban Development and Environment fell faster than government spending in general. So too did its Department of National Parks, which also has an important environmental role. These cutbacks have been neither economically efficient (the cutbacks do not reflect relative opportunity costs) nor consistent with a sustainable development path. Distribution of the reductions often reflects the ease with which they can be effected politically without major concern for their longer-term implications. Certainly the disproportionate cutbacks in health and education services in many developing countries will potentially constrain future growth potential. Likewise, the short-sighted cutbacks in environmental investments will certainly engender constraints to further development possibilities, as the recent experiences of Thailand bear witness.

Second, reductions in total domestic credit reduced credit availability to smaller rural investors. These reductions discouraged on-farm investment and thus failed to increase sustainable agricultural yields. When coupled with reduced investments in other agricultural projects, these reductions countered efforts to stabilize the agricultural frontier and promote intensive agricultural production. Farmers' responses frequently depend on the underlying system of land tenure. With an open land frontier, further deforestation and farming of marginal and fragile lands results. When tenure rights on nearby lands are well-secured, then the tendency is to mine existing lands in the absence of resources to secure more sustainable yields.

Third, "getting prices right" will not ensure sustained natural resource management if the underlying institutional structure does not enable economic agents to respond to the new price incentives. Uncertainty of land tenure regimes in all three countries poses serious obstacles to stabilizing agricultural production. With uncertain logging licensing and permit regimes, efforts to correct price distortions in forestry were ineffective. Pricing reforms were similarly frustrated in the water and energy sectors because government institutions could not implement and sustain the desired changes.

Even in light of these three points, a question still remains: Did these corrective policies, in the form of structural adjustment, improve the environment or make it worse? Thailand's experience is particularly instructive. Evidence presented in the Thai report suggests that structural adjustment reduced resource depletion and environmental degradation per unit of output but that as overall output increased, overall environmental quality declined.

Is this trade-off economically efficient or environmentally sustainable? The current design of structural adjustment packages emphasizes the rectification of government policy failures based on conventional economic criteria, but the underlying market failures related to the natural resource sector are not addressed systematically. Consequently, the trade-off between economic growth and environmental quality is not adequately addressed, and the long-term result is neither economically efficient nor sustainable. Only if the full social and environmental costs had been internalized in the output decision would such a trade-off be defensible.

Take this conclusion a step further. In the Thai case, there is little evidence to suggest that had market failures been corrected or mitigated, the pace of economic growth would have been slower. There are strong reasons to believe that the growth process could have been reinforced if traffic in Bangkok were flowing more freely, the air and water were cleaner, and infrastructure less of a bottleneck. New industries in waste reduction and management, waste treatment, recycling, environmental engineering, environmental auditing, resource rehabilitation, and reforestation could have sprung up to fill any slack created by reduced

What Are the "Right Prices"?

This study assumes that the "right prices" include the full social and environmental costs of production and consumption. It is clear that prevailing market prices do not reflect real costs, either environmental or social.

Market prices reflect the pattern of demand within the economy, which itself is a function of the underlying distribution of income and assets. A more equitable redistribution of income and assets within a society would certainly change both the overall level and pattern of demand, thus determining wholly new relative prices. This simple point illustrates the fact that there is nothing sacrosanct about the set of prices within an economy—in fact, they are endogenous and dependent on the conditions of supply and demand, which are changeable and are influenced by policy considerations.

For small open economies engaged in international trade, the prices used to guide domestic resource allocation are international border or shadow prices. International border prices are relative to existing patterns of demand and supply in the international arena. These prices are also determined by the distribution of assets and income across countries. Unless environmental costs are internalized in all producing countries, international border prices cannot reflect the full social and environmental costs of production and consumption. In addition, they may be distorted by trade policies and agreements among countries. In this sense, reliance on international border prices does not provide incentives for either domestic or international resource allocation to achieve sustained economic development.

investment in heavily polluting industries.

The Link Between Poverty and Environmental Degradation

Poverty is often described as both a cause and an effect of environmental degradation. All three studies affirmed that relationship, although in different ways. Further, the findings of each suggest that the relationship between poverty and the environment is complex and subtle.

Despite the fact that a precise causal link may be difficult to discern, three conclusions emerge: (1) environmental degradation poses a serious threat to the long-term security of poor households, (2) demographic growth rates aggravate the environmentally damaging impacts on the poor sectors, and (3) paradoxically, government efforts to address rural poverty have frequently aggravated environmental problems. The studies strongly suggest that sustainable management of natural resources must become a central element of efforts to improve the welfare of the poor. Concomitantly, the studies suggest that efforts to improve the welfare of the poor must be based on protection and restoration of the environment as a central tenet of government intervention.

The Côte d'Ivoire study found disparity in living standards between urban and rural areas and among different regions of the country in terms of household income and the quality of living conditions. Not surprisingly, according to most indicators, Abidjan's living standards are the highest, and the Savanna regions, with a disproportionate concentration of the very poor, are the most deprived. An unanticipated but significant finding is the relatively larger proportion of very poor households in the Eastern Forest region relative to the overall distribution of the population. This area is the original Cocoa Belt, where much of the country's initial timber harvest and agricultural expansion took place. Despite these real material advantages, current household income is below the national average. This situation may reflect recent declines in crop yields and farm income owing to the cumulative effects of soil degradation or local climate changes associated with the loss of forest cover. Recent mass migration from the region to virgin areas in western Côte d'Ivoire lends support to the hypothesis that unsustainable management of resources—characterized in this case by the effects of deforestation on soil quality and by agricultural mismanagement—leads to increasing poverty and, simultaneously, to further environmental degradation. It may be that the economic boom has run out of steam, with environmental degradation now at such a level that real incomes are declining, leading families to look for better prospects elsewhere.

Another troublesome aspect of the migration of farmers to the Western Forest region is their loss of livelihood security owing to a change in status under the indigenous land tenure systems. These new outsiders are typically obliged to become tenant farmers, often under insecure informal lease arrangements. Where migrants have settled in public forest reserves, their situation may seem even less secure, but the government frequently turns a blind eye to such illegal land use. In some cases, political pressures arising from high rural unemployment levels and heavy demand for agricultural land led the government to remove large areas from the public forest estate and accord legal tenure over them to squatters.

Other links to poverty and the environment are identified in Côte d'Ivoire: how deforestation has led to loss of nontimber products and related occupations, how the dependence of poor households on natural forests for fuel contributed to deforestation, and how urban poverty aggravates sanitation problems owing to the lack of facilities.

The Mexican study examined links between poverty and the environment in deforestation, water management, energy pricing, and general fiscal policy. The study concluded that there was a definite but complex link between poverty and natural resource degradation. With regard to deforestation, the primary link is political. Land clearing and settlement arising from legislation undoubtedly increased the pace of deforestation. But the problem is not simply one of unsustainable logging practices; settlers may not claim land until they remove all forest cover.

More generally, the Mexican study found no observable link between the mean level of household income in a community and the way it treats natural resources, including forests. Some social and economic factors impel poor communities to exploit resources in short-sighted ways; other forces encourage them to husband their natural patrimony.

As discussed previously, government efforts in Mexico include consumer subsidies for key commodities. Yet many of these subsidies, including water and energy prices, result in excessive use of natural resources and damage to the environment. The study suggests that removing such price distortions would benefit the environment and not significantly hurt the poor.

In Thailand, rural poverty has been partly alleviated by the expansion of agriculture in public forest reserves. Between 1950 and 1988, 108 million rai of forest land was cleared, and 90 percent of it was converted to agriculture. The availability of forest land during this period kept rural landlessness to low levels despite a doubling in the population. Rural poverty was also attenuated by the fact that agricultural income remained high despite a virtual stagnation in crop yields. Government actions to alleviate poverty and the urban-rural income disparity resulted in the destruction of forests in northeast Thailand. The deforestation contributed to widespread flooding, which ultimately led the government to declare a national ban on logging for export. This experience is an example of a poorly conceived trade-off of environmental assets for poverty alleviation.

Three factors mitigate the trend of slower agricultural growth, continued forest encroachment, and persistent rural poverty in Thailand. First, population growth fell dramatically over the past decade. Second, industrialization continues to attract migrants to urban areas, thus alleviating pressure on rural resources. The scale of rural-to-urban migration will remain relatively modest, however, so long as the government subsidizes capital-intensive industry. The third mitigating factor is the growth of rural industry, which may contribute significantly to rural off-farm employment, further alleviating pressure on rural natural resources. The relocation of industry to rural areas is expected to increase in response to overburdened infrastructure, congestion, and pollution problems in Bangkok and surrounding areas. But such relocation will bring other environmental challenges.

In all three case studies, the relationship between poverty and environmental degradation may be described as a vicious circle. Causal links vary, are often indirect, and work in both directions. A more surprising conclusion, although one consistent with the following discussion regarding the relation between adjustment and political economy, is that government efforts to address rural poverty often lead to inappropriate and short-sighted policies that in fact aggravate environmental degradation. In the long run, these poverty programs further endanger the long-term welfare of rural populations. The extent of environmental damage resulting from such policies depends largely on the resources available to the government to address poverty and on the country's underlying economic and political framework.

The Political Economy of Adjusting Countries and Environmental Degradation

These studies reveal that an important cause of policy failures in the natural resource sector is that the policies often reflected the interests of the most powerful sectors of a given society, not the interests of society as a whole. In this perspective, distribution of natural resources became an important method for preserving the social privilege of elites; they could extract rents from natural resources or distribute natural resources to the poor to attenuate growing social discontent.

The use of natural resources to preserve social privilege of the elites is striking in Côte d'Ivoire. Extraction of rents from the forestry sector became, to varying degrees during the country's postindependence history, a principal tool of patronage for the ruling elite. The institutional framework for regulating exploitation of forest resources and gaining title to new lands in the expanding agricultural frontier was weak and lent itself to political manipulation for the benefit of familial, tribal, and political clientele. The one-party political system in Côte d'Ivoire, which tolerated little political or social opposition for many years, effectively repressed any organized challenge to this politically motivated mismanagement of one of the country's most valuable natural resources.

In Mexico, a far more complex, yet more pervasive use of natural resources to maintain the prevailing political economy is apparent. Historically, the highly stratified structure of Mexican society, that is, a society characterized by a large sector of poor and a developed elite sector, has generated constant tensions within the country's corporatist political system. One important method for policymakers to attenuate demands by the impoverished has been to provide access to resources that do not require redistribution of assets or incomes. This response of increasing access of the poor to natural resources, based in the distribution of land following the Mexican Revolution, was expanded in recent years to include water, forests, and energy at below-market prices. Providing energy at prices one-quarter those on international markets and water, particularly to urban centers, at prices far below the real cost are now central ingredients in the terms of social peace established with competing sectors of Mexican society.

Although the political benefits of subsidizing access to these natural resources is reflected in the longevity of the ruling party, *Partido Revolucionaria Institutional,* the long-term economic consequences may be devastating. Consider, for example, the water subsidy benefiting the urban population, rich and poor, that has depleted the aquifers under Mexico City and extinguished springs in the Lerma valley. Similarly, subsidized petroleum prices have contributed to grave atmospheric pollution and encouraged development of capital- and energy-intensive instead of labor-intensive industries.

The decision to encourage expansion of the agricultural frontier in Thailand in the 1980s was, in part, a response to the growing social pressure exerted by the impoverished rural sector of that society. Instead of initiating basic changes in the unequal access to assets and income, policy makers decided to open the forests of northeastern Thailand to the poor farmers of the region. As pointed out in the Thai case study, income distribution inequalities grew during the period of adjustment. Although some environmental effects of the ensuing deforestation have already been felt, the long-term social and economic costs of liquidating natural assets to protect existing class relations are not yet fully clear.

Efforts to remove economic distortions and inefficiencies through structural adjustment programs may slowly encourage the elite in adjusting countries to give greater attention to the mismanagement of natural resources. Yet the fact that income distribution in Thailand— and in the other two countries as well, initial data would indicate— actually worsened during the adjustment period raises troubling questions about the impacts of adjustment on the environment of developing countries. For example, did growing distributional inequities occurring under adjustment accelerate distribution of natural resources to the poor in a short-term perspective of attenuating their social discontent? Did not adjustment policies tend to intensify the nonsustainable character of those countries' development approaches given that access to forest land was permitted but that little investment was made to stabilize the agricultural frontier through intensified production? There is no evidence to indicate that adjustment programs intentionally promoted these environmentally destructive practices with these short-term political objectives in mind. But there are strong grounds for concluding that adjustment programs allowed this historically established pattern of using the natural resource sector for short-term political gains to continue unchallenged.

Structural Adjustment and Institutional and Social Constraints

As noted above, one of the necessary conditions for achieving sustainable development is the correction of market and government policy failures in the natural resource sector. However, many countries encountered considerable difficulties in implementing structural adjustment reforms owing to institutional and/or social constraints.

Côte d'Ivoire, Mexico, and Thailand had different degrees of success in implementing policies of structural adjustment. Thailand was the most successful, largely because the adjustment program was an integral part of domestic planning and was in accordance with the country's underlying political and economic ethos. At the other end of the spectrum, Côte d'Ivoire experienced great difficulty in implementing reforms owing largely to the fact that both prior to and during adjustment, the government did not forge a consensus on the need to implement structural reforms. Consequently, various elite sectors vied with each other to protect their own particular interests instead of addressing the needs of the country as a whole. The broader public was not consulted or involved in the protracted adjustment effort, thus increasing social discontent as adjustment programs failed to improve citizens' social and economic well-being. The lack of consensus permitted continuation of economic and institutional rigidity and resulted in poor economic performance and the persistence of poverty. For example, continuation of the ambiguous legal system governing rural land tenure illustrates institutional failures that undermine implementation of agricultural and forestry reforms.

The Mexican case study shows that when the economy is badly managed, management of environmental resources is poor. Time and time again over the past 30 years, the Mexican government has used the resources of the natural environment to try to address social and political goals but has failed to meet basic development, social, distributional, and environmental challenges. During the past few decades, these short-sighted policies were translated into institutional arrangements that today discourage badly needed reforms.

This discussion of sustained development, debt and environmental degradation, an environmental Kuznets curve, and the environmental impacts of structural adjustment programs strengthens the view that poor macroeconomic management invariably results in unsustainable management of environmental and natural resources. The case studies reinforce the corollary that sound macroeconomic management is a necessary but not a sufficient condition for wise management of the natural resource sector. Sound environmental policies delivered through stable, predictable government intervention is an integral part of sound macroeconomic management. The studies provide ample evidence of why economic growth cannot be the single driving force of development. Left to its own logic, economic growth tends to destroy the conditions of production—that is, clean water, unpolluted air, uncontaminated soil, and a healthy work force—on which economic well-being depends. Economic policies, whether through structural adjustment programs or long-term development strategy, must be put at the service of and conditioned by social policy that promotes the long-term interests of the country. The conclusions highlight the fact that government policy failure as it pertains to the environmental sector is often caused by short-term political use of natural resources, often to attenuate underlying structural inequities. Use of social policy as a corrective on market failure must therefore guarantee promotion of the long-term sustainability of development strategies, not short-term political interests.

CHAPTER SIX ENDNOTES

1. J.R. Kahn and J.A. MacDonald, *Third World Debt and Tropical Deforestation* (State University of New York at Binghampton, 1990); J. Burgess, "Economic Analysis of Frontier Agricultural Expansion and Tropical Deforestation," University College, London, 1991.

2. James Gustave Speth, "Coming to Terms: Toward a North-South Bargain for the Environment," *WRI Issues and Ideas* (June 1989):3.

3. See, for example, Iona Sebastian and Adelaida Alicbusan, "Sustainable Development: Issues in Adjustment Lending Policies," World Bank, Washington, D.C., 1989.

RECOMMENDATIONS

by David Reed

A decade of structural adjustment programs has generated improvements in the economic performance of some developing nations, notably middle-income countries, but it has failed to produce improvements in others, particularly in low-income ones. Numerous questions, many still unanswered, have emerged during the past decade about the impacts of adjustment programs on the social and political fabric of adjusting countries. To these questions and concerns must now be added the conclusions derived from this study, that adjustment lending has had, at best, a random impact on the environment and, without qualification, that it has failed in placing adjusting countries on a sustainable development path. These conclusions lead us to affirm that a fundamental change is needed.

The recommendations offered in this closing chapter of the study call for reforms that extend beyond the specific design of adjustment programs themselves. For example, the recommendations encourage changes in the broader economic development strategies formulated within national planning institutions and international financial institutions. Further, the recommendations point out institutional changes that are required to integrate environmental policy reforms into the design and implementation of adjustment programs. This institutional focus is necessary because the institutions' operational assumptions themselves are constraints to integrating the environment in long-term development planning. In addition, the recommendations address the political foundations of adjustment programs because a fundamental shift is required in both adjusting countries and international financial institutions to guarantee that environmental issues are accorded a central place in development strategies.

Taken together, these recommendations call for a basic change in the conception and practice of structural adjustment lending. Their implementation requires the logic of promoting economic development and improving efficiency to be conditioned by broader environmental objectives and criteria. They require that international financial institutions place sustainability at the core of their policy prescriptions and hence that a reordering of investment priorities take place. Above all, these recommendations require that the empowerment of citizens be recognized as the linchpin of any efforts to protect the environment, locally and globally.

In formulating these recommendations, however, we have had to recognize that there are objective limits to what policy-based lending can accomplish in either its present or a reformed mode. There is no question that structural adjustment lending has been a privileged policy tool used to promote fundamental economic reforms during the 1980s and into the present decade. As such, it has had a pervasive impact on economic structures of scores of developing countries. Nonetheless, adjustment programs per se cannot correct the historical inequities between North and South, they cannot induce basic reforms in existing trade regimes, and they alone cannot reverse negative financial flows or induce extensive debt cancellation. Nor can adjustment programs change political arrangements and social systems within developing countries. But reformed structural adjustment programs can make fundamental and urgently needed contributions to improving the sustainability of development strategies. In this manner, the recommendations offered here can complement the improvements in the design of adjustment programs achieved during the past decade, and they can strengthen the call for further reforms in policy-based lending during the 1990s.

CHANGING THE POLICY FOCUS OF STRUCTURAL ADJUSTMENT

The policy changes recommended in this section reflect a trend that is already occurring in the focus and character of adjustment lending.

During the past few years, structural adjustment programs have shifted from correction of macroeconomic disequilibria to sectoral adjustment lending for two basic reasons. First, in some developing countries, the shift results from the success of previous adjustment programs in stabilizing fiscal and current account problems and improving macroeconomic management. In these countries, medium-term improvement in macroeconomic stability now requires efficiency gains and expansion of productive capacity to strengthen the supply-side response. Second, in numerous other developing countries, however, particularly resource-poor nations, the shift to sectoral lending is occurring because of protracted difficulty in achieving improvements in macroeconomic performance despite implementation of adjustment packages often over many years. In light of these problems, increasing sectoral productivity holds the best promise for improving these countries' macroeconomic stability. In the international financial institutions, this shift toward sectoral lending is reflected in the declining investments in structural adjustment loans (SALs) per se and in the growing resources of sectoral and hybrid loans; that is, loans that promote both policy reforms and expansion of productive capacity.

Recommendation 1. Priority must be given to poverty-alleviating economic strategies with a particular focus on stabilizing and strengthening the agricultural sector. Sound, sustainable management of rural natural resources depends on eliminating poverty-induced environmental damage. Reaching this objective requires implementation of a multifaceted package of policy reforms and investments that must include:

- budgetary reallocation to support the rural sector;
- redistribution of productive assests where appropriate;
- institutional reform and development, including reform of land tenure regimes and improvement of extension services;
- introduction of technological improvements to increase productivity, particularly of subsistence farmers;
- investment in human capital development;
- changes in national consumption patterns to encourage development of the nontradeable market; and
- price supports limited to an absolute minimum to encourage investment in the agricultural sector.[1]

Yet productivity and efficiency gains in the agricultural sector cannot improve at the price of environmental degradation. Thus to ensure protection and strengthening of natural resources, adjustment programs in the agricultural sector must:

- establish measurable environmental performance criteria;
- strengthen institutions to monitor the impact of economic activities on the natural resource base and correct policy shortcomings; and
- strengthen mechanisms for educating and involving local populations in sustainable management of natural resources.[2]

The overall purpose of this policy focus is to address the deepening poverty in rural areas that contributes to and is caused by severe environmental degradation. It is intended to reverse the disinvestment in the agricultural sector that was deemed necessary to fuel industrialization in many developing countries. This focus is designed to restore the economic vitality of the agricultural sector by redistributing productive assets as appropriate, expanding productivity of domestic and tradeable goods (with emphasis on the former) and stabilizing the agricultural frontier through intensified production. It must give particular attention to strengthening the role of women in the development process. This policy change must be sharply differentiated from antipoverty projects because it implies a fundamental change of objective in economic policy and social priorities, not simply the provision of short-term relief for the rural poor.

Recommendation 2. Structural adjustment lending, particularly sectoral programs, must begin operating on basic principles safeguarding sustainable use of resources. These principles must be applied by the international lending institutions and borrower governments within the context of individual countries. The principles should:

- guarantee that consumption of renewable resources does not exceed their regeneration rates;
- exploit nonrenewable resources at a rate that does not exceed the rate of development of renewable substitutes;
- ensure, through pollution minimization and control techniques, that industries' effluents and other by-products do not cause unacceptable damage to the absorptive capacity and other services provided by natural resources;
- protect natural resources that provide unpriced environmental goods

and services;

- ensure that sectoral reforms and investments internalize environmental costs and, when negative externalities are unavoidable, that adequate mitigation measures are included; and
- apply the precautionary principle—that is, reforms and investments should not be undertaken if the environmental costs and consequences are not known or are not calculable.[3]

As adjustment lending focuses more on sectoral reform than on macroeconomic change, it holds forth the promise of increased economic efficiency. The case studies demonstrate the fact that increased efficiency achieved through structural reforms may reduce resource depletion and environmental degradation per unit of output. But that increased efficiency may increase the overall demand for natural resources while also increasing the total waste from production and consumption. Consistent and rigorous application of the principles of sustainable resource use will considerably reduce the negative environmental externalities associated with expanded, although more efficient, production.

Recommendation 3. Sectoral adjustment lending during the 1990s must increase the attention given to rebuilding natural capital, restoring degraded natural resources, improving institutional capability for planning, and managing resource utilization.[4] The added attention to strengthening the supply-side response through adjustment programs can provide an opportunity to establish a better balance in the proportion of government resources given to developing physical, human, and natural capital. Over the past decades, the focus of productive investments was principally expanding physical capital, with secondary attention to developing human capital and virtually no consideration to natural capital. The case studies illustrate how environmental problems become economic constraints when expansion of a country's productive capacity is not accompanied by increased investments in the natural resource sector and in human resources to ensure better management of the resources.

Recommendation 4. A basic tool used in adjustment programs is expanding and liberalizing international trade. Despite the priority given to this aproach, structural adjustment programs have a relatively minor impact on the aggregate volume and structure of goods and services traded on a global level. For individual countries, however, promoting increased international trade through adjustment's policy reforms can have a significant impact on a country's economic structure.

By focusing on the tradeables sector, adjustment programs have the opportunity to bring the internalization of environmental costs into sharper focus. National level environmental policies are the primary vehicle for helping establish price mechanisms that reflect the full economic value of environmental products and services. Nonetheless, in the absence of the effective application of national environmental polices and standards to achieve full economic costing, structural adjustment programs should encourage internalization of environmental costs by:

- ensuring that expanded production of tradeables, promoted under adjustment programs, does not come at the expense of environmental degradation, that adequate provisions are included to facilitate internalization of environmental costs, and that production processes comply with accepted international standards, including the standards set by the multilateral development banks; investments should not be approved when internalization of environmental costs is not assured or when internalization of such costs would generate unacceptable rates of return; and

- ensuring that trade agreements that include countries participating in adjustment programs have adequate environmental protection clauses (e.g., Mexico's participation in the North American Free Trade Agreement).

International trade distorts environmental impacts because, as pointed out in Chapter 6, neither domestic nor border prices presently reflect the true costs of production. Integration of environmental costs into international commerce will require major changes in both the conception and practice of emerging trade regimes. The pace of change will depend on the commitment of the international community, including the official financial and trade institutions, to help create institutional and regulatory conditions under which environmental standards can be respected in a liberalized trading system. Four basic conditions must be put in place for trade regimes to apply environmental standards:

- standards must be developed to identify the potential negative environmental consequences of producing specific commodities;

- as production technologies are transferred from North to South, they should be subject to updated international standards of environmental protection; and
- transparency of decision making and adequate public disclosure mechanisms on all matters pertaining to the environment must be encouraged and expanded within trade regimes; and
- environmental dispute resolution mechanisms must be incorporated into new and existing trade agreements to promote fair and uniform practices with regard to environmental costing and to address problems caused by noncompliance with environmental protection standards.[5]

The official lending community must commit itself to supporting the creation of these conditions. To do so, the multilateral development banks must accept the fact that trade agreements can contribute to protecting the environment. In other words, lenders must move beyond the simplistic perspective that expansion of trade per se improves macroeconomic performance, which, in turn, will lead to improvements in a country's environmental performance.

INSTITUTIONAL REFORMS

Recommendation 5. Policy-based lending can support modest but important steps toward revising the existing System of Natural Accounts (SNA) which, in turn, can improve management of a country's vital natural resources. Sectoral loans should provide resources for:
- inventorying stocks of primary natural assets;
- establishing baseline data and data collection mechanisms for these resources;
- identifying anticipated pressures on natural resources and developing utilization models to ensure maintenance of stocks; and
- assisting in integrating environmental goods and services into the compilation of the country's national accounts with a view to directly adjusting the standard national income.

Developing a system of national income accounts (SNA) that integrates environmental services into national productivity remains a requisite for allowing policy makers to plan the rational use of environmental resources. Although important steps in developing national accounts have been taken by France, Norway, and other countries, major revision of the United Nations SNA remains beyond reach at the present time. Even with development of satellite accounts, adoption of uniform practices will take years. But correcting national accounting systems cannot wait; it must begin now, through incremental steps. The measures recommended above, if adopted and applied in each adjusting country, would contribute significantly to more effective natural resource management in the medium term while contributing to the long-term correction of national income accounting.[6]

Recommendation 6. Data collection for all development indicators affecting the environment must be improved, standardized, and made available to the concerned public. These indicators must include productivity in the natural resource sector as well as social indicators (e.g., income levels, distribution) that influence the environment. By providing technical assistance and financial resources, international financial institutions and bilateral aid agencies can take a vital part in helping establish adequate data collection systems.

One major obstacle faced by the research teams involved in this study was the lack of, or difficulty in gaining access to, data on both the environment and social issues that impact the environment. For example, although the terms of reference for the case studies explicitly called for an analysis of changes in income distribution during the adjustment process, government sources insisted that such information was not available, or they did not allow data to be given to the researchers. (Thailand was the exception. Its uniquely expansive and meticulous data on the economy and its 90 most important sectors were made available.)

Recommendation 7. A pressing area of need for institutional reforms is correcting land tenure regimes that facilitate extraction of rents, unstable tenancy rights, and destruction of natural resources. Legal reforms should spare no effort in protecting the rights of indigenous people, particularly in demarcating their territories and establishing their legal rights.

REFORMING THE PRACTICES OF OFFICIAL LENDING AGENCIES

Recommended changes for the World Bank, the International

Monetary Fund (IMF), and, by extension, the regional development banks (RDBs) are in four areas: integrating the environment into development planning, establishing an operational directive (OD) on sustainability, improving implementation capacity, and strengthening the international environmental incentive structure.

Integrating the Environment into Development Planning

8. Environmental issues must be integrated into the formulation of policy from which investment strategies of the international financial institutions are developed. Development strategies are formulated through three kinds of documents:

(a) Country Strategy Papers (CSPs)

The country strategy papers are the first venue in policy formulation whereby major changes can take place within the World Bank. The environment must become a central objective of sustainable development strategies, and no longer can it remain a mere limiting factor of economic growth. At a minimum, CSPs must address the impacts of macroeconomic reforms, changes in incentive and regulatory frameworks, and shifts in the status of the poor with regard to environmental resources. They must also document (de)capitalization of natural assets, thereby establishing a direct relation to the national accounts.

CSPs are significant because they set forth the Bank's development strategies for individual countries. These papers analyze the major development challenges in a country, its growth opportunities within a regional and a global context, major constraints in achieving these objectives, and the volume and composition of Bank lending. To date, CSPs have not addressed environmental issues except to the degree that a resource constraint (e.g., water) might impinge on economic growth.

(b) Policy Framework Papers (PFPs)

The IMF must make two immediate changes in PFPs, in which agreements for balance-of- payment lending are reached:
- The IMF must ensure that fiscal contraction, usually a central part of PFP's, does not fall to a disproportionate degree on agencies

responsible for regulating environmental performance or on infrastructure projects designed to improve natural resource management.

- The IMF must establish, as part of its measurable targets, guidelines that seek to prevent deterioration of income distribution, particularly the income status of the poor. As the case studies point out, when the rural poor need to find means of survival, they tend to increase destructive pressure on the environment. Particular attention must be given to the social safety nets, especially for rural populations, to guarantee that they are not deprived of productive assets and opportunities as macroeconomic stabilization is promoted. Their situation needs to be monitored by representatives of all affected social sectors.

Environmental issues are virtually absent from PFPs because the IMF has operated on the assumption that correcting macroeconomic imbalances is the best, if not the only, way to address environmental problems. No consideration has yet been given to the proposition, now documented by these studies, that adjustment can have negative long-term impacts on the natural resource sector. Nor has attention been given to the proposition that the adjustment process can benefit certain sectors while jeopardizing the economic and social well-being, particularly of the poor, in turn generating long-term environmental degradation. In this regard, the potential impacts of the poor's seeking means of survival through consumption of natural resources have also been ignored.

(c) Country Economic Memoranda (CEM)

A fundamental change is required in the role World Bank staff give to environmental issues in country economic reports. The Bank must take the initiative in summarizing problems in the natural resource sector, identifying environmental problems as of either policy or market origin, establishing the links of these problems with rural and urban poverty in addressing poverty, explaining long-term economic and social implications of these problems, and, above all, setting forth long-term action proposals for correcting the problems. Analysis of progress in directly reforming the SNA should routinely be included in these reports.

In some ways, country economic reports provide the most important platform for increasing the emphasis given to environmental issues in the formulation of Bank country policy. Whereas the two previous documents are for use exclusively by Bank and IMF staff and management or with recipient governments, CEMs are often shared and discussed with all official donors who may support development activities in a given country. Consultative group meetings and similar fora at which the CEMs are frequently used include assemblies of representatives of developing country governments, bilateral aid agencies, multilateral lenders, and agencies of the United Nations system. The meetings also signal priorities and planning objectives to the broader financial and development community.

Establishing an Operational Directive on Sustainability

Recommendation 9. Taken alone, amending policy formulation mechanisms in the Bretton Woods institutions and, by extension, the RDBs, to allow for inclusion of environmental issues will not provide adequate guarantees for correcting the present nonsustainable development approach. Commitment to protecting the environment must be translated onto an operational level best codified in a World Bank OD. Specifically, we recommend formulating an OD on sustainability that would be applied to both policy- and project-level lending.[7]

The OD on sustainability should ensure that macroeconomic and sectoral reforms strengthen the ability of an adjusting country to meet the needs of the present without endangering the ability of future generations to meet their needs. Because the concept of sustainability is relatively new to the Bank, it is not expected that the OD will be flawless or all-inclusive at the beginning. However, the OD should be implemented within 12 months from the date of publication of this study to halt forthwith the egregious departures from the basic principles of sustainability. It is expected that fine-tuning an OD on sustainability will be needed as experience is gained. Active cooperation with nongovernmental organizations from industrialized and developing countries is essential for its preparation and improvement. Although specific details need to be worked out, the OD should include, at a minimum, the following elements:
(a) Ensuring that restructuring the economy and expanding production

will maintain present stocks of natural capital by ensuring that renewable resources are not harvested faster than regeneration rates and that nonrenewable resources are not consumed faster than renewable substitutes are developed.

(b) Ensuring that expansion of industrial or agricultural productive capacity will respect the limits of a country's natural resource base in:

- protecting and using hydrological systems and water resources at sustainable levels by ensuring the integrity of aquifers, water catchment systems, riverine sources, and coastal marine areas; and
- protecting and using croplands, rangelands, and pastures at sustainable levels in the perspective of promoting food security by protecting against overexploitation, overgrazing, desertification, and erosion.

(c) Ensuring that a country's productive capacity will not generate wastes and emissions that exceed the environment's capacity to absorb such discharges now and that the environment's future absorptive capacity is not impaired by:

- ensuring against the discharge of pollutants in soil, water, and air beyond levels consistent with environmental and human health;
- ensuring against the increase in greenhouse gas emissions, acidification, and ozone-depleting chemicals beyond ecologically tolerable levels; and
- ensuring compliance with pertinent international conventions.

(d) Ensuring that expansion of a country's productive capacity, infrastructure, and transport capacity promotes:

- acceleration of the transition to use of renewable energy resources and
- supply-side expansion as a priority only after substantial demand-side gains through energy-efficiency and conservation improvements have been achieved.

(e) Ensuring that expansion of a country's productive capacity will not lead to extinction of plant and animal species.

(f) Ensuring that wealth generated through adjustment programs' economic reforms and efficiency improvements is distributed in such a manner that measurable goals in poverty reduction are reached so that poverty-induced pressure on natural resources is alleviated. The Operational Directive on Poverty Reduction (OD 4.15) establishes a sound framework to promote this goal. Special attention will be required, however, to assess and respond to the complex relationship between poverty and environmental degradation and to ensure that short-term poverty reduction is not accomplished at the price of weakening the natural resource base on which the productive capacity of the poor often depends.[8]

(g) Guaranteeing that governments move decisively to establish national accounting systems that integrate the natural resource sector into calculations of national income. The OD should assess country progress in establishing environmental accounts and integrating environmental goods and services into the compilation of national accounts.

ODs pertinent to the environment are now limited to project-level investments, as mandated in the Operational Directive on Environmental Assessment.[9] As a consequence of this shortcoming, the OD on sustainability must provide an umbrella framework applicable to both macroeconomic and sectoral reforms as well as to project-level investments.

Strengthening Implementation Capacity

Recommendation 10. Although Bank staff has been required to incorporate the general principles embodied in the concept of sustainability in preparing projects since 1984, it has not done so.[10] In fact, it is not possible to identify a single case in which the sustainability guidelines were applied to either project-level or policy investments.[11] Given the weaknesses, if not outright failure, in complying with existing policy, implementation of the OD on sustainability must be matched by significant improvement in quality control and supervision on an operational level. This imperative is further underscored by the growing problems in implementing projects of the Bank, which has experienced a "declining trend in reported performance, with a marked decline in the past few years."[12] Senior management must make a protracted commitment to ensuring that this shift in emphasis is effected at the operational level. To this end, we propose, at a minimum, reforming or strengthening the institutional capability of the World Bank and the IMF (and, by extension, the RDBs), in the following areas:

(a) Revising the following ODs to ensure that sustainability requirements are integrated into the formulation of country development strategies and that the status of natural capital is reported regularly in national accounts:

- OD 2.00 Country Economic and Sector Work
- OD 2.10 Country Strategy Papers
- OD 9.00 Processing of Investment Lending
- OD 9.10 Processing of Adjustment Lending (forthcoming).

These revisions should be operative no later than 12 months after publication of this study.

(b) Providing sufficient staff in sector and country operational divisions to improve their ability to address environmental issues that arise in project-level investments through proper environmental assessment and regular supervision.

(c) Shifting staff priorities and incentives, to improving the quality of Bank projects being implemented, representing commitments of approximately $140 billion.[13] Staff incentives and promotion should be contingent upon demonstrating the ability to identify and assess environmental challenges in project preparation, manage a project portfolio that has successfully addressed environmental challenges throughout project implementation, and prepare and supervise implementation of projects that contribute to enhancing the sustainability of countries' development strategies.

(d) Establishing an Environmental Quality Unit (EQU), possibly in the Central Operations Department (COD), to ensure that the design and implementation of Bank-financed projects fully respect the Bank's own environmental standards and those of the borrower government. The focus of the EQU will be to enhance environmental quality in Bank operations. In addition, the Bank should prepare periodic and systematic reviews and foster their incorporation of their conclusions into Bank work. It is important to upgrade the current inadequate mechanism for ensuring project quality, the Annual Review of Implementation and Supervision (ARIS), so that it becomes an effective tool for strategic planning.

(e) Creating a permanent environmental unit within the World Bank's Economic Development Institute to strengthen environmental training and capabilities of Bank staff and of borrowing government officials. Particular attention should be given to integrating environmental goods and services into the SNA and assessing environmental problems and impacts;

(f) Creating an environmental unit in the World Bank's Operations Evaluation Department that would provide comprehensive analysis of the sustainability and environmental impacts of Bank operations on both a project and a policy level.

(g) Establishing a separate environmental unit, adequately staffed with environmental economists and specialists, within the IMF to ensure that its macroeconomic operations are consistent with the sustainability requirements proposed above for the World Bank. In addition, the IMF should establish an evaluation unit that, in conjunction with the Bank's evaluation activities, would assess the environmental impacts of its macroeconomic interventions and correct its activities accordingly. As the IMF belatedly accepted the social dimension of its operations, it should now move decisively to address the environmental dimension of its activities.

Strengthening an International Environmental Incentive Structure

Recommendation 11. Following the precedent set in the 1970s by providing interest subsidies to International Bank for Reconstruction and Development (IBRD) countries through what was then known as the Third Window, externally supplied funds should be used to subsidize the incremental costs of environmental analysis and protection associated with structural and sectoral adjustment loans.[14] The Bank would manage these specially designated interest subsidies, which would cover activities required to ensure that no environmental damage is incurred through adjustment lending. These funds could be used specifically for:

- conducting analyses of the potential environmental impacts of adjustment lending operations prior to and during implementation;
- financing incremental costs of activities in sectoral investment programs that would prevent environmental damage; and
- financing the costs of new activities that would strengthen the environmental performance of sectoral programs.

Grants rather than interest subsidies should be made to International Development Association (IDA) borrowing countries for the same purposes.

Strengthening the evolving international environmental incentive structure will succeed only if financial resources and incentives do not conflict or compete with resources directed to core development activities. The proposed interest subsidies must be financed by additional resources.

CHANGING THE FOUNDATIONS OF ADJUSTMENT'S POLITICAL DIMENSION

Recommendation 12. This section of recommendations faces the essence of the political dimension of the environment-development problem: guaranteeing public vigilance over the planning and use of natural resources. The linchpin of any fundamental change in this area, and the basic recommendation offered herein, is guaranteeing timely public access to all information pertaining to the environment. This necessary change is of such importance that unless public involvement in managing the environment is drastically expanded—a change premised on access to information, fundamental improvement in the management of the local, regional, and global environment will continue to prove elusive.

The urgency of moving in this direction is underscored by the policy failure of both developing countries and international financial institutions in this regard. What are these failures? First, government policy relating to the environment is kept from public scrutiny and outside public debate in most developing countries. As the case studies illustrate to varying degrees, this lack of openness allows policy makers unrestricted leeway in determining how natural resources are to be used. Second, World Bank and IMF statutes require that all transactions remain confidential unless the borrowing country government divulges the terms and conditions of official agreements. In tandem, these two political constraints systematically deny the concerned public the opportunity of ensuring sustainable management of a country's natural patrimony.

The most immediate means of correcting this policy failure is to respect concerned citizens' demands for access to information from the multilateral financial institutions. Unquestionably this reform is urgently needed. The fact that IMF refuses to modify its information access policy, coupled with the still inadequate information policies of the World Bank, objectively reinforces their policy failures regarding the environment and perpetuates natural resource mismanagement by elites in developing countries. This counterproductive policy undermines the credibility of these institutions' other efforts to improve their environmental performance.

Even if that policy change were effected, it alone would fall short of correcting elites' stranglehold on the flow of information about development activities that affect natural resources. A far more comprehensive effort to democratize the public's knowledge about the status and planned use of natural resources in each country is required. Ultimately needed from every government is an environmental resource management plan (ERMP) that:

- identifies policy failures that have contributed to environmental degradation and pinpoints corrections that should be made in national and sectoral policies;
- sets forth proposals and investment plans for restoring the environment;
- articulates long-term strategies for sustainable management of natural resources that incorporate corrections in previous development policies;
- identifies institutional changes needed, including strengthening data collection, monitoring systems, national planning mechanisms, and legal reforms.[15]

Critical to the success of the ERMPs is their becoming part of the domestic social contract against which government representatives can be held accountable by the general public. To this end, long-term resource management plans must be borne of a broad public debate about the role of the environment in promoting the country's economic and social well-being. That is, ERMPs cannot be the product of a select group of national planners who may tend to reflect the interests of the elites; instead, they should result from a society-wide consensus on sound environmental management. An additional implication is that these resource management plans must be part of and further contribute to an ongoing public campaign to increase public knowledge and stewardship of a country's natural patrimony.

The international financial institutions are important in broadening the public discourse on the role of the environment in development strategies. They can contribute by encouraging governments to place the ERMPs in the public domain for extensive review and discussion. They can further use these plans, for example, as the basis for discussion in joint consultative meetings in which government representatives can be held accountable for their country's performance in the natural resource sector.

Within the international community, however, official lending institutions cannot be expected to bear sole responsibility for these changes. The U.N. system of development agencies, whose environmental performance remains largely hidden from public scrutiny, must assume increasing responsibility for establishing international standards of environmental performance.[16] To date, the U.N. system has not implemented integrated standards and guidelines for promoting sustainable development within its own agencies, not to mention with developing country governments. Further, the U.N. development system has not recognized the fact that in this age of global environmental crisis, new political requirements have emerged that, independent of any political persuasion or arrangement, demand invigorated public involvement in management of a country's and the planet's environmental resources. The United Nations must assume its leadership responsibilities in practice, not just in promise, for establishing standards of national environmental performance and broadening public knowledge of, and participation in, management of national environmental resources. To move in this direction, the U.N. system must begin by applying these standards to its own agencies and the activities it finances around the world. The very mandate of the United Nations in promoting security and equity should make it easier for the U.N. system to take action on these issues with clarity and decisiveness.

CHAPTER SEVEN ENDNOTES

1. Although these specific points are by and large consonant with the recommendations presented in the *World Development Report, 1990: Poverty*, that report does not address either the destructive impact of poverty-induced pressure on the environment or the environmental impacts of poverty-alleviating measures in rural areas. See World Bank, World Development Report 1990: Poverty (Washington, D.C., 1990).

2. The concept and practice of primary environmental care provides guidelines for promoting involvement of local populations in the management of natural resources. See, for example, *Supporting Primary Environmental Care Report of the PEC Workshop, Siena, Jan. 29-Feb.2, 1990* (Rome: Instituto Superiore di Sanitá, 1991).

3. Various versions of the precautionary principle were adopted by the U.N. Environmental Programme and environmental conventions as early as 1972. It was first endorsed as a principle to guide international environmental behavior by the second international North Sea conference in 1987. More recently, the ministerial declaration adopted at a meeting of the U.N. Economic Commission for Europe, on May 16, 1992, in Bergen, Norway, was formally signed by 34 member nations (although it was initially opposed by the United States), whereby the international stature of that principle was reaffirmed. The Bergen declaration states: "In order to achieve sustainable development, policies must be based on the precautionary principle. Environmental measures must anticipate, prevent, and attack the cause of environmental degradation. Where there are threats of serious or irreversible damage, lack of full scientific certainty should not be used as a reason for postponing measures to prevent environmental degradation."

4. See the work of Herman Daly, World Bank economist. Examples of relevant Bank publications include: *Towards an Environmental Macroeconomics (Washington, D.C., 1990); Ecological Economics and Sustainable Development* (1990); *An Historical Turning Point in Economic Development: From Empty-World to Full-World Economics* (1991).

5. Konrad von Moltke, "Trade and the Environment: Issues in Dispute Settlement," Report for the Office of Technology Assessment, Washington, D.C., 1992.

6. See, for example, S. El Serafy, "The Proper Calculation of Income from Depletable Natural Resources," in Y.J. Ahmad, S. El Serafy, and E. Lutz, eds., *Environmental Accounting for Sustainable Development: A UNEP-World Bank Symposium* (Washington, D.C.: World Bank, 1989); Robert Reppetto, "Accounting for Environmental Assets," in *Scientific American* (June 1992); S. El Serafy and Ernst Lutz, "Environmental and Natural Resource Accounting," in Gunter Schramm and Jeremy J. Warford, eds., *Environmental Management and Economic Development* (Baltimore: Johns Hopkins University Press, 1989).

7. Robert Goodland and Herman Daly made an important contribution to this recommendation through their article, "Approaching Global Environmental Sustainability," Society for International Development, Rome, 1992.

8. World Bank, *Operational Directive 4.01: Environmental Assessment* (Washington, D.C., 1991).

9. Ibid., p. 1.

10. World Bank, *Operational Manual Statement 2.36, Environmental Aspects of Bank Work* (Washington, D.C., 1984), pp. 2-4.

11. Interviews with World Bank staff, April-May 1992.

12. World Bank, *Bank Experience in Project Supervision* (Washington, D.C., 1992), p. iii.

13. World Bank, *The World Bank Annual Report 1991* (Washington, D.C., 1991), p. 193.

14. World Bank, *Annual Report 1975* (Washington, D.C., 1975), p. 14; *World Bank, Annual Report 1976* (Washington, D.C., 1976), pp. 7-8.

15. The World Bank's proposed Operational Directive on Environmental Action Plans (OD 4.02) could represent an important contribution in this direction. As presently drafted, however, it does not ask governments to analyze the nature and cause of environmental policy failures or identify what is needed to correct the failures.

16. Konrad von Moltke and Jenny Eckert, "United Nations Development Program and the Environment: A Nongovernmental Assessment," discussion paper for WWF-International, May 1992.

METHODOLOGIES USED IN THE ANALYSIS OF MACROECONOMY-ENVIRONMENT LINKS

MODELS FOR ANALYZING ECONOMY-ENVIRONMENT LINKS

This annex looks at alternative techniques for analyzing the macroeconomy-environment links and their use in the three cases studies. Several existing models were adapted for use in this study. Broadly speaking, they are intersectoral input-output models, less restrictive general equilibrium (CGE), models and those based on more limited macroeconomic models.

Input-Output Models

Input-output (I-O) models use information on the flow of resources among economic sectors to answer a range of questions in a medium- to long-term planning context:

- What are the implications of alternative growth paths on the demand for key commodities, such as energy, and key factors, such as labor?
- What are the regional implications of alternative development policies?
- If resources are likely to be limited for investment, which sectors are the "priority" ones that can benefit economic growth the most? The same question applies when key commodities (e.g., oil) are in short supply. I-O models identify key economic bottlenecks that need to be

cleared to obtain maximum efficiency from a given supply.

These models were adapted to examine the environmental implications of medium- to long-term economic strategies in developed countries. In principle, one could identify the key pollution outputs associated with economic activities, the key pollution abatement sectors, and the key constraints in terms of the sink capacity of the environment and incorporate them in an I-O framework to answer questions similar to those asked above—but with respect to the environment. Where should scarce investment resources be allocated if environmental and economic objectives are to be satisfied? And how should future economic development be influenced by environmental as well as economic constraints?

Lack of data is the essential difficulty with this approach. I-O tables exist for most developing countries, but they are often outdated, and rarely are there enough comprehensive and systematic data on environmental flows for their use in this modeling framework. The rigidity of the technique does not lend itself to the to use of partial and incomplete information.

General Equilibrium Models

I-O models incorporate restrictive assumptions about technology that are sometimes considered to lead to invalid conclusions. Nonlinear modeling techniques with a more flexible structure regarding the number of sectors and their relationships have been developed over the past 20 years. Such models, referred to as computable general equilibrium models, are now easily applicable with relatively limited computing equipment.

For environmental problems, the Stockholm School of Economics has made advances in recent years. Use of the CGE models for studying environmental impacts of economic development is a distinct possibility for developing countries. It may seem paradoxical that the CGE models should be more applicable than I-O models, but their flexible structure permits constructive use of limited data. Thus they could be used in analyzing the environmental impacts of economic policies in developing countries in the near future.

Although such models have promise, they are limited. The key problem is that many parameters of the models cannot be determined empirically with any real accuracy. Hence values have to be assigned on a somewhat arbitrary basis, and the results are then subject to considerable uncertainty.

This situation can be avoided to a some extent with sensitivity of the policy conclusions to the values of key parameters. Nevertheless, a broad area of uncertainty can remain.

Macroeconomic Models

The most frequently used models for economic management are undoubtedly the short-term macroeconomic models linking income, consumptions, investment, and other key aggregates.

These models are frequently used for forecasting short-term movements in the economy as well as for analyzing the implications of alternative fiscal and monetary policies. Such models are formally structured, with equations relating the movements of key variables and the latter divided into two groups: those whose values are determined within the model (endogenous variables) and those whose values are to be fed into the model from outside (exogenous variables).

Recently, however, analysis of alternative policies has been carried out in a less formal modeling framework. With the help of the World Bank and the International Monetary Fund, finance ministries in developing countries adopted an intersectoral accounting framework to look at the key questions relating to sectoral impacts of alternative policies. Such a framework, which can usually be set up in a spreadsheet, consists of projected national accounts for the economy by production sector and sectoral accounts for the government budget, the external account, the private account, and the monetary sector. Sectors can be added as needed. For example, in an analysis of the impacts of investments in the energy sector, an energy sector and a set of accounts for the key entities in that sector could be appended. The "model" consists of tracing the flow of funds among the sectors and ensuring consistency in the values of the variables. In terms of predicting future values of these variables, the distinction between the endogenous and exogenous variables remains, except that the endogenous variables are now determined by the accounting framework in the model, and the exogenous ones are determined outside the framework, including any that are forecast from other macroeconomic models.

Could such models be used for the analysis of environmental questions? Given their flexibility, the answer is almost certainly affirmative, partly in terms of the environmental impacts of economic policy, but more effectively in terms of the economic implications of environmental regulation. Forestry is an example. An accounting framework could be developed that relates stocks and flow of different timbers with the level of harvesting and the economic incentives for doing so. Each time policy changed (e.g., on export taxes, the exchange rate), its implications could then be worked out for this sector.

The more useful applications of such models, however, lie in dealing with the second link between the economy and the environment—that is, the economic impacts of environmental regulation. If taxes and charges are imposed on certain sectors of the economy for environmental reasons, the framework allows tracing through their implications on the government budget account, the external account, and the private sector.

APPLICATIONS IN THE THREE CASE STUDIES

In the three case studies carried out in connection with this study, it became clear that application of the methods described above would be difficult in most cases. The reason is mainly the lack of data and also of adequate models designed specifically to address the links of interest. As a small contribution to the research in this area, this study helped to develop some modeling capability in its adapting a CGE model for Thailand and developing an intertemporal forestry economy model for Côte D'Ivoire.

Yet it is clear from the studies that much can be achieved by an eclectic approach, applying simple models to answer specific questions (e.g., the effects of environmental controls on income distribution in Mexico). The data have sometimes been collected for other purposes, but they can be used for answering questions relevant to sustainable development goals.

All the case studies showed that revisiting the recent macroeconomic history of each country yielded some rewards. To look back at what happened and ask what the implications were for the environment has been a useful exercise. Moreover, it does not need a quantitative model to be useful (although such a model would help).

In sum, a modeling capability along the three lines described above should be developed. Doing so will take time, and the models used will depend on the questions asked. But it is always necessary to use simple models and to use one's judgment of economy-environment links in interpreting events and designing policies.

1. See for example I. Tchijov, and L. Tomaszewicz, eds., *Input-Output Modelling* (Berlin: Springer Verlag, 1985). For applications of I-O to environmental issues, see P. Nijkamp, *Theory and Application of Environmental Economics*, (Amsterdam: North Holland, 1977). I-O application techniques are closely associated with linear programming methods.

SUMMARY TABLES

1. MACROECONOMIC AND STRUCTURAL ADJUSTMENT POLICIES

AGRICULTURE

Country	Exchange Rate/Trade	Domestic Prices	Institutional Reforms	Public Sector Policies
Côte d'Ivoire	Simulated devaluation combined reduced subsidies on imported inputs with an export subsidy scheme. This policy was begun in 1987 but was only partially implemented. Export taxes were eliminated and producer prices of some export crops increased to reflect prevailing world prices.	Some domestic producer subsidies were eliminated and food crop prices and marketing liberalized.	Public agricultural agencies were restructured and state agricultural enterprises (sugar industry and agricultural banks) closed.	Export crops were diversified through promotional efforts of agricultural extension services. Public investment in agriculture sector declined.
Mexico	Series of exchange rate devaluations was established to increase international competitiveness. The Economic Solidarity Pact virtually fixed the exchange rate in 1988. Generalized trade liberalisation was undertaken. Import tariffs were gradually reduced and	Supported price adjustments altered price ratios among various crops (e.g., against maize and beans and in favor of oil crops, cotton, and sorghum). Subsidy on inputs, (pesticides, fertilizers, and	No major land reforms but the existing *ejido* system contributes to soil erosion owing to lack of transferability of rights, allocation of fragile lands, and "forced cultivation."	Public investment in agriculture declined both absolutely and relative to the average decline in the total public investment.

—continued

Country	Exchange Rate/Trade	Domestic Prices	Institutional Reforms	Public Sector Policies and Other Reforms
Mexico (cont'd)	export subsidies eliminated. Exports were diversified to reduce reliance on oil. Government entered into GATT, and Maquiladora program was established as a free trade experiment.	technology) were reduced and farm credit subsidy virtually eliminated by 1986.		
Thailand	Export taxes on many agricultural goods have been reduced, especially those on rubber and rice. Minimal import tax remains on fertilizers, but urea imports are subject to an additional 17% duty.	Farm price supports and input subsidies were recently introduced to promote production and improve farmers' welfare. Subsidized credit is a central component of government policy and is administered via a system of mandates, quotas, and interest rate ceilings. Some inputs are taxed (e.g., fertilizers). Irrigation water is provided free of charge and is an important subsidy to agriculture.	Free public forest land for agricultural expansion is the most significant subsidy to agriculture.	

FORESTRY

Country	Exchange Rate/Trade	Domestic Prices	Institutional Reforms	Public Sector Policies and Other Reforms
Côte d'Ivoire	Export taxes increased.	Concession and stumpage fees increased, but they remain small relative to total sector income, profits, and export taxes. New system of public auction of export licenses was initiated.	Protection of forest reserves was reinforced, management plans developed, and squatters resettled.	
Mexico	Devaluation and international trade agreements have secured high timber prices.	Credit subsidies and government loans for agrarian investments, including forestry, have been reduced.	Federal Agrarian Reform Law was amended in 1983, allowing a contract of partnership through participation for a 3-year maximum. Protected forestry zones: A series of regulations prohibited unauthorized change of land use, especially in basin areas. Authorities have intervened directly in reforestation projects. Boundary creation, land titling, and institutional consolidation: The World Bank Sectoral Loan 1991 was made conditional on achievement of these environmental objectives in the four poorest states.	Public expenditure on national parks and protected forestry zones declined as part of the stabilization package.
Thailand	Exchange rate has been kept near equilibrium values since 1984.	Low concession fees are invariant with respect to the area and the value of the concession. Stumpage fees vary by species. Royalties are levied on timber cut both inside and outside the forest reserves. Improvement fees (two times the royalty for teak and no additional royalty for nontimber species) are also levied on timber harvested from reserve forests.	Official ban on logging came into force in 1989.	

ENERGY AND TRANSPORT

Country	Exchange Rate/Trade	Domestic Prices	Institutional Reforms	Public Sector Policies and Other Reforms
Côte d'Ivoire		Consumer subsidy on electricity was eliminated to relieve pressure on fiscal deficits and encourage more efficient use of energy-intensive technology.		
Mexico		Energy prices were increased to reflect their marginal costs, and fuel subsidies were reduced.		
Thailand		Energy prices were raised in recent years to reflect opportunity costs (international prices) of imported oil. But the structure of petroleum prices has been distorted to reflect distributional and regional policy considerations (e.g., gasoline products are heavily taxed (85-105%), fuel oil and diesel taxes are low (1-10%), and LPG and kerosene are subsidized (6-13%)).		

Country	Exchange Rate/Trade	Domestic Prices	Institutional Reforms	Public Sector Policies and Other Reforms
Côte d'Ivoire	Membership in the West African Monetary Union precludes any devaluation; the nominal exchange rate is fixed relative to the French franc (CFA francs 50 = 1 FF). Import tariffs were harmonized and reduced (with some exemptions for certain industries). Import tariffs replaced quantitative restrictions. Export subsidy scheme was implemented at 20% of value added (subject to delays, only partial implementation).	Some producer and consumer subsidies were eliminated or reduced.	Public sector enterprises were restructured and privatization begun.	
Mexico	Series of devaluations contributed to the rapid growth of Maquiladora industries in the 1980s. In 1985, trade liberalization began and Mexico entered the General Agreement on Taxes and Tariffs. Equalization of environmental policies as part of the free trade agreement with the United States and Canada is currently under discussion.		Bureau of Urban Development and the Environment (SEDUE) was established, and a series of environmental regulations required companies to pay fines when emissions exceeded norms established for each process.	Many state-owned enterprises, IMF, and the World Bank provided financial support for reform.
Thailand	Successive exchange rate adjustments since 1984 have allowed Thailand to maintain a realistic exchange rate that has been fairly neutral to the industrial sector. Major revision of the import tariff structure in 1982 introduced lower and more uniform tariff levels. Investment and export incentives continued for export-orientated industries.	Minimum wages and interest rate ceilings have encouraged capital-intensive technologies in certain industries.	Section 19 of the Investment Promotion Act encourages promotion of projects to control environmental damage. Certain investments must be accompanied by an environmental impact assessment submitted to the National Environment Board for approval.	

WATER AND WASTE DISPOSAL

Country	Exchange Rate/Trade	Domestic Prices	Institutional Reforms	Public Sector Policies and Other Reforms
Côte d'Ivoire				No relevant reforms.
Mexico		Water fees are subject to reform as part of the financial restructuring program.		Financial restructuring by the National Water Commission involves less dependence on fiscal income and increased participation of the private sector through a system of credits and water fees. The World Bank and the Inter-American Development Bank will support various drinking water, irrigation, and drainage projects. Sewage treatment plants are under construction, many of them to be operated under private control.
Thailand				No relevant reforms.

2. ENVIRONMENTAL IMPACTS OF ADJUSTMENT

AGRICULTURE

Country	Environmental Issues	Environmental Impacts
Côte d'Ivoire	Land degradation and deforestation, loss of wildlife habitat, and biomass destruction on a massive scale result largely from clearing for agriculture, which has led to significant degradation of more than 75% of the original natural forest cover since 1940. An ambiguous and contradictory land tenure regime caused excessive land clearing, which is aggravated by rural poverty, rapid population growth and immigration, and the lack of alternative employment opportunities. Soil degradation is an increasingly serious problem in the densely populated and heavily cultivated Central and Eastern Forest Region (the original "Cocoa Belt"), arising primarily from extensive traditional cultivation of food crops.	Sectoral adjustment reforms were intended to reverse the historical bias against agriculture and the heavy reliance on coffee and cocoa exports by increasing producer prices, removing export taxes, and liberalizing markets. Although some of these reforms were implemented, resulting in improved terms of trade faced by rural producers, the increases in producer prices of coffee and cocoa were soon reversed, owing to dramatic declines in world prices of these crops. Cuts in producer subsidies for imported agricultural inputs were implemented. Environmental impacts are uncertain owing to the mixed record of reform. Declining returns on cash crops may stimulate more extensive production of food crops, leading to increased forest clearance and loss of natural environmental benefits. But expansion of cash crop farming, if successful, would also encourage increased forest conversion and land degradation.
Mexico	Soil erosion is increasing in scale and severity, particularly in areas of steep incline. Current estimates are that 71-98% of land suffers from accelerated erosion.	Adjustment policies, especially trade and exchange rate policies, have begun to reverse the earlier bias against agriculture. Improved terms of trade for agriculture will increase the demand for arable land but may also provide incentives for soil conservation and agricultural investments, depending on land tenure reforms and correction of price distortions in input and output markets. Promotion of perennial crops, such as coffee and fruit, for export has proved less damaging to soils than traditional cultivation of subsistence crops, such as corn and potatoes.
Thailand	Land clearance for agriculture has been a driving force of deforestation in Thailand. Crop yields on newly cleared forest land are high in the first 2-3 years under slash-and-burn agriculture; thereafter, yields fall as natural soil fertility declines, encouraging clearance of more land. Deforestation of increasingly marginal and fragile land has resulted in catastrophic landslides and floods like those in southern Thailand in 1988. About 50% of Thailand's relatively abundant land resources is affected by soil erosion, acidity, and salinity. The supply of irrigation water free of charge deprives the farmer of any incentive to conserve water and encourages overuse and waste, which result in environmental problems (waterlogging and salinization), inefficiency, and distributional problems (the worse-off rain-fed farmers subsidize the better-off irrigated farmers). Insecurity of land ownership deprives farmers of both access to credit and the incentive to improve and manage their land properly. Over 40% of agricultural land is occupied and farmed without recognized land title.	Export taxes on rice and rubber have distorted the farmers' choice against these two crops and in favor of maize, sugar cane, cassava, and other crops that are less protective of the soil. Dismantling export taxes on rice and rubber is likely to increase rubber export and raise domestic prices for both rice and rubber. More land would be agriculture, but maize, cassava, and sugar cane production would decline. The overall impact on the environment is ambiguous. On the one hand, the switch from maize, sugar cane, and cassava farming to rice and rubber will reduce soil degradation, but increased forest clearance for agriculture will result in loss of timber, secondary forest products, increased flooding and landslides, etc. Agricultural taxation has discouraged soil and water conservation by lowering the return on investments. Fertilizer taxes in the presence of an open forest frontier have distorted farmers' choice against intensification on existing farms and in favor of extension into new forest lands. Particularly high taxation of urea has biased fertilizer use in favor of nonnitrogen-based compound fertilizers that are less suitable for Thai soils. Government response to low fertilizer usage and the increasing need for intensification of agriculture has been to distribute subsidized fertilizers through the Marketing Organization of Farmers. But only a fraction of the government subsidy reaches farmers, and those who benefit are mostly the better off. Pesticide subsidies (either directly or through extension services) discourage integrated pest management, which is more labor intensive and less damaging to the environment than heavy pesticide use.

FORESTRY

Country	Environmental Issues	Environmental Impacts
Côte d'Ivoire	Deforestation of humid evergreen and semi-deciduous and transition forests has resulted in the loss of over 75% of the original forest cover since 1940. Estimates of the annual rate of deforestation are among the highest in the world, at about 6.5% during the 1980s. Deforestation results from inappropriate fiscal policy and concession terms in the forestry industry combined with an ambiguous and contradictory rural land tenure regime, which appears to encourage land clearing for agriculture as the principal means of acquiring secure title.	Public expenditure cuts have inevitably affected protection of public forest reserves, the agencies regulating the forestry industry, and government capacity to undertake research on improved forest management and to replant. Fiscal reform in the forest sector has doubled the proportion of economic rents appropriated by government, but from a low base. Stumpage fees based on logs extracted continue to favor high grading. Short concession periods discourage private investment in sustainable timber production and lead to neglect of secondary forest products and environmental damage. Reform of export licensing may reduce rent-seeking behavior, and elimination of preferential taxation of domestically processed timber products may reduce inefficiency of processing operations
Mexico	Estimates of temperate and tropical forests deforestation vary widely, from FAO's 1.3% per annum to regional studies reporting rates of over 25% per annum in some areas. The deforestation rate fundamentally depends on the incentives offered by laws governing resource property rights. The land may be private, social, or state owned. Deforestation is closely connected with the way these rights are defined and administered. Forest conversion for agriculture has been the norm for land appropriation. Breakdown of rural social conventions has hampered traditions of collective forest land management. Poverty alleviation through the provision of plots of land has contributed to destruction of virgin tropical forests. Restrictions on land use transactions reduce the profitability of forestry relative to agriculture (e.g., restrictions on the size of estates reduces potential economies of scale in forestry). Prohibition of sale, rent, and share-cropping prevents the transfer of land to more productive uses. Mortgage restrictions reduce the availability of commercial loans for capitalization and forestry investments.	Public expenditure for the two main public goods provided by the forests (i.e., protection of biodiversity and stabilization of drainage areas) was considerably reduced during the period of economic adjustment. Government failure to define clearly and enforce rural property rights has resulted in extensive appropriation battles and a system of incentives that discourages long-term investment in forestry compared to that for other land uses. The recent World Bank Sectoral Loan 1991 may partially correct this problem through its requirement for boundary creation, land titling, and institutional consolidation in four regions. Social objectives achieved by providing land to all farmers that request it has contributed to deforest-ation. It is not poverty that causes a change in the use of the land; it is government failure to use alternative policies for redistributing the wealth.

Country	Environmental Issues	Environmental Impacts
Thailand	Forests that covered over 50% of total land area 30 years ago now account for only 25% (1988). Uncontrolled logging and land clearing for farming are the main forces driving deforestation. Logging is now officially banned, but illegal logging continues. Destruction of watersheds and loss of biodiversity are becoming more important than the shortage of timber resources and fuel wood because the latter two are both tradeable and substitutable, whereas the former are not. Government failure to extract the full value of economic rents from timber harvesting has distorted investment incentives against reforestation by understating the true scarcity of both timber and standing forest. The incentive structure has clearly favored logging over management of forest land for nontimber products.	Timber concession fees have been too low to compensate society for the loss of a valuable and irreplaceable resource. They have also been invariant with respect to the area and value of concessions, creating an incentive for logging firms to accumulate vast holdings that they cannot harvest or police efficiently. The duration of timber concessions has been unrelated to the growing cycle of many tropical hardwoods. For example, timber concessions were awarded for 30 years despite the fact that tropical hardwoods have a 50-70-year growing cycle. Concessionaires with 30-year leases have no financial interest in the next crop and therefore do nothing to preserve long-term forest productivity. Timber stumpage fees also fail to provide incentives for efficient use and conservation. Not only have they been too low, but taxes based on timber harvested rather than on the marketable stand encourage high grading and damage to the remaining stocks. Royalties further compound the incentives for high grading and wasteful harvesting because log size is not a factor.

ENERGY AND TRANSPORT

Country	Environmental Issues	Environmental Impacts
Côte d'Ivoire	Electricity subsidies have encouraged excessive use of energy in industry and commerce, and they may have encouraged capital-intensive industrial technology.	Adjustment policies included removal of subsidies on electricity, leading to more efficient energy use.
Mexico	Fuel and electricity prices do not reflect social and environmental costs. Energy subsidies have resulted in the excessive use of energy, contributed to the public deficit, encouraged fuel intensity of technological processes in industry, and contributed to increased atmospheric pollution from the burning of fossil fuels.	Adjustment measures included price increases for public services and subsidy reductions. Energy prices reflecting more closely its marginal cost and the establishment of more competitive markets should promote more efficient resource use. But adjustments have not been targeted to environmental objectives.
Thailand	Industrialization and urbanization mean demand for more consumer durables, which are energy intensive and, by implication, pollution intensive. Air pollution and traffic congestion are two energy-related problems that affect the productivity and quality of life of people living in the BMR. Bangkok already exceeds the WHO guidelines for air pollutants, especially CO, SPM, and lead. An environmentally unsound energy mix and inefficient energy use combine to expose a large section of the population to serious environmental and health risks. The high lead content of gasoline is particularly worrisome because of its possible impact on children's learning capacity. Traffic congestion in urban areas is aggravated by the relatively low price of gasoline and low registration fees. In addition, whereas new vehicle sales are growing at spectacular rates, the supply of urban roads and public transport has hardly grown at all.	The structure of petroleum product prices has created perverse and inefficient patterns of fuel usage. For example, LPG subsidization has had the unintended effect of encouraging conversion of automobile engines from gasoline to LPG. Although this distortion has been reduced in recent years, there remains sufficient price distortion to encourage inefficient interfuel substitution. An increase in domestic oil prices to reflect world prices would have a general deflationary effect on the economy. The impact would generally be greater for industry than agriculture although total land use for agriculture would decline slightly. Exports and imports would both decline, but overall, a slight improvement on trade and current account balances is predicted. The model simulation is important for predicting the effect of a carbon tax on GDP growth and the balance of payments in the Thai economy. Overall, the environmental impact is likely to be positive.

INDUSTRY

Country	Environmental Issues	Environmental Impacts
Côte d'Ivoire	Industrial pollution is concentrated in and around Abidjan. Pollution is not considered a critical problem, although there is some concern about untreated organic pollution of lagoons and flushing of petroleum tankers that affect coastal and lagoon fisheries.	Environmental regulations are light and unevenly enforced. Public expenditure reduction may have affected government capacity to enforce existing regulations. But economic recession has slowed industrial expansion and hence may have alleviated pollution problems somewhat.
Mexico	The rapid expansion of the Maquiladora program has brought economic benefits but at considerable cost to the environment and the quality of life for inhabitants of the region. Different environmental regulations between the United States and Mexico may have encouraged the relocation of "dirty" industries to Mexico and may partially account for the rapid growth in the Maquiladora program.	Environmental regulation has largely been ignored. Companies have little incentive to modify their practices or equipment because the probability of being fined is low. SEDUE's budget limitations have forced it to adopt a negotiation policy instead of a strict regulatory policy. Negotiation is based on agreements with different industrial sectors to improve environmental control. It is hoped that the privatization program will lead to less environmental degradation because more funds will be available for investment in modern equipment. The environmental implications of trade liberalization are not yet apparent. Clearly, expansion of environmentally damaging industries is not desirable. And, introduction of environmentally acceptable production methods in response to the needs of meeting international market requirements will be positive. Ultimately, environmental impacts will hinge on whether international prices reflect the social costs of production.
Thailand	Many urban environmental problems relate to air and water pollution from industrial emissions and disposal of toxic wastes. Most industrial hazardous waste is dumped freely into rivers and landfills or is stored in drums onsite with little or no treatment. Degradation of the natural environment is directly related to haphazard development of tourism and tourist-related infrastructure. Discharges of untreated biodegradeable waste into public water bodies has reduced the dissolved oxygen in rivers below ambient standards.	Inadequate enforcement of regulations governing waste disposal means that the effective charge for waste disposal fails to reflect the true cost to the economy. In fact, industrial pollution is being subsidized. Failure to impose appropriate charges means that otherwise cost-effective resource recovery and recycling programs cannot be implemented. Domestic pricing distortions that raise the price of capital relative to labor may increase industrial pollution if capital-intensive technologies are more polluting than labor-intensive technologies.

WATER AND WASTE DISPOSAL

Country	Environmental Issues	Environmental Impacts
Côte d'Ivoire	Pollution of lagoons near Abidjan results from untreated domestic and industrial wastes. Increased salinity of lagoons owing to construction of interconnecting canals may have affected fisheries.	No significant impacts.
Mexico	Urban water pollution has become an increasing problem because population and economic growth increase waste discharges into rivers and lakes. In 1990, 30% of the population lacked access to adequate supplies of drinking water and 51% had no sewage system connection. This condition caused serious sanitary and health problems with waste water flowing onto streets. Construction of hydraulic works to supply urban populations with clean water reduced the volume of water available for irrigation. It also caused ecological devastation in the surrounding areas because lakes and rivers dried up. The existing subsidy to urban water users does not reflect the external costs to the surrounding areas. In addition, it benefits the upper classes in urban areas most and encourages excessive per capita usage.	The financial restructuring program launched by the National Water Commission will encourage rational water use through effective pricing and investments in treatment facilities. It is essential that the full external costs of urban water use be registered in the revised set of water tariffs for urban users. SEDUE will be responsible for setting and enforcing standards for municipalities and industries on the disposal of waste to water bodies.
Thailand		No significant impacts.

BIBLIOGRAPHY

Adjustment Lending: An Evaluation of Ten Years of Experience. Washington, D.C.: World Bank, 1989.

Adjustment Lending: How it Has Worked, How it Can be Improved. edited by Vinor Thomas and Ajay Chhibber, Washington, D.C.: World Bank, 1989.

Adjustment Lending Policies for Sustainable Growth. World Bank: Washington, D.C. 1991.

African Alternative Framework to Structural Adjustment Programs for Socio-Economic Recovery and Transformation (AAF-SAP). New York, N.Y.: United Nations, Economic Commission for Africa, 1989.

Ahmad, Yusef J., ed., *Environmental Accounting for Sustainable Development.* UNEP-World Bank. Washington, D.C.: World Bank, June 1989.

Akomian, J.E. "Etude sur le Regime Foncier Rural Ivoirien et les Problèmes Environnementaux Majeurs Qui en Découlent." Mimeographed, 1991.

Alagiah, George and Melvyn Westlake. "An Overdose of the IMF Medicine." *South*, February 1987.

Amelung, T. "Tropical Deforestation as an International Economic Problem." Linz, Austria: Egon-Sohmen Foundation Conference on Economic Evolution and Environmental Concerns, 30-31 August 1991.

Articles of Agreement of the International Bank for Reconstruction and Development. Washington, D.C.: IBRD, February 1989.

Articles of Agreement of the International Development Association—Accompanying Report of the Executive Directors of the IBRD. Washington, D.C.: IDA, September, 1960.

Articles of Agreement of the International Finance Corporation. Washington, D.C.: International Finance Corporation, July 1986.

Ayemou, A.O. "Analysis of Forest Management Strategies in Côte d'Ivoire: An Economic Model." Ph.D. diss. Urbana: University of Illinois, Urbana, 1989.

Bank Experience in Project Supervision. Washington, D.C.: World Bank, 1992.

Barbier, Edward B. *New Approaches in Environmental and Resource Economics: Toward an Economics of Sustainable Development.* London: International Institute for Environment and Development, 1988.

Barbier, Edward B., and Anil Markandya *The Conditions for Achieving Environmentally Sustainable Development.* London: International Institute for Environment and Development, 1989.

Baumol, William J. and Wallace E. Oates. *The Theory of Environmental Policy.* Cambridge: Cambridge University Press, 1988.

Berg, Elliott and Alan Batchelder. "Structural Adjustment Lending: A Critical View." Washington, D.C.: World Bank, 1984.

Betrand, T. "Thailand: Case Study of Agricultural Input and Output Pricing." World Bank Staff Working Paper no. 385. Washington, D.C.: World Bank, 1980.

Beyond UNPAAERD: From Talk to Action. New York, N.Y.: United Nations, 1991.

Broad, Robin. *Unequal Alliance: The World Bank, The International Monetary Fund, And The Philippines.* Berkeley: University of California Press, 1988.

Brown, Lester R. et al. *State of the World 1991: A Worldwatch Institute Report on Progress Toward a Sustainable Society.* New York, N.Y.: W.W. Norton & Co., 1991.

Burgess, J. "Economic Analysis of Frontier Agricultural Expansion and Tropical Deforestation." London: University College, 1991.

By-Laws of the International Bank for Reconstruction and Development. Washington, D.C.: IBRD, September 1980.

By-Laws of the International Development Association. Washington, D.C.: IDA, March 1981.

By-Laws of the International Finance Corporation. Washington, D.C.:

IFC, February 1980.

By-Laws of the Multilateral Investment Guarantee Agency. Washington, D.C.: M.I.G.A., June 1988.

"Children and Environment: A UNICEF Strategy for Sustainable Development." A UNICEF Policy Review, United Nations Children's Fund. New York, N.Y.: UNICEF, September 1989.

Chunanuntathem, S., S. Tambunlertchai, and A. Watlananukit, "Trade and Financing Strategies for Thailand in the 1980's." Working Paper no. 22. London: Overseas Development Institute, 1987.

Cline, William R., and Sidney Weintraub, editors, *Economic Stabilization in Developing Countries.* Washington, D.C.: The Brookings Institution, 1981.

Cobb, John B. and Herman E. Daly. "Free Trade Versus Community: Social and Environmental Consequences of Free Trade in a World with Capital Mobility and Overpopulated Regions." *Population and Environment: A Journal of Interdisciplinary Studies.* Human Sciences Press: Volume 11, Number 3, Spring 1990.

Cooper, Richard N. *Economic Stabilization and Debt in Developing Countries.* Cambridge, Massachusetts: MIT Press, 1992.

Cornia, Giovanni Andrea, *et al. Adjustment with a Human Face: Protecting the Vulnerable and Promoting Growth.* A Study by UNICEF, Vol. I. Oxford: Clarendon Press, 1987.

Cornia, Giovanni Andrea, *et al. Adjustment with a Human Face: Ten Country Case Study.* A Study by UNICEF, Vol. II, Oxford: Clarendon Press, 1988.

Conable, Barber. Address to the World Resources Institute, Washington, D.C., 1987.

Conable, Barber. "Development and the Environment: A Global Balance." Presented at Tokyo Conference on the Global Environment and Human Response Toward Sustainable Development, Tokyo, Japan, 11 September, 1989.

"Conservation Priorities for the Nineties." WWF-International: Meeting in Assisi. September 1986.

Cuarón, Alfredo. "Ecosistemas Tropicales y Primates." Ph.D. diss., San José: University of Costa Rica, 1989.

Daly, Herman E. "An Historical Turning Point in Economic Development: From Empty-World to Full-World Economics." Washington, D.C.: World Bank, 1991.

Daly, Herman E. *Ecological Economics and Sustainable Development.* Washington, D.C.: World Bank, 1990.

Daly, Herman E., "Towards an Environmental Macroeconomics." Washington, D.C.: World Bank, 1990.

Daly, Herman E., ed., *For the Common Good: Redirecting the Economy Toward Community, the Environment, and a Sustainable Future.* Boston: Beacon Press, 1989.

Diaz-Bonilla, Eugenio. *Structural Adjustment Programs and Economic Stabilization in Central America.* Economic Development Institute of The World Bank, an EDI Policy Seminar Report; Number 23. Washington, D.C.: World Bank, June 1990.

Dirzo, J. "Rescate y restauraci<n ecol<gica de la Selva de los Tuxtlas." *Ciencia y Desarroll.* no. 97, 1991.

Debt Bondage or Self-Reliance: A Popular Perspective on the Global Debt Crisis. Toronto, Ontario: GATT-Fly, 1985.

Demery, Lionel and Tony Addison. *The Alleviation of Poverty under Structural Adjustment.* Washington, D.C.: World Bank, 1987.

Dogsé, Peter, and Bernd von Droste. *Debt-For-Nature Exchanges an Biosphere Reserves: Experiences and Potential.* Paris: United Nations Educational, Scientific and Cultural Organization, 1990.

Economic Instruments for Environmental Protection. Paris: Organization for Economic Co-Operation and Development, 1989.

Economic Policies for Sustainable Development. Asian Development Bank.

Ehui, S.K. and T.W. Hertel. "Deforestation and Agricultural Productivity in the Côte d'Ivoire." *American Journal for Agricultural Economics.* 71(1989):3.

Environment and Development: Implementing the World Bank's New Policies. Washington, D.C.: Development Committee, July 1988.

Environmental Indicators: A Preliminary Set. Paris: United Nations Educational, Scientific and Cultural Organization, 1991.

Environmental Policy Benefits: Monetary Valuation. Paris: Organization for Economic Co-Operation and Development, 1989.

"Everything You've Ever Wanted to Know About Structural Adjustment But Were Afraid to Ask." Development Policy Unit. United Kingdom: Oxfam, February 1991.

From Crisis to Sustainable Growth. Washington, D.C.: World Bank, 1989.

Fossedal, Gregory. "IMF Conditionality, 1980-1991." Arlington, Virginia: Alexis de Tocqueville Institution, 1992.

Foy, George and Herman Daly. *Allocation, Distribution and Scale as Determinants of Environmental Degradation: Case Studies of Haiti, El Salvador and Costa Rica.* Environment Department Working Paper No. 19, Policy Planning and Research Staff. Washington, D.C.: World Bank, September 1989.

Financing and External Debt of Developing Countries: 1989 Survey. Paris: Organization for Economic Co-Operation and Development, 1990.

George, Susan. *The Debt Boomerang: How Third World Debt Harms Us All.* Boulder: Westview Press, 1992.

Gladwin, Christian H. ed. *Structural Adjustment and African Women Farmers.* Gainesville: University of Florida Press, 1991.

Global Economic Prospects and the Developing Countries. Washington, D.C.: World Bank, 1992.

Goldstein, Morris. *The Global Effects of Fund-Supported Adjustment Programs.* Occasional Paper No. 42. Washington, D.C.: International Monetary Fund, March 1986.

Goodland, Robert and Herman Daly. "Approaching Global Environmental Sustainability." Rome: Society for International Development, 1992.

Grootaert, Christiaan and Ravi Kanbur. *Policy-Oriented Analysis of Poverty and the Social Dimensions f Structural Adjustment: A Methodology and Proposed Application to Côte d'Ivoire, 1985-88.* Social Dimensions of Adjustment in Sub-Saharan Africa—Policy Analysis. Washington, D.C.: World Bank, January 1990.

Gwen, Catherine, Richard E. Feinberg, and contributors. *The International Monetary Fund in a Multipolar World: Pulling Together.* US-Third World Policy Perspectives, No. 13, Overseas Development Council. New Brunswick: Transaction Books, 1989.

Harte, John and Robert H. Socolow. *Patient Earth: The Problems of Urban Blight, Population Control, Resource Management, Conservation, the Ecological Impact of the Military, and Alternative Uses of Our Land.* New York, N.Y.: Holt, Rinehart and Winston, Inc., 1971.

Hartwick, John M. and Nancy D. Olewiler. *The Economics of Natural Resource Use.* New York, N.Y.: Harper & Row, Publishers, 1986.

Handbook of Economic Statistics 1990: A Reference Aid. Directorate of Intelligence. Washington, DC: Central Intelligence Agency, September

1990.

Handbook of International Trade and Development Statistics 1989.
United Nations Conference on Trade and Development. New York, N.Y.:
United Nations, 1990.

Holsen, John A. "An Overview of Structural Adjustment." International
Seminar on Structural Adjustment Policies in the Third World. Organized
by Bangladesh institute of Development Studies (BIDS), In collaboration
with World Institute for Development Economics Research (WIDER) The
World Bank, United Nations Development Programme in Dhaka, January
1990.

Hutaserani, S. and S. Jitsuchon. "Thailand's Income Distribution and
Poverty Profile and Their Current Situations." Bangkok: Thailand
Development Research Institute, 1988.

Jacobson, Jodi L. "Environmental Refugees: A Yardstick of
Havitability." *Worldwatch Paper 86.* Washington, D.C.: Worldwatch
Institute, 1988.

Kahn, J.R. and J.A. MacDonald. *Third World Debt and Tropical
Deforestation.* Binghamption, N.Y.: State University of New York at
Binghamption, 1990.

Kanbur, Ravi. *Poverty and the Social Dimensions of Structural Adjustment
in Côte d'Ivoire.* Social Dimensions of Adjustment in Sub-Saharan Africa -
Policy Analysis. Washington, D.C.: World Bank, March 1990.

Khan, Mohsin S. and Malcolm D. Knight. *Fund-Supported Adjustment
Programs and Economic Growth.* Occasional Paper No. 41. Washington,
D.C.: International Monetary Fund, November 1985.

Killick, Tony. *The Quest for Economic Stabilisation: The IMF and the
Third World.* London: Heinemann Educational Books, 1984.

King, Robert E. and Helena Tang. *International Macroeconomic
Adjustment, 1907-92: A World Model Approach.* World Bank Discussion
Papers No. 47. Washington, D.C.: World Bank, February 1989.

Kolko, Joyce. *Restructuring the World Economy.* New York, N.Y.:
Random House, 1988.

Krugman, Paul R. *Has the Adjustment Process Worked?* Washington,
D.C.: Institute of International Economics, October 1991.

Leonard, Jeffrey H. *Are Environmental Regulations Driving U.S. Industry
Overseas?* Washington, D.C.: Conservation Foundation, 1984.

Le Prestre, Philippe. *The World Bank and the Environmental Challenge.*
London: Selinsgrove Susquehanna Associated University Press, 1989.

Maass, J.M. and S. García Oliva. "La conservacion de suelos enzonas tropicales." *Ciencia y Desarrollo.* 15(90) (1990).

Mahar, Dennis J., ed. *Rapid Population Growth and Human Carrying Capacity: Two Perspectives.* World Bank Working Papers, No. 690, Population and Development Series, No. 15. Washington D.C.: World Bank, January 1985.

Mans' Impact on the Global Environment: Assessment and Recommendations for Action. Report of the Study of Critical Environmental Problems (SCEP), Sponsored by the Massachusetts Institute of Technology. Cambridge: Massachusetts Institute of Technology Press, 1970.

Mathews, Jessica Tuchman. "Nations and Nature: A New Look at Global Security." Twenty-First J. Robert Oppenheiment Memorial Lecture, August 12, 1991. Los Alamos, New Mexico. Washington, D.C.: World Resources Institute, 1991.

McNamara, Robert. *The McNamara Years at the World Bank: Major Policy Addresses of Robert S. McNamara 1961-1981.* Washington, D.C.: World Bank, 1981.

Meadows, Donella H., et al. *The Limits to Growth: A Report for the Club of Rome's Project on the Predicament of Mankind.* A Potomac Associates Book. New York, N.Y.: Universe Books, 1972.

Morrisson, C. "Balancing Adjustment and Equity." *OECD Observer* 172(1991).

Mosley, Paul, et al. *Aid and Power: The World Bank and Policy-Based Lending.* London: Toutledge, 1991.

Mukela, John. "The IMF Fallout." *Africa Report.* January-February, 1987.

Nelson, Joan M., ed. *Fragile Coalitions: The Politics of Economic Adjustment.* Overseas Development Council. New Brunswick: Transaction Books, 1989.

Operational Directive 4.01: Environmental Assessment. Washington, D.C.: World Bank, 1991.

Operational Manual Statement 2.36, Environmental Aspects of Bank Work. Washington, D.C.: World Bank, 1984.

Our Common Future. World Committee on Environment and Development. New York, N.Y.: Oxford University Press, 1987.

Panayotou, Theodore. "The Economics of Environmental Degradation: Problems, Causes and Responses." Development Discussion Paper no. 335. Boston: Harvard Institute for International Development, 1990.

Panayotou, Theodore. and C. Parasak. "Land and Forest: Projecting Demand and Managing Encroachment." Bangkok: Thailand Development Research Institute, 1990.

Panayotou, Theodore and C. Sussangkarn. *The Debt Crisis, Structural Adjustment and the Environment: The Case of Thailand.* Washington, D.C.: WWF-International, 1991.

Panayotou, Theodore, P. Kritiporn, and K. Charnpratheep. "Industrialization and Environment in Thailand: A NIC at What Price?" *TDRI Quarterly Review*, 5(3)(1990).

Partnership for Sustainable Development: A New U.S. Agenda for International Development and Environmental Security. Washington D.C.: Environmental and Energy Study Institute Task Force, May 1991.

Pearce, David W., Anil Markandya & Edward Barbier. *Blueprint for a Green Economy: A Text for the Next Election.* For the UK Department of the Environment. London: Earthscan Publications Ltd., 1989.

Pearce, David W., and R. Kerry Turner. *Economics of Natural Resources and the Environment.* Baltimore: Johns Hopkins University Press, 1990.

Pearce, David W., ed. *Sustainable Development and Cost Benefit Analysis.* London: International Institute for Environment and Development, 1988.

Pearce, David W., ed. *The MIT Dictionary of Modern Economics.* Camberage: MIT Press, 1986.

Plant, Roger. *Sugar and Modern Slavery.* London: Zed Books, 1987.

Please, Stanley. *The Hobbled Giant: Essays on the World Bank.* Boulder, CO: Westview Press, 1984.

Population Resources and the Environment: The Critical Challenges. London: United Nations Population Fund, 1991.

Program Performance Annual Report: First and Second Structural Adjustment Loans. Washington, D.C.: World Bank, 1988.

"Program Performance and Audit Report Thailand—First and Second Structural Adjustment Loans (Loans 2097-TH and 2256-TH)," Report no. 6085. Washington, D.C.: World Bank, 1986.

Rau, Bill. *From Feast to Famine: Official Cures and Grassroots Remedies to Africa's Food Crisis.* London: Zed Books Ltd., 1991.

Reichmann, Thomas M. "Experience with Programs of Balance of Payments Adjustment: Stand-By Arrangements in the Higher Trenches, 1963-72." International Monetary Fund Staff Papers.

Repetto, Robert. "Accounting for Environmental Assets." in *Scientific American* (June 1992)

Repetto, Robert. *The Forest for the Trees? Government Policies and the Misuse of Forest Resources.* Washington, D.C.: World Resources Institute, May 1988.

Repetto, Robert, eds. *Wasting Assets: Natural Resources in the National Income Accounts.* Washington, D.C.: World Resources Institute, 1989.

Restructuring Economies in Distress. Washington, D.C.: World Bank, 1991.

Ribe, Helena, ed. *How Adjustment Programs Can Help the Poor: The World Bank's Experience.* Washington, D.C.: World Bank, 1990.

Schneider, Keith. "Military Has New Strategic Goal in Cleanup of Vast Toxic Waste." *The New York Times*, August, 5, 1991.

Schneider, S.H. "Tropical Forests and Climate." *Climate Change.* London: Kleuver Publishers, special issue 19(1-2) (1991).

Schramm, Gunter and Jeremy J. Warford, eds. *Environmental Management and Economic Development.* Baltimore: Johns Hopkins University Press, 1989.

Sebastian, Iona and Adelaida Aligbusan, *Sustainable Development: Issues in Adjustment Lending Policies.* Policy and Research Division, The World Bank. Environment Department Divisional Paper No. 1989-6. Washington, D.C.: World Bank, October 1989.

Sicular, T. ed. *Food Price Policy in Asia.* Ithaca, N.Y.: Cornell University Press, 1989.

Social Indicators of Development 1990. World Bank Publication. Baltimore: Johns Hopkins University Press, 1990.

Speth, James Gustave. "Coming to Terms: Toward a North-South Bargain for the Environment." Washington, D.C.: *WRI Issues and Ideas.* June 1989:3.

The State of the Environment. Paris: United Nations Educational, Scientific and Cultural Organization, 1991.

Statistics and Policies: ECA Preliminary Observations on the World Bank Report: Africa Adjustment and Growth in the 1980s. Addis Ababa: United Nations, 1989.

Sterner, T. "Factor Demand and Substitution in a Developing Country: Energy Use in Mexican Manufacturing," in *Scandinavian Journal of Economics.* 91(4)1989.

Structural Adjustment, Agricultural Development and the Poor: Lessons from the Malawian Experience. Managing Agricultural Development in Africa, MADIA Discussion Paper 9. Washington, D.C.: World Bank,

December 1989.

Structural Adjustment Lending: A First Review of Experience Washington, D.C.: World Bank, 1986.

Sub-Saharan Africa: From Crisis to Sustainable Growth. Washington, D.C.: World Bank 1989.

Supporting Primary Environmental Care Report of the PEC Workshop, Siena, Jan. 29-Feb.2, 1990. Rome: Instituto Superiore di Sanit", 1991.

"Thailand: Managing Public Resources for Structural Adjustment." World Bank Country Case Study. Washington, D.C.: World Bank, 1984.

"Thailand: Pricing and Marketing Policy for Intensification of Rice Agriculture." World Bank Country Study. Washington, D.C.: World Bank, 1985.

"Thailand: Rural Growth and Employment." Washington, D.C.: World Bank, 1983.

The Third Report on Adjustment Lending: Private and Public Resources for Growth. Washington, D.C.: World Bank, 1992.

Thornes, J.B., ed. *Deforestation: Environmental and Social Impacts.* Chapman and Hall, 1991.

Trade and Development Report 1990. United Nations Conference on Trade and Development. New York, N.Y.: United Nations, 1990.

Trairatvorakul, P. "The Effects on Income Distribution and Nutrition of Alternative Rice Price Policy in Thailand." Report no. 45. Washington, D.C.: Food Policy Research Institute, 1984.

Vaggi, G. et al. *From the Depth Crisis To Sustainable Development.* New York, N.Y.: MacMillan, 1992.

von Moltke, Konrad. "Trade and the Environment: Issues in Dispute Settlement." Washington, D.C.: Office of Technology Assessment, 1992.

von Moltke, Konrad and Jenny Eckert. "United Nations Development Program and the Environment: A Non-governmental Assessment." Gland, Switzerland: WWF-International, May 1992.

Wheeler, Joseph C. *Development Co-operation: Efforts and Policies of the Members of the Development Assistance Committee.* Paris: Organization for Economic Co-operation and Development, December 1990.

"Working Documents, ACP-EEC Joint Assembly, Report of the Working Party on Conditions for Implementing the Structural Adjustment Policy under Lome IV and the Effects Thereof on the Conditions for Implementing the Structural Adjustment Policy under Lome IV." Brussels: Africa, Caribbean, Pacific-European Economic Community, 1992.

The World Bank Annual Report 1975. Washington, D.C.: World Bank, 1975.

The World Bank Annual Report 1976. Washington, D.C.: World Bank, 1976.

The World Bank Annual Report 1991. Washington, D.C.: World Bank, 1991.

World Development Report 1980. Washington, D.C.: World Bank, 1980.

World Development Report 1988. Washington, D.C.: World Bank, 1988.

World Development Report 1989: Financial Systems and Development. World Development Indicators. London: Oxford University Press, 1989.

World Development Report 1990: Poverty. World Development Indicators. The World Bank. London: Oxford University Press, 1990.

World Development Report 1991: The Challenge of Development. World Development Indicators. The World Bank. London: Oxford University Press, 1991.

World Economic Outlook: A Survey by the Staff of the International Monetary Fund. World Economic and Financial Surveys. Washington, D.C.: International Monetary Fund, 1990.

World Economic Survey 1990: Current Trends and Policies in The World Economy. Department of International Economic and Social Affairs. New York, N.Y.: United Nations, 1990.

Yao, J., Y. Kouadio, J. Akomian, and O. Angoran. "Structural Adjustment and the Environment: The Case of Côte d'Ivoire." to World Wide Fund for Nature. Abidjan: Côte d'Ivoire, 1992.

Zuckerman, Elaine. "Compensatory Programs: Redressing Social Costs of Adjustment." Washington, D.C.: World Bank, 1989.